GUANGDONG-HONG KONG-MACAO GREATER BAY AREA

Planning and Global Positioning

GUANGDONG–HONG KONG–MACAO GREATER BAY AREA

Planning and Global Positioning

Chief Editor

GUO Shiping
Shenzhen University, China

Editors

LI Cheng
Shenzhen University, China

JI Jie
ZHAO Genhong
Shenzhen Institute of Information Technology, China

World Scientific

NEW JERSEY · LONDON · SINGAPORE · BEIJING · SHANGHAI · HONG KONG · TAIPEI · CHENNAI · TOKYO

Published by

World Scientific Publishing Co. Pte. Ltd.

5 Toh Tuck Link, Singapore 596224

USA office: 27 Warren Street, Suite 401-402, Hackensack, NJ 07601

UK office: 57 Shelton Street, Covent Garden, London WC2H 9HE

Library of Congress Cataloging-in-Publication Data
Names: Guo, Shiping, editor.
Title: Guangdong-Hong Kong-Macao Greater Bay Area : planning and global positioning /
    chief editor, Guo Shiping, Shenzhen University, China, editors, Li Cheng, Shenzhen University,
    China, Ji Jie, Zhao Genhong, Shenzhen Institute of Information Technology, China.
Other titles: Guangdong, Hong Kong, Macau Greater Bay Area
Description: New Jersey : World Scientific, [2021] | Includes bibliographical references and index.
Identifiers: LCCN 2020006490 | ISBN 9789811218675 (hardcover) | ISBN 9789811218682 (ebook)
Subjects: LCSH: Regional planning--China--Guangdong Sheng. | Regional planning--China--
    Hong Kong. | Regional planning--China--Macau (Special Administrative Region)
Classification: LCC HT395.C552 G8356 2021 | DDC 307.1/1609512--dc23
LC record available at https://lccn.loc.gov/2020006490

British Library Cataloguing-in-Publication Data
A catalogue record for this book is available from the British Library.

《粤港澳大湾区: 规划和全球定位》
Originally published in Chinese by Guangdong People's Publishing House
Copyright © Guangdong People's Publishing House, 2017

For any available supplementary material, please visit
https://www.worldscientific.com/worldscibooks/10.1142/11779#t=suppl

Desk Editor: Tan Boon Hui

Typeset by Stallion Press
Email: enquiries@stallionpress.com

Printed in Singapore

Preface

The Guangdong–Hong Kong–Macao Greater Bay Area Brings New Opportunities for China

It was on March 5, 2017 that Premier Li Keqiang first proposed in the "Report on the Work of the Government" that China would study and formulate the development plan for the city clusters in the Greater Bay Area of Guangdong, Hong Kong and Macao, making the Greater Bay Area a reality and elevating it to the status of national strategy. If we view the New York, San Francisco and Tokyo Bay Areas as the models of global economic development in bay areas, then the first bay area economy in China — the Guangdong–Hong Kong–Macao Greater Bay Area which emerges from the Pearl River Delta will become a pilot area in China's endeavor to develop the bay area economy, so there'll be some new chances for China to promote this economic development model elsewhere. Guangdong will no longer be called "Guangdong Province", but "Guangdong City Clusters". On March 22, 2018, Premier Li Keqiang, in his "Report on the Work of the Government" at the 1st Session of the 13th National People's Congress, incorporated the Guangdong–Hong Kong–Macao Greater Bay Area into the government's work proposals for 2018. He suggested that the development plan of the Guangdong–Hong Kong–Macao Greater Bay Area be formalized, promulgated and implemented to comprehensively promote mutually beneficial cooperation between the Mainland, Hong Kong and Macao.

It is envisioned that the Guangdong–Hong Kong–Macao Greater Bay Area will become the largest Bay Area Economic Belt in the world.

The Greater Bay Area of Guangdong, Hong Kong and Macao includes the cities with the best and most promising development potentials in China. We can evidently see that nine cities in the Pearl River Delta have enjoyed some world-shaking achievements in economic development: Guangzhou has overtaken Singapore, Shenzhen has overtaken Hong Kong, Zhuhai is comparable to Florence in Italy, Foshan has overtaken Amsterdam, Dongguan has overtaken Las Vegas, Zhongshan has overtaken Geneva, Huizhou has surpassed Bremen in Germany and Zhaoqing is comparable to Liverpool in England. It is quite certain that once the Greater Bay Area of Guangdong, Hong Kong and Macao is established, it will surely surpass the three major bay areas of the world, namely, the New York, San Francisco and Tokyo Bay Areas.

The Greater Bay Area of Guangdong, Hong Kong and Macao Has the Support of Financial Centers

One of the greatest advantages of the world's three major bay areas resides in their financial centers. Tokyo is an international financial center, New York has an international financial center on Wall Street and San Francisco's financial sector is also highly developed. Obviously, the robust economic development of the great bay areas is impossible without strong financial support, because it is these financial centers that provide huge financial support for the economy of the great bay areas, and the cost of fund utilization is the lowest there. Compared with the three recognized great bay areas in the world, the Guangdong–Hong Kong–Macao Greater Bay Area possesses obvious financial advantages. First of all, as an international financial center, Hong Kong has been providing financial services for the world, especially Asia. In the future, Hong Kong will provide strong financial support to the Guangdong–Hong Kong–Macao Greater Bay Area. Second, as a regional financial center, Guangzhou has played an important role in serving the Pearl River

Delta region. Third, as another regional financial center, Shenzhen's financial status is not inferior to that of Beijing and Shanghai. Shenzhen's stock exchange, private equity funds, risk management and risk investment funds, venture capital funds and so on are at the forefront of China. In conclusion, Hong Kong, Guangzhou and Shenzhen are the three major financial centers that can provide continuous financial support to the Guangdong–Hong Kong–Macao Greater Bay Area, as well as to the Pan-Pearl River Delta region.

Greater Bay Area also offers new opportunities for the development of Guangdong's financial sector and even for that of the whole country. There are two regional financial centers in Guangdong Province — Shenzhen and Guangzhou. They provide financial services to the Pearl River Delta, and they could also play an important role in the proposed Greater Bay Area. First, Shenzhen and Guangzhou could become the financial backup bases for Hong Kong. And with the establishment of the Greater Bay Area of Guangdong, Hong Kong and Macao, Hong Kong, Macao, Shenzhen and Guangzhou can be linked together. Hong Kong's inclusion into the Greater Bay Area makes it a financial base not just serving the bay area but also providing financial services across the country. At the same time, Hong Kong, with its status as an international financial center, could become an offshore center for RMB offering services for foreign RMB account settlements. As for Shenzhen and Guangzhou, their proximity to Hong Kong means the two cities could act as a backup for Hong Kong's financial services. In addition, many banks in Hong Kong do have arrangements with the two cities for account settlements in Shenzhen and Guangzhou. Similarly, many securities companies in Hong Kong could also settle their accounts in Shenzhen and Guangzhou. Second, Shenzhen and Guangzhou can help Hong Kong integrate into the Guangdong–Hong Kong–Macao Greater Bay Area. Almost all the world-renowned financial institutions have their Asian headquarters established in Hong Kong. They all hope to provide financial services for China through Hong Kong. However, the financial system of Hong Kong is different from that of the Mainland, and there are also differences in the *modus operandi* of the financial services. Relying solely on

Hong Kong often produces unsatisfactory results. It is believed that if Hong Kong invests in the Mainland's financial sector through Shenzhen and Guangzhou as "transit bases", it will reap good rewards and produce beneficial outcomes.

The Guangdong–Hong Kong–Macao Greater Bay Area is Founded on the Bases of Openness and Freedom

The most important common feature among the New York, San Francisco and Tokyo bay areas is their open economy. Goods and services can freely enter and exit the bay areas. In addition, capital, people and other factors of production can move freely in and out of the bay areas. There is also optimum allocation of resources and economic benefits of the highest level. The efficient harbor, port and air service systems, well-developed foreign trade coupled with relatively low trade barriers and minimum tariffs and capital controls form the foundation for the development of the open economy in the three major bay areas. In addition, the management offices of the three major bays have emphasized the role of an "invisible hand" in guiding and controlling market orientations and risk prevention. Furthermore, the three major bays are closely linked to the international market and are engaged in the international division of labor at multiple levels. Clearly, the three bay areas represent important nodes for the world's value and supply chains.

Compared with the other city groups or clusters and economic zones in China, the Guangdong–Hong Kong–Macao Greater Bay Area is the most open area in China. First of all, Hong Kong is the most open free trade port in the world. Most commodities can enter and leave Hong Kong with the exemption of tax. People from 170 countries or regions can enter Hong Kong without a visa, and its foreign exchange regulation and control is also very lax. Likewise, Macao's economy is also very open and its foreign exchange control is relatively lenient too. It exempts visa requirements for citizens from nearly 130 countries and regions, and people come in and go with convenience and relatively little restrictions. Another point to note is the position of the Pearl River Delta — the economic hinterland of Hong Kong and Macao. Again, the Pearl River Delta has always adopted an open trade policy. The vast majority of trade is foreign trade. Guangzhou has long been the hub of South China's foreign trade and Shenzhen is a show house for China's opening up. Generally speaking, Guangdong, Hong Kong and Macao play a leading role in China's foreign trade and opening-up endeavor and they are essentially poised to develop into a world-class bay area.

The Greater Bay Area of Guangdong, Hong Kong and Macao Will Form a Great and Strong Powerhouse Radiating its Energy and Influence

As the most important bay area economy in China, the economy of the Greater Bay Area will become a powerful driving force that influence the whole country. The benefits generated will never simply be a mathematical "one plus one equals two" result but the beneficial effects will be multi-fold and will amplify further. The Guangdong–Hong Kong–Macao Greater Bay Area may be divided into three structural levels or regions, forming the differentiated superposition effects. The core level consists of the nine cities in the Pearl River Delta plus Hong Kong and Macao, commonly referred to as the "9 + 2 urban agglomeration or city clusters". According to preliminary estimates, the total economic output of this core region in 2016 exceeded 9.11 trillion Yuan, about US$1.37 trillion, of which 9 cities in the Pearl River Delta contributed nearly 6.8 trillion Yuan, and the economic outputs of the 9 were approaching the economic scale of the world's developed bay areas. The second level mainly consists of underdeveloped cities in the Guangdong Province, including Shanwei, Shantou, Jieyang, Heyuan, Yangjiang and other towns of Guangdong. At present, they remain underdeveloped, but they provide a vast hinterland for the Guangdong–Hong Kong–Macao Greater Bay Area. The third level of the proposed Greater Bay Area extends to Fujian, Guangxi, Hainan and Jiangxi — the regions which depend on the resources of the southeastern coastal bay areas, with the main regions of the Guangdong–Hong Kong–Macao Greater Bay Area as their core, the Xiamen Bay Area as the eastern wing and the Northern Bay Area as the western wing, forming the development setting of "one core leading two wings flying together", while at the same time driving the development of Hunan, Guizhou, Yunnan and Sichuan.

The economic belt of the Greater Bay Area, once established, will provide wider space and more opportunities for the further development of Guangdong's economy. As national science and technology centers, Shenzhen and Guangzhou could provide scientific and technological support to the aforementioned areas. As for the competitiveness in science and technology, Shenzhen ranks first among Beijing, Shanghai and Shenzhen. China's industry is currently moving toward Industry 3.0 and Industry 4.0. It therefore urgently needs the support and backing of scientific and technological advancements. The huge demand for science and technology means the huge expansion of markets for the development of science and technology in Shenzhen and Guangzhou.

Since Shenzhen and Guangzhou are China's logistics centers, the manufactured goods across the Greater Bay Area can be shipped through these two cities. Yantian Port in Shenzhen is one of the largest ports in the world, with one of the highest single-port container throughput wharf terminals in the world. The speed of loading and unloading of goods is very fast, which means that Yantian can provide maritime transport easily and efficiently for these areas. Guangzhou Port is the largest and most comprehensive hub port in South China, and it can also perform the same function.

In addition to the aforesaid advantages, the Greater Bay Areas will attract an increasing number of cultural programs and talents to Shenzhen and Guangzhou, the national hubs for cultural industry. The two cities are the biggest cultural trading exchange markets in China with a very high degree of marketization of cultural industries. More and more people involved in cultural activities and within the culture circle will flock there to seek jobs. It follows that with the Greater Bay Area taking shape, their cultural industries will develop and expand further.

Guo Shiping

Director, Professor and Doctoral Supervisor

Institute of Contemporary Finance, Shenzhen University,
Shenzhen, China

About the Chief Editor

Guo Shiping, Director, Professor & Doctoral Supervisor, Head of Contemporary Finance Institute at Shenzhen University, guest professor at Sydney University, part-time professor at Peking University, Tsinghua University etc., Consultant of Shenzhen government.

About the Editors

 Li Cheng, Contemporary Finance Institute, Shenzhen University. Li Cheng, Doctor of Economics, postdoctoral fellow at Shenzhen University China Special Economic Zone Research Center, researcher at Shenzhen University Contemporary Finance Research Institute, Master of Statistics and Financial Maths at Rutgers University, visiting scholar at Japan Hannan University during September 2015 to February 2017. He has participated in the following projects: TISA Rules Changes and Development Study, Influences of International Service Business Agreement Changes to China and Strategies China Should Take, High Standard Rules Leading Development of Qianhai, Global Positioning of the Belt and Road Initiative China's Development Strategies and Oversea Investment, etc.

 Ji Jie, Shenzhen Institute of Information Technology. Ji Jie, Doctor of Economics of Regulation at Liaoning University, Economist, works at Shenzhen Institute of Information Technology. She has co-edited one book, completed four vice ministerial and municipal level projects and published seven core journals. She has won the first prize of Guangdong Province Colleges E-Teaching Competition.

Zhao Genhong, Shenzhen Institute of Information Technology. Zhao Genhong, Doctor of Economics at Liaoning University, associate professor at Shenzhen Institute of Information Technology. His major research field is national macro-economic regulation and regional economic development. He has published over ten research articles, including five articles in core journals and two in CSSCI journals. He has participated in 2009 Ministry of Education Financial Crisis Confrontation project "Impact of International Financial Crisis on China's Equipment Manufacturing Industry and Its Countermeasures", projects that aiming at solving the issue of revitalization of the Northeast old industrial bases, including "Research on Accelerating the Countermeasures of National Central Cities" "Research on Supporting the Comprehensive Revitalization of Fiscal Policies in the Liaoning Old Industrial Base" "Research on Active Participation in the Coordinated Development of Beijing, Tianjin and Hebei", etc. He has also participated in editing the teaching book of higher education's National Economics.

Contents

Chapter 1

Introduction

Guo Shiping* and Wang Dong[†]

*Shenzhen University
†Lingnan University

Global regional economic integration is the global background for the proposed Guangdong–Hong Kong–Macao Greater Bay Area economy. The concept of regional economic integration may be defined in the following terms: In order to safeguard common economic and political interests, two or more countries or regions adjacent to each other, through inter-governmental treaties or agreements, formulate common policies and measures to implement and make them uniform — so as to transfer partial sovereignty of some countries to others for the establishment of common institutions — to exercise supranational powers and forces on a long-term and stable basis, to carry out economic adjustment and to effect and form economic and even political alliances.

At the 5th meeting of the 12th National People's Congress in 2017, Premier Li Keqiang announced that a Guangdong–Hong Kong–Macao Greater Bay Area economy would be established, thus bringing good news to these regions.

On July 1, 2017, Hong Kong Special Administrative Region Chief Executive Carrie Lam Cheng Yuet-ngor, Macao Special Administrative

Region Chief Executive Fernando Chui Sai on and Director of the National Development and Reform Commission He Lifeng and Ma Xingrui, Governor of Guangdong Province, jointly signed the "Enhancing Guangdong–Hong Kong–Macao Cooperation and Promoting Greater Bay Area Framework Agreement" in Hong Kong. The signing ceremony was witnessed by President Xi Jinping.

Global regional economic integration is the global background for the proposed Guangdong–Hong Kong–Macao Greater Bay Area economy. The concept of regional economic integration may be defined in the following terms: In order to safeguard common economic and political interests, two or more countries or regions adjacent to each other, through inter-governmental treaties or agreements, formulate common policies and measures to implement and make them uniform — so as to transfer partial sovereignty of some countries to others for the establishment of common institutions — to exercise supranational powers and forces on a long-term and stable basis, to carry out economic adjustment and to effect and form economic and even political alliances.[1] Regional economic integration brings economic growth that is not simply represented by the mathematical equation of 1 plus 1 equals 2; the integration brings a "multiplier" effect which is amplifying.

I. The Background for the Establishment of the Guangdong–Hong Kong–Macao Greater Bay Area

The Greater Bay Area of Guangdong, Hong Kong and Macao is composed of Guangzhou, Shenzhen, Zhuhai, Foshan, Huizhou, Jiangmen, Dongguan, Zhaoqing and Zhongshan — nine cities in the Pearl River Delta — and two special administrative regions, Hong Kong SAR and Macao SAR. It covers an area of about 56,000 square kilometers and has a total population of about 66 million.

In the process of regional economic integration of Guangdong, Hong Kong and Macao, Hong Kong and Macao are well known as international metropolises, and compared to Guangdong, are obvi-

---

[1] Kang Xueqin: *Research on Sub-regional Economic Integration in the Growth Triangle of Guangdong, Hong Kong and Macao*, China Social Science Press, 2014.

ously in advantageous positions in corporate financing, company management and information technology. However, the economic development of Hong Kong and Macao is limited by shortage of land space and the lack of natural resources. This can be overcome by exploiting rich natural resources, labor force, land and other factors of production in Guangdong. The Greater Bay Area is established against the backdrop of economic, political and social considerations.

(A) *Economic background*

The most direct motivation driving the establishment of economic integration is the need to overcome the problem of economic bottlenecks faced by each party. For Guangdong, the teething issues are the rising cost of factors of production, insufficient driving force for upgrading industrial production and manufacturing structures as well as a serious homogeneity of production. In the case of Hong Kong, the biggest problem lies in the limited space and the rising land prices, thereby forcing the manufacturing industries to move out of Hong Kong. This in turn has resulted in the "hollowing out" of Hong Kong's industries. On the contrary, real estate tycoons in Hong Kong have made use of capital gained with rising land prices to control and monopolize industries that affect people's livelihoods. Such monopolies make it difficult for small and medium industries to expand. Excessively high land prices impose higher costs upon the start-up companies and has seriously hampered their long-term development and affected the returns of high-tech industries, industries related to cultural activities as well as other high-risk industries with long periods for returns, thus exacerbating the "hollowing out" of Hong Kong industries. As for Macao, it is too dependent on the gambling and tourism industries, and these industries (gambling especially) do impact negatively on society. This is therefore one major problem that must be addressed and overcome.

Since China's reform and opening-up, Guangdong Province, Hong Kong and Macao have ushered in a period of rapid development. This has also been the result of the closest cooperation between the Guangdong Province, Hong Kong and Macao.

Since then, the cooperation between the three places has undergone the following four phases:

(a) 1979–1982 was a period of pilot or experimental cooperation. During this phase, capital from Hong Kong and Macao SARs (mainly from family-controlled enterprises) was invested in the areas of tourism, entertainment and other sectors.

(b) 1984–1992 was a period of industrial cooperation, with the so-called "shopfront with a rear factory" model of economic development in the Pearl River Delta.

(c) 1993–1999 was a period of enhanced cooperation. The economic "soft landing" of the Pearl River Delta — which was affected by the Asian financial crisis — plus the return of Hong Kong and Macao to the motherland, spurred the economic cooperation between the three areas to new heights. During this phase, huge amounts of capital from Hong Kong and Macao poured into the financial, housing and other sectors of Guangdong.

(d) Comprehensive cooperation occurred post 2000. Since 2000, there has been less reliance by Guangdong on Hong Kong and Macao. There is now little "one-way" dependence. Guangdong has begun to take on parts of the service industries of Hong Kong, and gradually, Guangdong, Hong Kong and Macao have become an integrated economic entity in which the three are interdependent.[2]

An important item in the outline of the 11th Five-Year Plan is to actively participate in international and regional economic cooperation mechanisms and organizations; to be actively involved in multilateral trade and the formulation of investment regulations in order to promote a new international economic order. It has been proposed in the outline of the 12th Five-Year Plan that we should

---

[2] Zhou Yunyuan: *Research on the Economic Developments of Guangdong, Hong Kong and Macao — the Trend Moving Away from Imbalance Towards Integration, Guangdong, Hong Kong and Macao Regional Cooperation Research Series*, China Social Science Press, 2011.

adhere steadfastly to the combined and coordinated expansion of opening-up and regional development. We should promote "opening-up" along the coastal, inland and border areas to form regional openings to bring about a situation of complementary advantages, division of labor, cooperation and balanced coordination in economic developments.[3] On June 29, 2003, the Central Government and the Government of the Hong Kong Special Administrative Region signed the "Closer Economic Partnership Arrangement between the Mainland and Hong Kong" in Hong Kong; and on October 17, 2003, the "Closer Economic Partnership Arrangement between the Mainland and Macao" was signed by the Central Government and the Macao Special Administrative Region in Macao. CEPA and the "Arrangement for Closer Economic and Trade Relations between the Mainland and Macao" are different from the cooperation between developed countries and sovereign developing countries in the now defunct Trans-Pacific Partnership Agreement (TPP). The regional cooperation between Guangdong, Hong Kong and Macao is based on the development model that emphasizes Chinese characteristics under "one country, two systems". We are of the opinion that this model provides valuable experience for the diversified development of humankind.

In 1997, the Asian financial crisis engulfed Thailand, and swept many countries and regions in Asia. International capital retreated from Hong Kong and other major Asian capital markets. However, in the 2008 subprime mortgage crisis, although Hong Kong did suffer from the crisis, it also became a safe haven for capital inflow from around the world. Hong Kong therefore consolidated its position as a world financial center. Hong Kong's stronger risk management ability is closely related to the economic prosperity of Chinese Mainland. In addition, a series of agreements made with the Mainland, plus CEPA and others, have enabled Hong Kong — with the full support of the Mainland — to concentrate on seizing the opportunities arising from the process of economic development

---

[3] Suggestions of the Central Government on Planning the 12th Five-Year Plan for National Economic and Social Development, *Wenhui Bao*, 7th edition, March 17, 2011,

between Chinese Mainland and the world and to become versatile enough to respond to all sorts of international challenges.

Since the implementation of CEPA, Guangdong, Hong Kong and Macao have achieved some progress in regional economic integration. However, problems still exist in the financial sector. First, the phenomenon of the cross-border RMB cash flow outside banking system is still prevalent. Second, the settlement of bills is monotonous, and the advantages of real-time payment systems are not obvious. Third, the banks of Guangdong Province are lagging behind in introducing overseas foreign financial institutions to participate in the banks' equities. Additionally, the banks of Hong Kong has not yet carried out any substantial operation in participating in the equities of the banks of Guangdong. Fourth, the cooperation between the regulatory authorities is at a low level, showing a lack of institutional innovation, cooperation and coordination in the financial sector.[4] The root cause of this kind of problem stems from the "obstacles or barriers of economic cooperation" between the two sides caused by two different systems under the framework of "one country, two systems", which brings us to the political backdrop of our discussion of the Guangdong–Hong Kong–Macao Greater Bay Area.

(B) *Institutional and legal background*

After 1997, Hong Kong and Macao returned to the motherland. However, as special administrative regions, Hong Kong and Macao are quite different from Chinese Mainland in their economic and legal systems. Economically, Hong Kong and Macao — being single tariff zones — are independent of the tax regulations of the mainland. Macao's legal system is based on "continental law", while Hong Kong's legal system — though under the guarantee of the Basic Law — will continue to be based on the common law system

---

[4]Zhou Yunyuan: *Research on the Integration of Economic Developments of Guangdong, Hong Kong and Macao* (*Guangdong, Hong Kong and Macao Regional Cooperation Research Series*), China Social Science Press, 2011.

and be governed by Hong Kong's local laws such as regulations and customary laws. Hong Kong's legal system is therefore totally different from the Mainland legal system. After more than 30 years of efforts, the Chinese legal system has improved greatly, but there is still room for improvement concerning the legislation on some major industries (such as the service industry) in Hong Kong and Macao. In order to seek judicial coordination and cooperation and pave the way for regional economic development, the Central Government has sought to formulate a series of laws adapted to the objective conditions of Guangdong, Hong Kong, Macao and China's national conditions and circumstances. The State is attempting to formulate regulations and to promulgate laws that would bring China in line with, or "connect" with international economic policies, as well as integrating Guangdong, Hong Kong and Macao into the "Belt and Road" Initiative. Meanwhile, in order to further strengthen the economic ties and cooperation between Guangdong, Hong Kong and Macao, the Hong Kong and Macao governments have also tried to overcome the obstacles of the existing administrative systems to facilitate and realize the free flow of products and factors of production in the Greater Bay Area. Action is taken to reduce the differences arising from the "one country, two systems" between the two sides. One example is by providing maximum preferential treatment and more incentives and conducive conditions.

(C) *Social background*

In international law, the border of a country is defined by the boundary dividing one country's territory from that of another: it refers to the limit of the boundaries of one country's territory and its unoccupied territory, or that of its territories and its high seas, national airspace and perceived outer space. Borders are boundaries where sovereign states exercise their sovereignty or suzerainty. People on both sides of the border have formed their own unique customs, social norms, languages and cultures under their respective sovereignties. The dominant "shielding effect" of the boundary is reflected chiefly in the psychology of alertness between the two sides of the boundary and the resultant trade barriers.

With the march of economic globalization, this dominant effect and the consequent trade barriers are gradually waning. However, human beings are social animals and because of factors such as national honor and other social attributes, in their collective consciousness, they will gradually transform the explicit shielding effects like trade barrier built on protectionism into implicit ones. In other words, because of differences in psychology (ethos), culture, customs, language and ideology and value systems, there arise concomitant differences in action, behavior and other distinctions. Within the Greater Bay Area of Guangdong, Hong Kong and Macao, Guangdong is geographically adjacent to Hong Kong and Macao. Around 80% of Hong Kong and Macao compatriots are ancestrally from Guangdong Province. As the shared dialect of the Hong Kong and Macao Special Administrative Regions, Cantonese is used by half of nearly 80 million people in Guangdong Province, which is the main Cantonese-speaking heartland in Chinese Mainland.[5] The similar demographic characteristics and language systems weaken the implicit shielding effect between Guangdong, Hong Kong and Macao. However, due to the colonial rule of Britain and Portugal in the past and the setbacks experienced by China on its journey of socialist construction, cultural differences do exist between the two SARs and the mainland. Upon the return of the two SARs to the motherland, the "one-country, two-systems" mode of governance brought into sharp relief the differences between the three places. The implicit "shielding" effect caused by differences in cultural and value systems could be attributable to conflicts between Western capitalism and socialism with Chinese characteristics. And to a certain extent, these conflicts and barriers prevent close cooperation in economic and social matters among the three parties in the Greater Bay Area.

---

[5] Data from the Guangdong Provincial People's Government. http:www.gd.gov. cngdgksqgmrkyy201303/t20130312_ 176012 htm.

II. Strategic Significance of Establishing the Guangdong–Hong Kong–Macao Greater Bay Area

Since the return of Hong Kong and Macao to their motherland, the Central Government has placed great importance on the construction of a mechanism of cooperation between Guangdong, Hong Kong and Macao. With reforms and opening-up, the economic and trade relations between Guangdong, Hong Kong and Macao have gone through four stages of continuous enhancement and strengthening. At the 5th Session of the 12th National People's Congress, held on March 5, 2017, Premier Li Keqiang, in his Report on the Work of the Government, proposed that "we should promote further cooperation between the Mainland and Hong Kong and Macao, and conduct studies to formulate a plan about the Greater Bay Area of Guangdong, Hong Kong and Macao's groups of cities (city clusters) in an agglomeration development, taking into account the unique strengths of Hong Kong and Macao, thus elevating their status and functions in contributing toward China's national economic development and opening up." What this signified is that the economic cooperation between Guangdong, Hong Kong and Macao entered a new phase from 2017; that is, it has since been elevated from regional economic cooperation to a national strategy.

(A) *Economic significance*

Generally, the modes of cooperation between parties under "semi-closed" boundary conditions include the channel or passageway type, the entry port type and the cross-border type of economic development.[6] Based on the cooperation extended by the three (Guangdong, Hong Kong and Macao) cities in the past, it can be said that the mode was one of semi-closed cross-border coopera-

---

[6] Zhang Jianzhong, Zhang Bing, and Chen Ying: "Border Effect and the Regional Model for Cross-border Economic Cooperation — Taking Southeast Asia as an Example", *Human Geography*, Vol. No. 1, 2002, pp. 8–11.

tion. This mode of cooperation was characterized by a trend toward economic integration in which factors of production interplayed with one another. The border cooperation mode, based predominantly on trade and commerce, often fails to meet the needs of economic development of all parties. Therefore, the countries involved generally utilize ports of entry or entry points for the purpose of expanding the scope of business, and they establish the region where the entry points are located as a free trade and development zone, integrating cross-border trade, markets and investments, and forming an agglomeration of industries in the area of cross-border economic cooperation.[7] From the perspective of economic strategy, the establishment of the Guangdong–Hong Kong–Macao Greater Bay Area helps to form a comprehensive and open economic system with greater efficiency in resource allocation in Guangdong, Hong Kong and Macao. This Greater Bay Area provides a window for external communication, and propels the integration of the Pearl River Delta region into a new development phase.

In recent years, the Guangdong Province has undergone large-scale industrial restructuring. While it is vigorously upgrading the traditional industries, it is also accelerating the construction of high-tech industries represented by cloud computing and artificial intelligence and advanced services based on mobile Internet. The areas west of the Pearl River, where development lagged behind in the past, will gradually, following the completion of the Hong Kong–Zhuhai–Macao Bridge and other infrastructures, become more prosperous. This region is expected to become the third largest economic growth area in Guangdong after Guangzhou and Shenzhen. As far as Guangdong enterprises are concerned, the establishment of the Guangdong–Hong Kong–Macao Greater Bay Area will enable them to make full use of the highly internationalized advantages of Hong Kong and Macao. It is easier to raise funds from

---

[7]Zhang Xuhua: "The Construction of Cross-border Economic Cooperation Zone and Analysis of the Strategies of Cross-border Cooperation with China", *Asia-Pacific Economics*, Vol. No. 4, 2011, pp. 108–113.

world capital markets, and additionally, the process of internationalization of these corporations or enterprises will speed up as they make use of the advantages of technology, management and services of Hong Kong and Macao. In this way, they would be able to further expand their international markets. At the same time, since Guangzhou and Shenzhen are strategically located along the "Maritime Silk Road", in the framework of the Greater Bay Area of Guangdong, Hong Kong and Macao, strategic importance will also be gained by the two cities. As such, the two cities play positive and important roles in the economic development of the Pearl River Delta as well as that of the "Maritime Silk Road". As for Hong Kong, the city's companies have always had great abilities in fund raising, project operation and management, and they should be able to — with the development of infrastructure construction in Eastern Guangdong — play complementary roles to promote the "Belt and Road" Initiative by easing the serious problems of internal competition produced by economic homogenization of the industries of Guangdong, Hong Kong and Macao. At the same time, in the strategic plan regarding the world economy laid out by the Central Government, Hong Kong would be "taking a free ride" by "riding on the wings of economic boom" as more development opportunities open up.

(B) *Political significance*

From the political perspective, a major obstacle preventing the further enhancement of the cooperation between Guangdong, Hong Kong and Macao lies in the distinctly different political systems of Guangdong, Hong Kong and Macao, under the "one-country, two-systems" framework. There exist obvious administrative "borders" and consequent "shielding effects". The establishment of the Greater Bay Area of Guangdong, Hong Kong and Macao represents an innovative effort to break political barriers between them in a real sense, chiefly by playing the economic card. Of course, every "innovation" meant to break the political barriers will face opposing views and dissent. For instance, the construction of the Hong Kong West Kowloon High-speed Railway Station raises the question of whether Mainland personnel or officials could exercise law enforcement powers in Hong Kong. There are wide differences of opinion. On another issue, one of the key points in the construction of the Guangdong–Hong Kong–Macao Greater Bay Area is to strengthen cooperation between Guangdong, Hong Kong and Macao on high-tech industries typically involving big data, cloud computing, artificial intelligence, virtual reality, etc. It is therefore incumbent upon the Central Government to formulate special policies in view of the objective conditions of the three parties taking into consideration the high land price and opportunity costs in Hong Kong and Macao, which impede the research and development of high-tech industries. It is safe to say that the Guangdong Province possesses good industry and basic infrastructure and has in place a comprehensive system of scientific research and development as well — all of which are essential attributes required to support large numbers of high-tech talents and professionals in high-tech research and development. However, Guangdong lacks top-notch universities and institutions of higher learning and outstanding individuals in the scientific and technological areas. This state of affairs has caused shortfalls and insufficiency in research funding compared to that obtained or available in Beijing and Shanghai. In contrast, Hong Kong and Macao have many top international colleges and universities that have adopted the teaching systems of the West. At the same time, intellectual property rights are better protected in Hong Kong and Macao since their intellectual property laws are more comprehensive. It follows that academic and scientific research results can be commercialized in good time to bear profits. Thus, it can be seen that, politically speaking, the Greater Bay Area of Guangdong, Hong Kong and Macao will play strategically leading and innovative roles in serving the economy — creating more opportunities for the development of other regional economic entities and innovative enterprises in the future. Indeed, this will herald a new chapter in China's economic development.

For China, the establishment of the Greater Bay Area of Guangdong, Hong Kong and Macao means that the policy of reform and opening-up implemented since the 3rd Plenary Session of the 11th Central Committee will enter a new phase. Today, China has become the second largest economy in the world, and an indispensable part of the world economy. As an important hub of the "Belt and Road" Initiative, the political role of Guangdong, Hong Kong and Macao will also change from a "water diversion channel or conduit" for external capital and technology transfer in the early stage of opening-up to a "mentor" providing valuable experience for China's economic development. Since the reform and opening-up, in the light of the complex world political and economic situation, China's foreign policy has been "slanted" toward "maintaining a low profile while working hard to achieve our national goals". As the reform and opening-up policy enters a new phase, China as a great country now bears the responsibility and possesses the ability to show an objective and feasible road of peaceful development for the benefit of less-developed countries modeled on its own development process, and in due course, China's political vistas will become more open too.

(C) *Social significance*

The tourism industry of Guangdong, Hong Kong and Macao has its own characteristics. Guangdong Province boasts of rich tourism resources. There are nine 5A scenic spots (tourist attractions) in the territory (as of 2016). These are Guangzhou Chimelong Tourist Resort, Shenzhen Overseas Chinese City Tourist (OCT) Resort, Guangzhou Mount Baiyun Scenic Area, Meizhou Meixian County's Yannan Fei Tea Field Scenic Area (also known as Meizhou Yannanfei Chatian Vacation Village), Guanlanhu Leisure Tourist Resort in Shenzhen, Subterranean River Tourist Area in Lianzhou in Qingyuan, Shaoguan Renhua Mount Danxia Scenic Area, Foshan Qiaoshan Scenic Spot and Huizhou's Luofushan Scenic Spot, while the domestic 4A tourist attractions number 61. Additionally, Guangdong Province has 7 national historic and cultural cities, namely Guangzhou, Chaozhou, Foshan, Zhaoqing, Meizhou, Zhongshan and Leizhou, and 16 provincial historic and cultural cities. As a well-known international city, Hong Kong is the transportation hub of the Asia-Pacific region. It has Victoria Harbor, Asia's biggest and world's third largest seaport, as well as many famous landmark attractions. It has been lauded as the "Pearl of the Orient". Hong Kong is unique because of the influence of British culture. The combination of Chinese and Western cultural styles holds a strong attraction for domestic and foreign tourists. Macao is rich in Portuguese culture. It has more than 20 historical buildings and structures including the ruins of St Paul's, A-Ma Temple and so on. Macao is the only legal gambling area in China, housing plenty of unique and colorful entertainment centers, a fact that gives the biggest advantage to Macao's tourism industry.

In recent years, with the growth of China's economy and the increasing degree of opening-up to the outside world, more and more Chinese nationals have chosen to travel abroad. Although Guangdong, Hong Kong and Macao are different from each other, there are many strong competitors from other parts of the world. For example, with visa exemption granted to Chinese nationals by South Korea, the casinos on Jeju Island, South Korea have successfully diverted some tourists from Macao to Jeju. The relaxation of visa requirements for tourists from the Mainland granted by developed countries such as Japan, the European Union and the United Kingdom has also had a great impact on Hong Kong's tourism industry. The establishment of the Greater Bay Area of Guangdong, Hong Kong and Macao will mean that the three places will complement each other's strengths in the tourism industry, thus creating a synergistic effect in the cultural field. The integration and development of tourism in the Greater Bay Area not only is of great economic significance but will also foster mutual interactions and enhance the understanding among the peoples of Guangdong, Hong Kong and Macao and help to close the gaps caused by misunderstanding and prejudice against one another.

III. Global Positioning of the Guangdong–Hong Kong– Macao Greater Bay Area Economy

With an open economic system, efficient resource allocation, a strong external cohesion effect and developed international networks, the economy of the Guangdong–Hong Kong–Macao Greater Bay Area has become an important growth center that drives the global economic engine and is a pioneer in promoting technological revolution. Currently, among the three famous bay areas of the world, New York Bay Area has created Wall Street, the Bay Area of San Francisco has created Silicon Valley — the world innovation center — and the port-vicinity economy of Tokyo Bay Area has contributed to about one-third of Japan's total economic output. According to the statistics of 2015, the GDP of 11 cities in the Guangdong–Hong Kong–Macao Bay Area was twice that of San Francisco Bay Area, close to the level of New York Bay Area. The import and export trade value was about US$1.5 trillion, roughly three times that of Tokyo Bay Area, and the container throughput of regional ports was 72 million standard containers (TEUs), which was 5.5 times the total of the three bay areas.[8]

Examining the development experiences of the New York, San Francisco and Tokyo Bay Areas, we recognize that the purpose of establishing the Guangdong–Hong Kong–Macao Greater Bay Area is to enhance the international competitiveness of the Greater Bay Area, as was the purpose of the other bay areas or regions of the world. According to Michael Porter, the factors affecting a country's or a region's competitive edge or advantage include factors of production, conditions of demand, performance of related and supporting industries, strategy, structure and competitors. The government should play a catalyzing role in this process, encouraging and even pushing enterprises to strive for competitive advantages, and creating an environment "conducive to advantageous industries" rather than directly creating "advantageous industries". The

---

[8]Yan Pengli: "The Greater Bay Area of Guangdong, Hong Kong and Macao: New Iconic Landmark for All-round Opening-up", *Environmental Economics*, 2017, pp. 64–67.

root cause for the establishment of "advantageous" industries and the competitiveness of enterprises is innovation, which is the cumulative result of various technological breakthroughs.[9] Viewed this way, a core function and role of the Greater Bay Area of Guangdong, Hong Kong and Macao is to guide enterprises toward high-tech manufacturing whereupon these enterprises shall use their leading-edge technological strengths — rather than traditional comparative strengths or advantages — to play the role of leading innovators by transforming scientific research achievements and high-tech industries into a position of competitive advantages among the regional economies of the world.

In addition to technological innovation, creating financial centers, business centers and transportation hubs are also important goals for constructing the Guangdong–Hong Kong–Macao Greater Bay Area. In order to make the Greater Bay Area a world financial center, one key point lies in the extent or degree of internationalization of the RMB. On the one hand, China should actively foster cross-border innovations in finance and gradually carry out cross-border RMB business transactions between financial institutions in Guangdong and that of Hong Kong and Macao. On the other hand, it should make full use of the subsidized infrastructure projects associated with the "Belt and Road" Initiative for countries along the route and try to set up relevant overseas funds based on RMB. The core of a business center is the service industry, and a mature professional service industry cannot be separated from the development of the convention and exhibition industries, tourism and the training of professionals. Objectively, transportation hubs are formed because of their geographical location and transport conditions. Within the Greater Bay Area, there are two free ports, Hong Kong and Macao; two special economic zones, Shenzhen and Zhuhai; and three free trade "pilot fields", Nansha, Hengqin and Qianhai's Shekou. They do seem to possess the fundamental conditions for constructing a world-class bay area and logistics center. However, we

---

[9] Michael E. Porter: *Competitive Advantage: Creating and Sustaining Superior Performance*, Free Press, 1985.

must admit that at this stage, there are still some gaps and shortcomings of the Guangdong–Hong Kong–Macao Greater Bay Area as compared to the regional economic entities of the New York, San Francisco and Tokyo Bay Areas, which have been in existence for many years. The main problem is not the lack of funds and technology but the difficulty in achieving complete interconnection between Hong Kong, Macao and the Mainland under the two political systems and three tariff systems. Moreover, among the cities in the urban agglomeration (city clusters) between Guangdong, Hong Kong and Macao, there is still a lack of clear "division of labor" acceptable to all. Although none of them wants to be the "back garden or backyard" of the others, the highly homogenized problems brought about by unclear positioning of the cities within the Bay Area will produce too much internal competition as well as loss through attrition in the development of the Greater Bay Area, thus hindering its economic construction.

IV. The Strategic Relationship Between the Greater Bay Area and the "Belt and Road" Initiative

Regional economic cooperation between Guangdong, Hong Kong and Macao has progressively deepened with China's reform and opening-up and has achieved fruitful results. And thanks to the policy of "one country, two systems" and the new development opportunities brought about by China's accession to the WTO, the level of cooperation between Guangdong, Hong Kong and Macao has reached a new high. At the same time, with the rapid development of other regional economic regions in China, such as Shanghai's Pudong New Area and Xiongan New Area, and their increased internationalization, the prior comparative advantages of Guangdong, Hong Kong and Macao economic sphere are gradually waning. Within the Greater Bay Area, Guangdong Province has firmly established its position in the manufacturing and modern service industries by utilizing its resources after many years of economic development modeled upon the concept of "shop front and factory at the rear". However, with the rise in labor cost, and the constraints of resources and environment, the traditional regional economic cooperation model between Guangdong, Hong Kong and Macao is facing new challenges. For Hong Kong, the rapid development of emerging cities in the mainland, especially Shanghai, has forced Hong Kong's traditional industry to transform and upgrade in order to meet the challenges. For Macao, its gambling industry is a double-edged sword. On the one hand, entertainment venues bring a large number of domestic and foreign tourists to Macao and make great contributions to the rapid development of the local economy. On the other hand, the singularity of Macao's economic model and the problems associated with externalities brought by the gambling industry are driving Macao inevitably toward diversification in its industrial structure.

In addition, although the rapid development of other regional economic entities in China has made great contributions to China's economic growth, with the passage of time, the developments of these economies have reached a relative saturation point, making the marginal benefits of domestic infrastructure production factors gradually decline, possibly even leading to the phenomenon of inefficiencies because of diseconomies of scale. In order to judiciously solve the serious issue of domestic overcapacity, the Chinese government, on the one hand, has adopted the policy of opening up a new economic growth point in Xiongan New Area (radiating it to the surrounding areas through various means) so as to help increase the marginal benefits of production factors and advance the development of the surrounding areas together. This is the policy of "those who get rich first help to make others rich". The spillover effect of the important cities not only spurs the development of the surrounding cities but also causes local house prices to increase, and this can effectively alleviate high housing price in the first-tier cities and the surplus of buildings in the second-tier and third-tier cities. On the other hand, the Chinese government has proposed the "Belt and Road" Initiative top-level, national initiative, the direct economic purpose of which is to oversee the existing overcapacity in the country and to transfer advantages in technological knowhow to the less developed areas, and such measures will not only promote local economic development but also produce a bigger market for domestic economies and enterprises.

The implementation of the "Belt and Road" Initiative cannot be separated from the interactions and cooperation with other countries along the "route" of the "belt" and because many private enterprises in the mainland are used to focusing on the domestic market, their intention or motivation to internationalize is often not strong. In response to the "Belt and Road" Initiative, they will find that the accounting systems, legal systems, social commitment and duties and so on are different from those of the local countries (along the route), resulting in increased risks of their operations abroad. In contrast, many organizations and institutions in Hong Kong and Macao have gained international recognition for their rich experience in dealing with international business affairs. If we regard the Greater Bay Area of Guangdong, Hong Kong and Macao as the "bridge" of the "Belt and Road" Initiative, then one end of the bridge will connect the world and act as an important platform in the opening-up process of China's "Belt and Road" Initiative, so that enterprises within the Greater Bay Area will be able to "move out" in a pragmatic, down-to-earth or steadfast way — and achieve a win–win situation with the market as the leading factor — while the other end of the bridge will connect the southern part of China, the vast hinterland in the central and western regions. This means the Greater Bay Area acts as an "epicenter" of Chinese economic growth with economic activities radiating to cover the development of the Pearl River Delta, further driving the economic development of the central and western regions, helping to redress the developmental imbalance between the eastern and western parts of China and reducing the income gap between the rich and the poor and hopefully achieving "common prosperity" in the real sense of the word.

Chapter 2

Comparison between the Economies of the Guangdong–Hong Kong–Macao Greater Bay Area and Other Bay Areas of the World

Ji Jie* and Pan Feng†

*Shenzhen Institute of Information Technology
†Shenzhen University

The impact of the three major bay areas on the world economy is tremendous. The establishment of the world's fourth largest bay area economy in Guangdong, Hong Kong and Macao will also have a huge impact on the economy of the Pearl River Delta and that of China as a whole. There are similarities between the economies of the Guangdong–Hong Kong–Macao Greater Bay Area and the other bay areas of the world; nonetheless, each bay area does possess unique characteristics.

The impact of the three major bay areas on the world economy is tremendous. The establishment of the world's fourth largest bay area economy in Guangdong, Hong Kong and Macao will also have a huge impact on the economy of the Pearl River Delta and that of

21

China as a whole. There are similarities between the economies of the Guangdong–Hong Kong–Macao Greater Bay Area and the other bay areas of the world; nonetheless, each bay area does possess unique characteristics.

I. Similar Experiences of Economic Development in the Three Great Bay Areas of the World

As economic entities borne out of their spatial and geographical uniqueness, the world's major bay areas share similar features in addition to having distinctive characteristics of their own.

(A) *Prerequisites for Greater Bay Area development*

By definition, a bay area is endowed with close proximity to the sea; being close to the sea is only one of the many fundamentals that constitute the prerequisites for the development of the bay area economy.

(1) *Geographical advantages of the bay areas*

The favorable geographical location and abundant natural resources, especially port or harbor resources, are the innate advantages bay area economies possess. For the growth of the bay area economy, efforts should be made to foster the development of regional port groups or clusters and promote competition and cooperation among ports within the same economic region. Therefore, taking advantage of the port openness and making use of complementarity of advantages and difference of functions are not only the primary conditions but also the main strengths responsible for the economic development of bay areas.

(2) *Population advantage of the bay areas*

Population is an advantage of bay area economies. The population provides human resources: people with higher education levels and skilled labor. It is the population advantage and abundant manpower that ensure the continuous development of the economy of the bay areas. The population and density of the whole metropolitan area, the higher quality of the work force, education of the elites and skilled labor are rightly considered as advantages possessed by the population. It is opportune for the government to formulate relevant policies for training, re-education and exchange of people, attracting talented and skilled professionals in order to enrich human resources and increase human resource reserves in these bay areas.

(3) *Good infrastructure and well-developed traffic and transport network of the bay areas*

In general, there are good and convenient transport systems in the bay areas, and shipping, freight, aviation, subways, railways, etc., are integrated into a huge network. Good infrastructure greatly enhances the overall economic development of the bay areas.

(4) *Inclusive, all-encompassing cultural characteristics*

The bay areas are generally pluralistic, open and inclusive in the cultural milieu. Because of their unique geographical advantages and status as transportation hubs, bay areas generally accommodate people from all over the country and even from all over the world, thus providing opportunities for the bay areas to display different cultures. Although different cultural groups have different backgrounds, the atmosphere is one with fair and equal opportunities, encouragement of innovation and tolerance to failure. This atmosphere has resulted in the inclusiveness and openness of the culture of the bay areas. For example, the San Francisco Bay Area is a melting pot of multiculturalism. Starting with the "gold rush" a long time ago, San Francisco began to welcome immigrants of different ethnicities from many countries. Ethnic settlements gradually formed. San Francisco has ethnic minority settlements such as Little Italy, Little Japan, Little

Mexico, Chinatown. Cultures and traditions have been maintained for a long time in these little ethnic enclaves. Similarly, the Bay Area of New York and the Bay Area of Tokyo encourage a multicultural atmosphere as well.

(B) *System of division of functions within the Greater Bay Area*

There are inherent differences within the cities of any bay area economy as to the types and availabilities of resources. In order to promote a well-balanced and healthy development of cities within the bay area, the division of functions of local governments is the key to the competitive edge of the bay area economy. Different functions of the economy are assumed by different sub-areas. Their economies and resources complement each other; they collaborate in the division of functions and complement each other via staggered, differential and complementary development so as to advance the overall prosperity of the bay area.

The general pattern of the division of functions in each region or sub-area of the bay area is that the bay area should first select the industries with lower production factor costs to be the dominant industries of the relevant city according to its own resources and obtain comparative benefits by means of trade flow and other means within the cities. At the same time, the development of each city is not only dependent on the available resources, but also on the creation of each city's own comparative advantages. The creation of the so-called comparative advantages, including economies of scale, cumulative effects on economy and so on, becomes the dominant direction in which division of labor and cooperation among cities will be headed. In addition, if the resource endowment of a city is poor, this shortcoming can be mitigated via implementing appropriate economic development policies by establishing a competitive industry organizational structure, so as to coordinate the development of the cities within the area. In this way, the overall economic prospects of the bay area are improved.

Taking Tokyo Bay Area as an example, we see that this bay area is composed of cities and regions such as Tokyo, Saitama and Kanagawa prefectures. Most of the cultural and educational institutions, government administrative offices, accommodation and catering services, wholesale and retail industries, real estate, financial and insurance industries are concentrated in Tokyo, which is the political and economic center. Tokyo, together with London and New York, are the world's three major financial centers. Tokyo is the economic, political and cultural center of Japan and one of the most important world economic centers.

The Kanagawa Prefecture is one of the four major industrial bases of Japan, and it is also the logistics and industrial center of Japan. With suburbanization and urbanization in areas around Tokyo, some industries and their functions are gradually moving away from the central urban areas, thus making the locality of regional functions in the Kanagawa Prefecture evidently more important. Yokohama is Japan's second largest city in which many headquarters of corporations, state administrative organs and many cutting-edge industries are located. As the center of heavy industries, Kawasaki is another important city in the Kanagawa region. Its R&D and manufacturing functions are more clearly evident. The functions of Yokohama and Kawasaki Ports complement each other, providing services for finished products and raw materials for corporations. With the expansion of port advantages within the bay area, the Kanagawa Prefecture has become the gathering place of the logistics industry and other industries in the Tokyo metropolitan economic sphere.

Saitama Prefecture has a highly developed transportation network. As a transportation center and sub-(second) capital, it is one of the most important transportation hubs in eastern Japan. Additionally, it has taken over some of the "transferred" government functions. This is also in line with its regional position as an agglomeration place for business, leisure, government agencies, accommodation and catering services, etc.

(C) *Cross-regional coordination and integration mechanism*

The development of a bay area requires coordination with local governments to form cooperative alliances, and a cross-regional integration mechanism is thereby necessitated. Generally speaking, the bay area economy consists of a "city sphere" or metropolitan area, comprising a central city (one or more) and several adjacent regional cities, which are closely linked both economically and socially. The metropolitan group of cities is an area that interacts with other such metropolitan groups, spanning many regions, with a tendency or inclination toward becoming integrated. These metropolitan groups (city spheres) are interdependent and exert mutual restrictions or constraints. Any given metropolitan group is also highly dependent on the functions of the cities. In order to develop the economy of the bay area and create a beneficial or a virtuous cycle, local governments need to form cooperative or collaborative alliances, transcend the idea of regionalism, establish a unified and open market system, form a rational and integrated structural plan, improve the legal security system, and prosper and develop together, thus forming a "combined force" in a particular region. Specifically, this "combined force" is manifested in the following:

(1) *Making full use of the mechanism of government-market-society unity*

The formation of a bay area economy depends not only on the functioning of the market mechanism but also on the influence of the government and the society. Therefore, in the process of economic development, the bay area needs to make full use of the resource allocation function of the market, the planning and decision-making function of governments, and the supervisory and promotional functions of the society. The market-led mechanisms chiefly include the following aspects: the establishment of specialized regional markets, transfer of industries (driven by changing market forces, i.e. costs of factors of production), the promotion of cooperation among enterprises in the area, regional development (the core of which consists of factors of production and markets for products), etc. The government-led mechanism mainly involves formulating industrial policies, administrative planning and management, investment and financial policies, etc.

(2) *The mechanism of government-market-society unity*

The tripartite mechanism coordinates the development of the urban economy and ecological environment, and it "transcends" the development of the times in the sense that it is ahead of its time. In view of the social background at the relevant time, this tripartite mechanism focuses on the future development of the social economy and coordinates the development of the metropolitan economy. For example, under the restriction and supervision of Japan's "Capital Sphere Preparatory and Readiness Law", the Capital Sphere Planning was introduced and amended five times. At the same time, this Capital Sphere of Japan also issued a large number of regulatory documents on the layout plan pertaining to the promotion of industrial clusters, industrial restrictions and the plans for transfer of the functions of the Capital, etc. Many aspects were covered, including the population distribution and road map layout of the Capital Sphere of "one Capital, three Prefectures", environmental protection, transportation layout, urban spatial function layout, etc. The five amendments of the "Capital Sphere Preparatory and Readiness Law" made by the Japanese government resulted in the formation and development of the Tokyo Capital City Sphere. San Francisco Bay Area also passed the Urban Planning Act, and the three unofficial local planning programs in New York also bolstered the overall development of the region.

(3) *The setting up of governmental and non-governmental organizations that link and interact with each other within the bay area*

The classic case of a non-governmental organization is the cross-regional New York City Group of the US. The New York City Government and NGOs, such as the New York Regional Planning Association (RPA) and the New York Metropolitan Area Commission, are the main regulatory bodies under the New York Metropolitan Area Management and Planning Program. Close collaboration between the government and NGOs has played a pivotal role in the development of the New York metropolitan area. It is a prominent feature of NGOs that they exist to supplement the management and administration of local governments without supplanting their powers. New York metropolitan area NGOs have always played an active role in the scientific planning and policy formulation of the metropolitan area.

Japan has also set up various official bodies such as the Construction Bureau, General Affairs Bureau and Overall Urban Preparation Bureau to oversee the construction of the Tokyo metropolitan area. The object is to oversee all matters pertaining to the Capital Sphere, especially regional socioeconomic developments. The unit responsible for regional planning for future development is the Tokyo Metropolitan Policy Planning Bureau. Tokyo Bay Area Authority is responsible for port maintenance, construction, transportation and other matters within the coastal areas of the Tokyo metropolitan region. In order to eliminate the inherent conflicts in the Tokyo–Yokohama Industrial Zone — for the three major ports of Kawasaki, Tokyo and Yokohama — the bay area has set up the Tokyo–Yokohama Industrial Zone Port Association, which usually meets once every 2–3 months to plan and coordinate port-related works.

The Bay Area of San Francisco has established a semi-official coordinating body of public–private partnership — the Bay Area Commission Economic Research Institute — which is dedicated to overseeing and maintaining the economic vitality and competitiveness of the bay area. It is tasked mainly with coordinating the division of labor, cooperation between governments and scientific research institutions and coordinating their developments. In addition, the leading bodies of the Bay Area Commission Economic Research Institute and the Association of Bay Area Governments (ABAG) have established a cordial partnership to jointly support the economic development of the bay area.

(D) *Industry, education and research driving the scientific and technological innovations*

Within the bay area economy, scientific and technological innovation is the common feature of all industrial developments, and also the key factor for the development of enterprise agglomeration. Educational and scientific research and development facilitate outward expansion. Upgrading the industrial structure requires advances in technological innovation, strengthening of scientific research and development functions as the main factors in attracting industries and forming links between industry, academic and research institutions. Technological innovation provides technical support for product enhancement, development of new products and improvement of product quality and performance. In this way, the competitive advantage of enterprises shall be assured within the same industry. Scientific and technological innovations are the best and most effective paths in promoting industrial upgrading and sustainable development of the bay area economy.

One outstanding feature of scientific and technological innovation is the agglomeration of high-tech industries based on the collaboration between industry, education and research. High and new technologies are necessary for industrial development, but the research and development of high and new technologies may not be ably buttressed by the industry's own level of knowledge and scientific research. Though scientific research institutions and universities have abundant talents and knowledge resources, they lack large amount of funds to invest in research and development of new and high technologies — and lack of funding is a common problem. Through the platform of Industry–(Higher) Education–Research collaboration, the close coalition between university–enterprise and that between scientific research–enterprise can better solve the bottlenecks of the development of high-tech industries. At the same time, through a series of financial funding and associated or matching policies, it is possible to help foster the extension of the innovation chain, from creativity all the way to the ultimate industrialization (Figure 1).

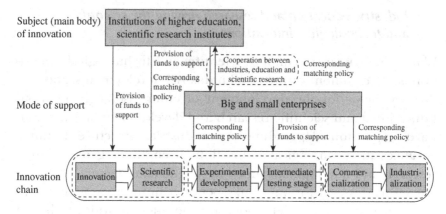

Figure 1.   The integration of industries, education and R&D.

All the three major bay areas emphasize the importance of the role of scientific and technological innovation, realizing that scientific and technological progress is the driving force of economic development. Hence, the bay areas make great efforts to facilitate the upgrading of the industrial structure: the further integration of industry, academia and research institutions strengthens the transformation and innovation of industrial technologies.

Japan's Industry–Education–Research structure is dependent on the rise of the third scientific and technological revolution, especially the extensive development of the electronic information technology and Internet, which explicates that the direction of development of Tokyo Bay Area shall be the combination of Industry–Education–Research based on scientific and technological innovation. The basis for the development of the innovation-driven science and technology industry is increasing the number of research institutions and universities in the core city areas. The important condition for the gathering of scientific and technologically innovative people in the Tokyo metropolitan area is that the number, scale and proportion of postgraduate and university students in Tokyo, Kanagawa and Saitama prefectures are constantly increasing (see Table 1). Industrialization of science and technology requires a large number of educational and scientific research resources to provide personnel and knowhow. In addition to

Table 1. Changes in number of the institutions of higher learning in Tokyo through the years 2002–2010.

Number of Institutions	2002	2003	2004	2005	2006	2007	2008	2009	2010
Institutions of higher learning	162	164	171	176	184	187	189	192	196
Proportion of total (%)	23.6	23.4	24.1	24.2	24.7	24.7	24.7	24.8	25.2
Number of students	100,2268	1,010,968	1,010,219	1,030,398	1,027,245	1,015,311	1,024,371	1,039,600	1,060,521
Proportion of total (%)	36	36.1	36	35.9	35.9	36.2	36.2	36.5	36.7

Source: Japan National Transport Bureau (Capital Sphere White Paper, 201).

colleges and universities, there are also many research institutes and large enterprises within Tokyo Bay Area, including NEC, Canon, Mitsubishi Chemicals, Mitsubishi Heavy Industries, Mitsubishi Electric, Sony, Toyota Research Institute, Fujitsu, Toshiba and so on. Institutions in Tokyo Bay Area have strong R&D and management capabilities, precisely because these R&D institutions possess strong capacities in industrial innovation.

For San Francisco Bay Area, its agglomeration of reputable colleges and universities and advanced research institutes — with large talent pools and excellent entrepreneurial innovation capabilities — renders it a winner in economic development.

San Francisco Bay Area is a world-class research center with a large number of universities, research institutes and laboratories. As the most innovative area in the world, the region has made significant scientific breakthroughs since the second half of the 20th century. The Bay Area is the birthplace of nine world-renowned research institutions, including University of San Francisco, Stanford University, University of California at Davis, Lawrence Livermore National Laboratory, Ernest Orlando Lawrence Berkeley National Laboratory, NASA Ames Research Center, Sandia National Laboratory and Stanford Linear Acceleration Center.

Many prominent development corporations and private sector research centers are located here, earning for the Bay Area a reputation as a high-tech industry area in the world. It is the center of the world, the birthplace of high technology and the incubator of bio-engineering. The Bay Area has more pioneering biotechnology and high-tech companies than the rest of the United States. More recently, San Francisco Bay Area has also been regarded as the leading US communications and multimedia center.

San Francisco Bay Area is also recognized as having high-quality human resources. Its labor force is the most skilled and most highly educated in the United States. The bay area not only leads in the fields of engineering technology, mathematics and natural sciences but also has the top graduate programs in social sciences and humanities. The creative and intelligent graduates from these colleges and universities have formed a huge talent pool for the bay area (Figure 2).

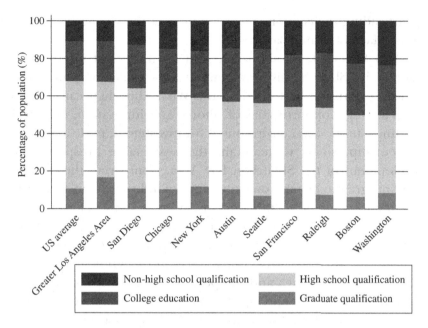

Figure 2. Education levels of San Francisco residents.

Source: "Economic Evaluation Report of San Francisco Bay Area", "San Francisco Bay Area Economic Commission Report" (October 2012).

II. Lessons Learned and Other Revelations upon Examining the Experiences of the World's Three Great Bay Areas for the Development of the Guangdong–Hong Kong–Macao Greater Bay Area

For convenience, we shall "downsize" the Guangdong–Hong Kong–Macao Greater Bay Area by focusing on the Shenzhen Bay Area and proceed to discuss what lessons we could learn or what revelations we could discover by studying the three major bay areas of the world. There are two reasons for doing so: first, in the integration of Guangdong, Hong Kong, Macao into the Greater Bay Area, the integration of Shenzhen and Hong Kong represents the main thrust of the "merger"; second, from the perspective of economic development trends, Shenzhen is likely to become the leader in spearheading the economic development of the Guangdong–Hong Kong–Macao Greater Bay Area.

As a Special Economic Zone and an important international trading city, Shenzhen is now at an advanced stage of reform, continuous expansion and opening up. What Shenzhen can do is to grasp strategic opportunities of reform and innovation, constantly creating a more open environment for investment, trade and entrepreneurship, so as to maintain the sustainable prosperity and development of the Shenzhen Bay Area. Comparing the development progress and common experience of industrial transformation and development of the three major bay areas and specifically learning from the characteristic features and advantages of the world's developed bay area economies, including the headquarters economy of New York Bay Area, the science and technology finance of San Francisco Bay Area and the port economy of Tokyo Bay Area, Shenzhen could refer and tap into the said experiences of the three bay areas for the future development of its bay area.

(A) *For industrial upgrading and transformation development*

It can be seen from the successful development of the three bay areas that the key elements of economic development in most bay areas are high-tech, service-oriented manufacturing, high-end development, the promotion of the strategy of developing cultural industries and the development of production and modern services. At the same time, the transformation of the mode of corporate and enterprise production and the private economy and non-profit sectors also play an important role toward their success.

(1) *What experiences could we learn from an industry-led and industry-driven model of economic transformation for the Greater Bay Area economy*

There are generally three pathways for the evolution of the industry-led and industry-driven economic model of the bay areas, described as follows:

Pathway 1: Structural upgrading as the driving force

In this pathway, the successful transformation is affected by promoting and driving upscaling or upgrading of industries. This is done by taking appropriate measures to encourage the extension of the production chain by upgrading the traditional model of industrial production.

Pathway 2: Fostering technological innovations

Steps are taken to promote and encourage industries with comparative strengths and advantages toward technological advances and innovation to bring about the transformation driven by the upgrading of industrial capacities.

Pathway 3: Transformation driven by emerging industries

This transformation is achieved by introducing new ideas and discarding obsolete ones and by "taking another road or making new approaches" by encouraging and supporting the development of emerging industries to lead and drive the economy.

(2) *Revelations and lessons learned from the economic model of the bay area that is jointly driven by industrial and spatial transformations*

Through the case studies of economic development in the bay areas, it can be discovered that the simultaneous optimization of the spatial layout and transformation plays a decisive role in the urban development of the bay area economy. In the evolution process of the economic model of the bay areas, the synchronous optimization of industrial and spatial layouts and that of the location of industries — in consideration of the economic development — have become the key factors. There are two lessons to be learned from the evolution process of such an economic model: (1) industrial transformation should be conducted concomitantly — via adjustments — with spatial transformation.

(2) The other lesson is the need for industrial and urban transformations when adjusting for urban spatial structures.

(3) *Lessons to be learned: Bay area economic model led by urban government strategic planning*

During the economic evolution of the world-renowned bay areas, besides spatial and industrial transformations, governmental strategic planning plays a decisive and fundamental role. For example, Tokyo and New York formulated realistic urban strategic plans in the early stages of their bay area economic developments. They determined the progressive objectives of urban transformation and development, thus providing macropolicy and institutional assurance for the full and mature development of the bay area economy.

(B) *For promoting the innovation of science and technology finance*

The main corpus or subject of the financial environment in the San Francisco Bay Area is the developed venture capital investment, which integrates financial capital with new and high-tech industries, providing the necessary financial resources for the economic and industrial development of the bay area. The well-developed scientific and technological financial system also gives necessary and sufficient financial assurance to the high-tech and innovative technology industries in Silicon Valley. Relatively speaking, the Shenzhen Bay Area needs to constantly "renew" its industrial structure, upgrade traditional industries and raise the levels of high-tech manufacturing in its industries. A sound scientific and technological financial system is therefore indispensable. For the integration of science, technology and finance, Shenzhen could learn from the following experiences:

(1) *Innovation incubators and angel investment model*

Generally, venture capital investments encompass three stages in the development of high-tech enterprises: seeding stage (for

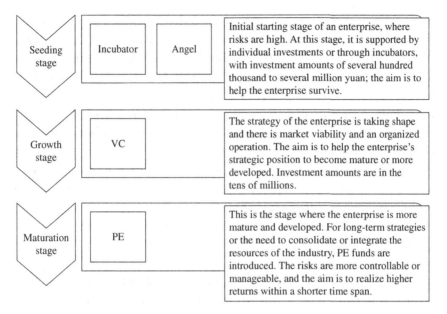

Figure 3. Categories of investment for start-up venture capital investment and the three phases/stages.

newly established enterprises or start-ups), growth stage and maturation stage. The corresponding types of venture capital are angel investment, VC venture capital investment and PE private funds (Figure 3).

The service organization specializing in science and technology entrepreneurship is the incubator. It helps to reduce the cost of the entrepreneurship and improves the efficiency by providing production, R&D and infrastructure services for start-ups. Depending on the different, actual leading institutions, this incubator organization can generally be divided into government-led (business-oriented), research institutes-integrated and independent enterprise categories.

At present, Shenzhen's government-led incubator, also known as science and technology entrepreneurship service center, is mainly tasked with giving support to small and medium-sized science and technology enterprises. It aims to cultivate an entrepreneurial atmosphere in the region and assumes the functions of publicizing policies, coordinating enterprise research and information communication. It is administratively subordinate to the regional science and technology bureaus and adopts the organizational model of public institutions. The infrastructural capital of enterprise incubators, daily operating expenses and incubation funds are allocated by the treasury; however, this single source of funds limits the further development of business incubators.

In the seeding phase, the common denominator of the incubator model and angel investment is that the acquisition of the enterprise ownership is not the investment purpose of both. The main objective is to expand and grow the enterprise through services and investment and to withdraw through appropriate ways — after realizing returns on the investment. Therefore, the mode of operation of the business incubator should be to be able to attract angel investment institutions through preferential policies. Angel investments and incubators are each independent under this mode. The bay area uses incubators as a medium to establish a platform for cooperation between start-ups and angel investment institutions in order to promote and attract diversified sources of funding. Through the collaborative development of angel investment and business incubators, the risks faced by the angel investment can be reduced and the investment functions of the incubator can be enhanced.

(2) *Encouraging scientific and tech enterprises to be proactive in carrying out financial innovation*

The capacity of the bay area is to create wealth while being relatively strong. There is therefore good and dependable financial support from venture capital in the bay area. The production efficiency of high-tech industries in the bay area is the highest among all economic sectors, and this fact allows a large number of households (families) and enterprises to accumulate wealth through scientific and technological practitioners and enterprises in the bay area. Additionally, high-tech industries possess strong risk tolerance and strong investment demands and can be taken as a reliable and "natural" source of venture capital. An illustration: high-tech enterprises represented by Intel have set up venture capital institutions by virtue of their management ability, knowledge and skills, which in turn stimulate and enrich the venture capital industry. Science and technology companies from Shenzhen should take the cue and take the initiative to delve into the financial sector, and the government can also give guidance and incentives in this regard.

(3) *Establishing specialist science–technology banks*

Innovative high-tech enterprises are high-risk enterprises, and science and technology banks could become the chief provider of financial services to these high-tech enterprises and venture capital. San Francisco Silicon Valley Bank is representative of the science and technology banks providing credit services for start-ups and venture capital. With its capital advantages, it has also become a shareholder or partner of venture capital. It has established closer ties with the venture capital industry, strengthened investment cooperation and forged a common development and effective "coalition", sharing profits and information with the said venture capital industry.

On August 2012, SPD Silicon Valley Bank, which focused on serving science and technology innovation industries, was established in Shanghai. It was the first science and technology bank with independent legal (juridical) person status approved since 2007. Silicon Valley Bank Co. Ltd. and Shanghai Pudong Development Bank Co. Ltd., were the two major shareholders, each holding 50% of the equities of SPD Silicon Valley Bank. The function of science and technology banks includes offering venture loans and collecting interest in the early stage of enterprise establishment, acquiring part of the enterprises' options or warrants according to agreement, and then exercising specific options when the enterprise is acquired or listed, or selling equities to obtain prior returns.

In view of the fact that the finance and banking sectors of the Shenzhen Bay Area are more established, we would suggest that

Shenzhen form its science and technology bank to facilitate the marriage between finance and tech industries.

(4) *Establishing Shenzhen's version of SBIC*

The San Francisco government has strongly and actively supported the venture capital industry, and it has created a good development environment to provide for start-ups. For the purpose of industrialization and encouraging high-tech development, the government has come up with a series of policies and laws to foster the development of the venture capital industry, including preferential tax rate on profit of venture capital, establishing the small business investment company system (SBIC) and giving access to institutional investors. These steps have markedly improved the development environment of the venture capital industry.

Shenzhen municipal government can learn from some of San Francisco's practices, specifically including:

(i)   *Promoting an atmosphere conducive to venture capital.* We can set up pilot funds for venture capital specifically for small and medium-sized technological enterprises at the municipal level, encourage "social capital" to set up venture capital companies, venture capital management companies, etc. — all within the Shenzhen Bay Area. We should encourage domestic and foreign venture capital companies to use their private capital to set up venture capital institutions and equity investment companies and implement preferential taxation to encourage the further development of venture capital.

(ii) *Establishing the Shenzhen version of SBIC.* Shenzhen SME Service Department could establish SME investment companies in the form of public–private partnership with various investment institutions, including private investors, pension funds and banks to establish Shenzhen's own SBIC. This SBIC shall carry out venture capital investments for small and medium-sized high-tech enterprises (Figure 4).

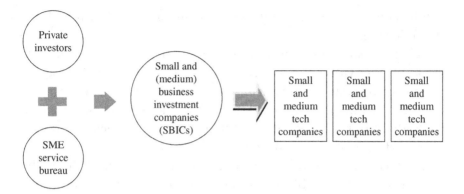

Figure 4. The SBIC model of investment.

(C) *For the strategy of headquarters economy development*

The development of the headquarters economy of New York Bay Area is at the forefront of the world. Some of its established development experiences can provide some reference for how we expand the headquarters economy for Shenzhen Bay Area.

(1) *Improving urban infrastructure and the central business district environment*

Good infrastructure and a conducive central business district (CBD) environment in New York are important conditions for attracting headquarters economy. Manhattan is the CBD of New York City, with a total area of 57.91 square kilometers. Manhattan's CBD spans old and midtown Manhattan Island. The famous blocks are Greenwich Street and Fifth Avenue. On Wall Street, which is less than 1.54 kilometers long and which covers an area of less than 1 square kilometer, over a hundred large companies' headquarters, dozens of exchanges, insurance companies and big banks are gathered. As a financial CBD area, it provides hundreds of thousands of jobs, and this area has the highest employment density in the world.

To attract more enterprises to move their headquarters to Shenzhen, we need to improve the CBD environment. The government should continue to strive to create a more beautiful, clean, comfortable and conducive living environment, which can include the following:

First, we should establish and improve the internal traffic network of the CBD, the pedestrian traffic system, and make it pedestrian-friendly by enhancing the "walking experience" within the CBD. In addition, we should strengthen the connectivity between the pedestrian traffic system and public transport — such as the subways and bus stations. More attention should be paid to the hierarchical or categorized planning and construction of the highway transport in the CBD, so as to ensure the smooth flow of traffic in the main internal roads and the urban network of expressways.

Second, efforts should be made to diversify the functions of the CBD. Facilities such as exhibition halls, business hotels and high-end entertainment venues are to be introduced in the CBD to meet the business needs of corporate or enterprise headquarters and the personal needs of employees in order to ensure the vitality of the CBD.

Third, an ecological community should be established. The existence of an ecological community in the periphery of CBD will gradually create a natural, clean, comfortable and healthy living environment.

Fourth, the construction of an urban transport system must be properly planned and effective implementation should be ensured. The traffic and transport systems of intelligent cities must be developed in a stepwise and progressive manner, and the management and construction of the transport system should be strengthened.

(2) *Improving the supporting services of authentication, certification, verification, accreditation, etc., and personnel packages required for the development of headquarters enterprises*

First, we should implement "green channel or passageway" for headquarters enterprises and we must perform a good job in serving enterprises headquartered in Shenzhen. For the headquarters enterprises stationed, the "green channel" system is to be formulated and implemented by the government's management agencies. The headquarters enterprises are identified, welcomed and recognized by the government as such. Procedures are simplified, the "green card" certificates issued and the headquarters enterprises assisted in handling various approval, certification and verification procedures and various preferential and incentive policies should be introduced to make them feel welcome. We would propose setting up special service organizations for enterprises headquartered in Shenzhen, providing regular door-to-door service to assist enterprises in solving their existing problems.

The second aspect is to increase the pace for the training, introduction and exchange of personnel in headquarters enterprises. We will speed up the training and recruitment of senior project management personnel and international business personnel commensurate with the characteristics of the headquarters economy and industries, as well as helping to train and bring in specialized professionals in accounting, auditing, law, consultation, exhibition, planning, real estate, networking and other fields, so as to better serve the construction of the headquarters economy. Help will be provided to corporations/enterprises to familiarize themselves with Shenzhen's environment, establish personal networking and business relationships, contacting colleges and universities and providing training for their employees if necessary. Additionally, relevant policies should be formulated to facilitate the entry, residence and travel into Hong Kong, Macao and Taiwan to expedite procedures for senior managers in Shenzhen headquarters and to strengthen economic and trade ties with personnel from other areas.

(3) *Establishing and optimizing a fair and just legal system and environment*

Shenzhen Bay Area should learn from the legal systems and environment of the advanced bay areas. It should speed up the process of integration with international laws and regulations and management, so as to become a stalwart of globalization, standardization and specifications by providing a unified and fair legal environment for the headquarters of multinational corporations to implement their global competition and development strategies. Laws and regulations should be reviewed and modified if found to be in conflict with WTO rules or regulations of international management. We should also strengthen the enforcement and protection of intellectual property rights, encourage headquarters to speed up technological innovation and transformation of achievements and set up intellectual property protection consultation, rights protection and specialist property rights trading institutions specifically serving the headquarters. In addition, we should continue to broaden the investment areas of private enterprises in Shenzhen, simplifying the application, verification and approval procedures for stationing the headquarters of private enterprises. We must also strengthen the protection of the legitimate interests of private enterprises, giving them equal treatment as with other enterprises in investment and financing, taxation, land use, foreign trade and export, and gradually removing discriminatory and unreasonable legal and institutional red tape against private enterprises. This is to ensure fairness and to maintain the stable development of the private enterprises in Shenzhen. Relevant departments also need to further strengthen the complaint management of investment enterprises in Shenzhen, and they must listen regularly to their problems — reflected during the process of application, verification and approval, establishment, production and operation of the enterprises. The concept and idea of "service" must be appreciated and understood; improving services includes strictly prohibiting administrative law enforcement departments from "delegating" part of their power to intermediary agencies such as to levy or impose compulsory charges or illegal fees.

(D) *For port economy development in the Greater Bay Area*

After more than 30 years of development, Shenzhen's port industry has made considerable progress, but there are still disparities compared to the ports of Tokyo Bay Area. Learning from the development experiences of Tokyo Bay Area will enhance further development of Shenzhen Port.

(1) *Strengthening the coordinated development of port clusters within the Greater Bay Area and realizing intensive development*

We need to implement and promote seamless collaboration among major ports, accelerate the planning and construction of infrastructure and engineering works, carry out and optimize supporting projects, port management and logistics service network mechanisms. We have to optimize the allocation of port resources, development of ports, create advantages for agglomeration of ports and develop intensive production shorelines with ports, industries and warehouses. Government departments could introduce special controls to prevent vicious competition and to avoid duplication of construction as far as possible. In this way, the ports within the Greater Bay Area will possess their own characteristics, thus realizing differential competition and staggered and complementary development. Cooperation between the ports brings about obvious benefits to all parties involved, which may include increasing the rate of returns on port investment, expanding the economic scale of the ports, reducing the operating costs and increasing the profitability of the ports. Other benefits include coordinating port utilization, thus stabilizing port operation; accelerating the development and transfer of technology, thus improving the efficiency of use; jointly investing in equipment and other services, such as communication, staff training and inland warehousing services. Other important services include marketing, transportation links, financing, software development and maintenance, stocks, supply and so on. The aforementioned collaborations serve to reduce risks and improve service quality in overall port operations.

(2) *The development of bay area port clusters requires the dilution of the administrative divisions of the government*

The development of the bay area port groups or clusters is not solely for the benefit of each port but also for the objective of allowing the bay area to adapt to the competition of international shipping and freight markets. In this regard, each of the ports from the clusters will have to play its specific role. In the integration of port resources among major regional ports in the world, the advantages of the geographical location and industrial agglomeration play an obviously pivotal role. The development of the port economy needs to overcome or circumvent the restrictions of regional administrative demarcations: this is important in order to coordinate development with the natural attributes and economic "rhythms" of port groups, to integrate port resources in market competition, to consolidate the leading status of hub ports and to enable small or non-major ports and feeder ports to play their auxiliary roles. We need to formulate and improve coastline utilization and port cluster development planning and further strengthen the division of labor within port groups. We seek to promote the coordinated development of the ports as a whole and to form economies of scale while complementing each other.

(3) *The scientific development of regional port groups (clusters) requires establishing an appropriate and sound or effective organization and management model*

We can explore the establishment of a Guangdong, Hong Kong and Macao Port Authority to manage the coordinated development of port clusters within the Greater Bay Area. The premise the establishment of this institution is that the collaborating parties must internalize the concept of the "win–win situation and mutual benefit". This concept replaces confrontation with cooperation, proprietary intentions with willingness to share, and rigid and fierce competition with flexible accommodation. On this basis, a slowly evolving and expanding community of common and shared interests will be created. This "community of shared interests" needs to work at attaining the common long-term interests of all parties involved in the cooperation; they shall have to take this community as the meeting point to transform external antagonism into the exchange of mutual interests within the community. The New York–New Jersey Port Authority of the United States belongs to such interested community organizations, at least to a certain extent.

(4) *Developing aggressively a diversified seaport economy with high-level industries*

Comparing the diversified port economy of the Tokyo Bay with Shenzhen Bay, it is incumbent upon Shenzhen Port to learn from the development experience of Tokyo Port. By taking advantage of the structural transformations in land, sea and aviation developments, Shenzhen should take an aggressive and vigorous stance in developing its multifarious port economy in areas such as international trade, port logistics and ocean shipping. It also needs to further enhance its international transit capacity as well as strengthen its status as an international container hub port. Additionally, Shenzhen Port should attempt to accelerate the development of supply chain management, cross-border e-commerce and other new businesses and develop R&D outsourcing, software outsourcing, data services and others. It must also strengthen its trade control functions and work toward "exporting" more capital, management, services and technology.

III. Comparing the Industry Competitiveness of the World's Three Great Bay Areas with the Guangdong–Hong Kong–Macao Greater Bay Area

Industry competitiveness otherwise known as International Industry Competitiveness, refers to the competitiveness of a particular industry in one country or region relative to the same industry in other countries or regions in terms of production efficiency, capability of meeting market demands, sustained profitability and so on. The following is an index or indicator evaluation system set up from various sectors or domains and perspectives both at home and abroad to systematically analyze the overall position of the Guangdong–Hong Kong–Macao Greater

Bay Area in the development of industrial competitiveness in the frontline domains at home and abroad.

(A) *Comparing industry competitiveness with typical foreign bay areas*

In accordance with the overall policy direction of the economy of the Guangdong–Hong Kong–Macao Greater Bay Area, the focus of economic construction of the Greater Bay Area is to cooperate with Hong Kong and Macao to build the Guangdong–Hong Kong–Macao Greater Bay Area. It is upon this basis that the industrial competitiveness of the Greater Bay Area and other internationally renowned bay areas is compared.

(1) *Comparing the occupied land area: The Greater Bay Area of Guangdong, Hong Kong, Macao is the largest and Tokyo Bay Area is the smallest*

The area of New York Bay Area is 21,481 square kilometers and that of San Francisco Bay Area is 17,932 square kilometers. Tokyo Bay Area has the smallest land area at 13,548 square kilometers. In comparison, the Guangdong–Hong Kong–Macao Greater Bay Area has the largest land area of 56,500 square kilometers (Figure 5).

(2) *Gross domestic product (GDP): Tokyo Bay Area has the largest GDP, while San Francisco Bay Area has the smallest*

However, the rate of increase of GDP is fastest in the Greater Bay Area of Guangdong, Hong Kong and Macao.

GDP is the best indicator of a country's economic situation. The bay area with the largest GDP is Tokyo Bay Area, while the smallest is San Francisco Bay Area. On GDP growth, the growth rate of Guangdong, Hong Kong and Macao is the highest, while that of Tokyo Bay Area is the lowest — in fact, it is showing negative growth.

Unit: Square Km

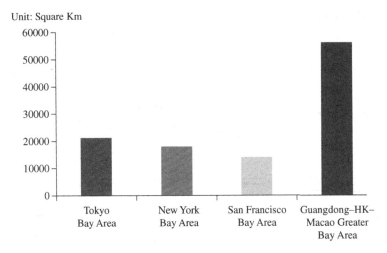

Figure 5. Comparing the land areas of the four bay areas.

Tokyo Bay Area has the largest share of national GDP and San Francisco had the smallest; Tokyo Bay Area has the highest GDP density or concentration and San Francisco Bay Area has the lowest. Tokyo, New York and San Francisco Bays are relatively close to each other in terms of GDP per capita, while the corresponding values for the Guangdong–Hong Kong–Macao Greater Bay Area are relatively small, but the GDP growth rate is relatively large. In terms of GDP per square kilometer and the rate of GDP growth, the Greater Bay Area of Guangdong, Hong Kong and Macao ranks 1st. From these indicators, we would conclude that the Guangdong–Hong Kong–Macao Greater Bay Area belongs to the emerging Bay Area economy. The Greater Bay Area is at the stage of rapid growth, but its economic strength is relatively weak though.

The GDP of Tokyo Bay Area is the largest of the four bay areas. In 2012, the GDP of Tokyo Bay Area was US$1987.6 billion. In terms of the share or proportion of the total GDP in each bay area, Tokyo's GDP accounted for 58% of the total, while Kanagawa, Chiba and Saitama prefectures accounted for 18%, 12% and 12%, respectively.

Unit: US$100 million

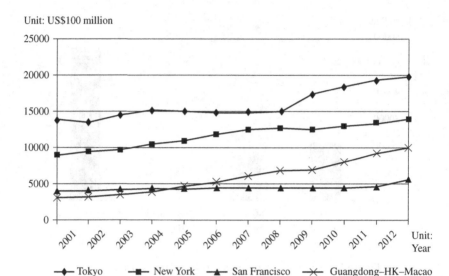

Figure 6. Comparing the GDPs of the four bay areas.

The GDP of New York Bay Area is second only to that of Tokyo Bay Area. In 2012, New York Bay Area GDP was US$1358.4 billion, i.e. 68.34% that of Tokyo Bay Area GDP.

The GDP of San Francisco Bay Area is far behind that of Tokyo and New York Bay Areas. In 2012, the GDP of San Francisco Bay Area was US$556.4 billion. By the composition of the Bay Area GDP, the GDP of the San Francisco–Oakland–Hayward metropolitan statistical area was US$360.4 billion, accounting for 64.77% of that of the total Bay Area, and this is the core component of the Bay Area economy. Compared with the Tokyo and New York Bay Areas, the GDP of San Francisco Bay Area was only 27.99% and 40.96%, respectively (Figure 6).

Before 2005, the GDP of the Guangdong–Hong Kong–Macao Greater Bay Area was close to that of San Francisco Bay Area, but it soon surpassed it, ranking 3rd. In 2012, the GDP of the Guangdong–Hong Kong–Macao Greater Bay Area was US$1009.5 billion. Therefore, catching up with and surpassing New York Bay Area could be regarded as the short-term objective of economic growth of the Guangdong–Hong Kong–Macao Greater Bay Area, while catching up with Tokyo Bay Area may be regarded as its long-term objective.

(3) *Comparison of industrial structure: New York Bay Area has the highest degree of industrial upgrading and advance, while the Guangdong–Hong Kong–Macao Greater Bay Area has the lowest*

Within a country or region, at different stages of economic development and points of the development timeline, the industrial sectors constituting the national economy will be different, and their contributions to economic growth would also differ. Hence, use could be made of certain industrial structure indicators to gauge the economic development stage of a country and region. Generally speaking, the GDPs of the four major bay areas mainly comprise tertiary industries. The proportion of the value added of the tertiary industries is more than 75%, across the board while the proportion of the value added for the primary industry is very small (Figure 7).

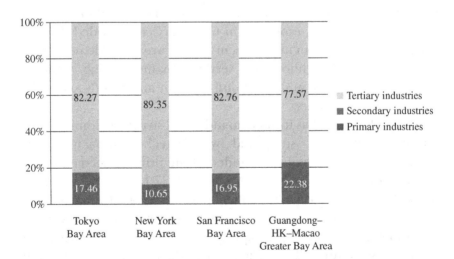

Figure 7. Proportion of value added for various industries in the four great bay areas for the Year 2012.

Among the four bay areas, New York Bay Area has the largest proportion of tertiary industries. In 2012, the proportions of value added of the primary, secondary and tertiary industries in the New York Bay Area were in the ratio of 0:10.65:89.35. The New York Bay Area was the earliest area to initiate the industrial revolution among the four bay areas, and its industrial revolution process was completed by the early 20th century. Since then, the bay area's industrial structure continued to undergo adjustments and upgrading. By the second half of the 20th century, the service industries became the main driving force of economic development. Of these industries, real estate, finance, insurance, professional and technological services, health and medical care, and wholesale and retail are the most important industries in New York Bay Area.

San Francisco Bay Area is dominated by service industries, but the high-tech manufacturing industry does play an important role as well. In 2012, the proportions of value added for the primary, secondary and tertiary industries in San Francisco Bay Area were 0.28:16.95:82.76. In the 1980s and 1990s, the main driving force behind economic growth was the development and manufacture of computer hardware. By the late 1990s, the momentum shifted to greater dependence on the provision of services rather than the production of goods, especially in many services provided through the Internet. The main industries in the bay area include real estate, professional and technological services, manufacturing, financial insurance, wholesale and retail, information and health and medical care, among others.

Tokyo Bay Area has formed an industrial structure dominated by tertiary industries — supported by high-tech manufacturing. In 2012, the proportions of value added of the primary, secondary and tertiary industries in Tokyo Bay Area were 0.27:17.46:82.27. After the Second World War, Tokyo, Yokohama, Kawasaki and Chiba in Tokyo Bay Area developed robustly in heavy industries, propelling rapid economic growth through export trade. After the oil crisis, the industrial structure of Tokyo Bay Area gradually shifted from capital-intensive industries to technology-intensive industries. High-tech industries and service industries have become the main driving force of the bay area economy. Into the new millennium, the economy of the bay area mainly consisted of service industries, wholesale and retail, manufacturing, real estate, finance and insurance industries. From 2001 to 2010, the proportion of value added for the manufacturing industry showed a downward trend, from 17% to 13%, while that for the real estate industry, communication industry and service industry was on the rise. The financial and insurance industry remained relatively stable, accounting for 8–10% of the value added of the industries.

The proportion of the secondary industries in the Greater Bay Area of Guangdong, Hong Kong and Macao is comparatively large, and this fact reflects obvious regionalization characteristics. In 2012, the proportions of value added for the primary, secondary and tertiary industries in the Greater Bay Area were 0.04:22.38:77.57. Relatively speaking, the proportion of the secondary industries is larger than that of tertiary industries. This is mainly because Shenzhen's secondary industry has a large proportion of value added (44.3%), and the tertiary industry has a relatively small proportion of value added (55.6%). There are obvious differences within the industrial structures of the Guangdong–Hong Kong–Macao Greater Bay Area, which is due to the difference of comparative advantages between Hong Kong and Shenzhen. Since the onset of the reform and opening-up — spanning 40 years — Shenzhen's economic growth has been largely spurred by a huge number of exports of manufactured products. The proportion of value added of secondary industry in GDP has been more than 50%, followed by the financial industry, wholesale and retail and real estate industries. Hong Kong, with its unique geopolitical location and comparative advantages, developed very strong import and export trade services, transportation and warehousing industries, as well as financial, insurance and information industries in a free investment environment.

Regarding major industries, the industrial structures of the New York, San Francisco and Tokyo Bay Areas are comparatively similar, while the industrial structure of the Guangdong–Hong Kong–Macao Greater Bay Area has obvious industrialization and regional

Table 2.   Main industries of the four bay areas.

Bay Area	Main Industries
New York Bay Area	Real Estate, Finance and Insurance, Professional and Technological Services, Health and Medical Care, Wholesale and Retail
San Francisco Bay Area	Real Estate, Professional and Technological Services, Manufacturing Industry, Finance and Insurance, Wholesale and Retail, Information Services and Health Care
Tokyo Bay Area	Services, Wholesale and Retail, Real Estate, Manufacturing, Finance and Insurance and Communication Media
Guangdong–HK–Macao Greater Bay Area	Industrialization, Import and Export Trade, Finance, Wholesale and Retail, Real Estate, Transportation, Warehousing and Mail, Information Transmission, Computer Services and Software

Sources: US Bureau of Labor Statistics, US Department of Commerce, Bay Area Association, Bay Area Census, Cabinet Office of Japan, Shenzhen Bureau of Statistics and Hong Kong Bureau of Statistics.

characteristics (Table 2). The difference in the industrial structure reflects the different stages of economic development and different developmental modes. The New York, San Francisco and Tokyo Bay Areas, each having undergone industrial transfer and upgradation in their industrial structure, have completed the industrial development stage during which the manufacturing industry was the main driving force for growth, and their current industrial structure has become more and more "mature". Their economic development is now mainly driven by real estate, financial services, high-tech industries and wholesale and retail industries. The most important industries in the Greater Bay Area of Guangdong, Hong Kong and Macao are industrialization (industrials) and import–export trade. In Shenzhen, the main industry is industrialization while Hong Kong's import and export trade services represent its most important industry.

(4) *Comparison of labor quality: San Francisco Bay Area
has the highest level of education for its labor force*

The San Francisco Bay is one of the most "highly educated" areas in the United States, second only to North Carolina, Boston and Washington. In San Francisco Bay Area, 46% of the labor force has undergraduate degrees (bachelor degree) or above; this figure was 42% in New York Bay Area and 28% for US national on average. We can see that with such high-quality labor, San Francisco Bay Area has great advantages. This advantage stems from two factors as follows:

First, the high concentration of venture capital in San Francisco Bay Area. In the late 1990s, more than 30% of venture capital investment in the United States was in San Francisco Bay Area, and it has now risen to more than 40%. The concentration of the venture capital drives the development of technology-intensive industries and increases the demand for quality, highly educated, scientific and technological personnel. Second, both public and private research institutes in the bay area have stepped up their investment in R&D, creating a greater demand for well-educated people (Figure 8).

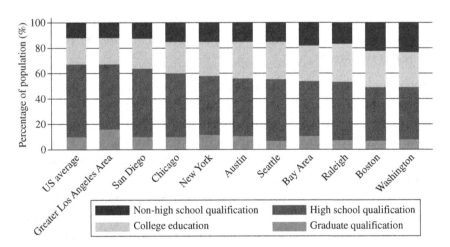

Figure 8. Educational levels of employees of US metropolitan statistical areas.

Source: "San Francisco Bay Area Regional Economic Assessment Report", "San Francisco Bay Area Council Economic Institute Report" (October 2012).

Table 3. Distribution of the top 100 universities in the four great bay areas, 2012–2013.

Bay Area	Number of Universities in the Top 100	Name of University
Guangdong–HK–Macao Bay Area	0	—
Tokyo Bay Area	1	Tokyo University
San Francisco Bay Area	3	Stanford University, University of California, Berkeley, University of California, Davis
New York Bay Area	2	New York University, Rutgers University

Source: Top 100 Universities in the World 2012–2013, published by the *Times Higher Education Supplement*.

According to the *Times Higher Education Supplement's* "Top 100 Universities in the World 2012–2013" ranking, two of the top 100 universities were located in New York Bay Area, three in San Francisco Bay Area and one in Tokyo Bay Area (Tables 3 and 4).

(5) *Comparing strengths in enterprise innovation: Tokyo Bay is the strongest, the Guangdong–Hong Kong–Macao Greater Bay Area is the weakest*

Global technology innovation companies are mainly located in the Tokyo and San Francisco Bay Areas, while the numbers of such companies in New York Bay Area and the Guangdong–Hong Kong–Macao Greater Bay Area are relatively small. According to the "Top 100 Global Innovative Enterprises (Institutions) in 2012" released by Thomson Reuters, there were, respectively, 20, 8, 1 and 0 such enterprises in the Tokyo Bay, San Francisco Bay, New York Bay and Guangdong–Hong Kong–Macao Greater Bay Area. The differences among global innovation enterprises in the four bay areas are very obvious and glaring; this situation to some extent reflects the relative strengths in the technological innovation of each bay area.

Table 4. Distribution of the world's top 100 innovative enterprises (organizations) in the four bay areas in 2012

Bay Area	Number of Such Enterprises	Name(s) of the Corporations/Enterprises
Greater Bay Area of Guangdong, HK and Macao	0	—
Tokyo Bay Area	20	Fuji Film, Fujitsu, Brothers Industrial Company, Ricoh, Canon Corporation, FANUC, Olympus, Hitachi, Honda Automobiles, JATCO, Mitsubishi Electric Co., Mitsubishi Heavy Industry Company, Shin-Etsu Chemical Industries, Sony Corporation, TDK, Toshiba, NEC, Toyota Motor Company, Nippon Steel Sumitomo Corporation, Nippon Telephone and Telegraph (NTT).
San Francisco Bay Area	8	AMD, Altera, Apple, Google, Intel, Marvell, SanDisk and Xilinx
New York Bay Area	1	Avaya

Source: Thomson Reuters' release of the "Top 100 Global Innovative Enterprises (Organizations) in 2012".

Tokyo Bay Area is an important source of innovation for the world. Innovation enterprises there focus mainly on machinery, automobiles and electronic products. Mitsubishi Heavy Industries, Toyota Motor Company, Sony and Canon are representative of the innovation enterprises and corporations.

Silicon Valley in San Francisco Bay Area is the world's center for technological innovation. Ever since the 1970s, it has become an agglomeration area for global computer and Internet companies. The most famous corporations in the world, such as Google, Apple, Intel and HP, are headquartered in the San Francisco Bay Area. In terms of the number of patents granted, San Francisco Bay Area has the most patents approved and granted in all the metropolitan statistical areas in the United States, far more than New York Bay Area and the Los Angeles Metropolitan Statistical Area. The number of patents accounted for 15.2% of all patents in the United States, which proves beyond a doubt that San Francisco Bay Area has very high technological innovation strength. The Bay Area of San Francisco is the pillar upon which American technology is leading the world.

New York Bay Area is another technological innovation center in the United States, second only to the Bay Area of San Francisco. In terms of the number of patents and the proportion of patents granted to the whole country, New York Bay Area is also a strong leader in tech innovation in the United States.

The reason why there are no enterprises listed among the Top 100 in the Greater Bay Area of Guangdong, Hong Kong and Macao is that Hong Kong's economy is dominated by services and international trade, and technology-intensive industries are not the mainstream industries in Hong Kong. Compared to the other developed areas, the innovative capacities of Shenzhen's enterprises are also in a relatively weak innovation stage. Technological innovation in Shenzhen is mainly functional innovation and innovation in external appearance, while breakthrough innovations or innovations of a fundamental nature are relatively lacking.

(6) *Size or scale of the headquarters economy: The Tokyo Bay Area is the biggest*

Bay areas are the most important and diversified business centers or headquarters for economic agglomerations in the world. Many of the biggest and fastest growing international enterprises or corporations are headquartered in the bay areas. Driven by the effects of the headquarters economy, these enterprises gradually develop into new industrial chains in areas including energy, food, clothing, consumer goods and technology. Companies in the bay areas make full use of the opportunities and advantages of the strong regional connections to constitute the wealth of the Fortune 500 that accounts for an increasing share of global GDP growth. In San Francisco Bay Area, 30 companies belong to the Fortune 500 of the United States and 10 companies belong to the Fortune 500 in the world, including the world-famous Apple, Google, Oracle, Intel and others. New York Bay Area has 18 global top 500 companies, 45 national top 500 companies, 16 of the largest Forbes-listed private companies and 24 of the fastest growing companies. Last but not least, Tokyo has 47 Fortune 500 companies too, including Toshiba, Honda and Sony corporations.

(7) *Venture capital investment volume: San Francisco Bay Area is the highest and the Guangdong–Hong Kong–Macao Greater Bay Area is the lowest*

On June 22, 2017, Shawn Randolph, President of the Economic Research Institute of San Francisco Bay Area Commission, said in the report of the Institute of Comprehensive Development and Research on "Global Innovation Growth Poles: Shenzhen and Silicon Valley" that in the past 3 years, San Francisco Bay Area absorbed 45–50% of the total investments in the United States, with a large number of venture capital located in and around San Francisco and its Bay Area, and the Boston–New York–Washington Corridors accounted for more than 40% of the global venture capital. It is evident that fostering and encouraging venture capital promotes the development and growth of science and technology innovation enterprises. It can be clearly seen that the abundant venture capital and financial system for science and technology present in San Francisco Bay Area have boosted the prosperity of the Silicon Valley. In contrast, China's per capita venture capital investment is relatively low.

Overall, the top 500 companies headquartered in Tokyo Bay Area have higher business turnovers and greater total assets than the other three bay areas, but the top 500 companies headquartered in San Francisco Bay Area have created bigger turnovers with lower total assets as represented by high-tech Internet companies such as Apple, Google and Intel. Compared with the other industries, such as communication equipment and automobile engineering, Internet companies rely much less on fixed assets, and their profit models tend to be more diversified. Advertising revenue, search engine ranking, software application sharing and even technology patents are all sources of profits for the business.

(B) Comprehensive evaluation of the competitiveness between typical foreign bay areas and the Guangdong–Hong Kong–Macao greater bay area

Using the method of quantitative comparative analysis, we discover that the four bay area economies have their own strengths in different indicators. In order to comprehensively evaluate the competitive advantages of each bay area, the following evaluation system is established to compare the Guangdong–Hong Kong–Macao Greater Bay Area with typical foreign bay areas.

(1) Design of the bay area economic evaluation system

Based on the intended function and nature of the bay area economies and the availability and comparability of combined data, the development dimensions of the bay area economies can be summed up into four systems of influence or impact, *viz* influence of scale or size, influence of benefits, influence of openness and influence of innovation. The four dimensions of evaluation are explained in Table 5.

(2) Methods of assessment/evaluation and choice of indicators

This comprehensive evaluation is conducted using the analytic hierarchy process or AHP. The analytic hierarchy process involves gathering the elements associated with the decision-making process and breaking them down into objectives, criteria, schemes and others. Based on that, the qualitative and quantitative decision-making methods are used in evaluation. The special characteristic of AHP is making use of less quantitative information to "mathematicize" the thinking process during decision-making — in light of and upon the basis of the intrinsic nature, influencing factors and their internal relations in complex decision-making problems — thereby providing a simple decision-making method for complex

Table 5. Four dimensions to evaluate the bay area economies.

Dimension to be Evaluated	Dimension Explained	Relevant Indicators
Impact of scale	This is mainly concerned with the total volume of the sizeable industrial development and the total amount or volume of the factors. Combined with the availability of data, the total scale or size of factors is mainly related to the land and population sizes.	Gross GDP of the bay areas; land size; population size; the scale or size of industries, etc., in areas under the radiation effect.
Impact (influence) of benefits	Mainly includes structural upgradation and input–output efficiency indicators.	Weightage or proportion of tertiary industries; per capita output; average land output (per square kilometer).
Influence of openness	This influence mainly includes the openness of trade and policies on the openness of the environment in the bay area.	Dependence on foreign trade; number of multinational corporations; amount of foreign capital investments obtained and so on.
Innovation influence	This mainly covers technological innovation and product R&D indicators.	R&D investment as a proportion of GDP; the number of invention patents; total exports of new products, etc.

decision-making problems with multi-objective, multi-criteria or "structure-less" characteristics. AHP is especially suited for situations where the results of decision-making are difficult to quantify directly and accurately.

Based on the above criteria of the four dimensions for the bay area economy and the availability of data, the index–indicator system for comparing the Greater Bay Area of Guangdong, Hong Kong, Macao with the three well-known bay areas is shown in Table 6.

Table 6. System of evaluation indicators for bay areas.

Variable	Indicators
X1	GDP (US$100 million)
X2	Population (in 100,000)
X3	Total occupied land area (square km)
X4	Population density (per square km)
X5	Per capita GDP (US$)
X6	GDP growth rate (%)
X7	Proportion of tertiary industries (%)
X8	Global financial center index
X9	Number of top 100 universities
X10	Number of world's top 500 companies
X11	Number of the most innovative companies of the world
X12	Number of overseas tourists (in 10,000)

(3) *Evaluation process and analysis results*

The specific steps for the Principal Component Analysis (PCA) are as follows:

(i) Standardization of raw data.
(ii) "Extracting" or "weighting" of "common factors" (or "components"). According to the Scree Plot (see Figure 9), the eigenvalues of the first three common factors are significantly larger than those of the latter ones, and the eigenvalues change steadily from the fourth common factor onward. The cumulative contribution rate of the first three common factors is 100%. Therefore, the first three common factors or components are more appropriate for "weighting".

From Tables 7–9, we can see that the GDP, total population, population density, GDP growth rate, position in the top 500 enterprises of the world and the number of most innovative enterprises have a higher load or weightage on the first common factor (component). These are the core factors for the economic development of the bay area and can be said to be

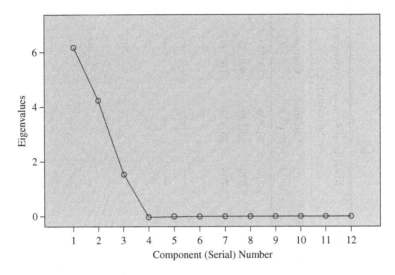

Figure 9. Scree plot of principal component analysis.

the competitive strength of the economy of the bay area. The proportion of the tertiary industry, the index of the global financial center and the number of overseas tourists have a higher load or weightage on the second common factor or component. These indicators show the peripheral competitiveness of the industrial development of the bay area, and we could say they represent the competitive potential of the economy of the bay area. Total occupied land area, per capita GDP and the number of top 100 universities have a higher weightage on the third common factor, and these indicators depict the corresponding supporting environment for the industrial development of the bay area. They contribute to the "competitive" environment of a bay area.

(iii) Computing the score of common factor: using the Common Factor Score Coefficient Matrix, the formula for each factor score is as follows:

$$F1 = 0.209X1 + 0.244X2 - 0.037X3 + 0.065X4 + 0.047X5 \\ + 0.023X6 + 0.010X7 + 0.046X8 - 0.245X9 + 0.216X10 \\ + 0.131X11 - 0.030X12$$

Table 7.   Explanatory total variance.

Component	Initial Eigenvalue			Extracting Sum of Squares and Substituting			Rotational Sum of Squares and Substituting		
	Total	Variance (%)	Cumulative (%)	Total	Variance (%)	Cumulative (%)	Total	Variance (%)	Cumulative (%)
1	6.202	51.685	51.685	6.202	51.685	51.685	4.320	35.996	35.996
2	4.249	35.409	87.095	4.249	35.409	87.095	3.976	33.129	69.125
3	1.549	12.905	100	1.549	12.905	100.00	3.705	30.875	100.00
4	0	100	100	—	—	—	—	—	—
5	0	100	100	—	—	—	—	—	—
6	0	100	100	—	—	—	—	—	—
7	0	100	100	—	—	—	—	—	—
8	0	100	100	—	—	—	—	—	—
9	0	100	100	—	—	—	—	—	—
10	0	100	100	—	—	—	—	—	—
11	0	100	100	—	—	—	—	—	—
12	0	100	100	—	—	—	—	—	—

Table 8. Rotatational component matrix.

Z score	Components		
	1	2	3
X1	0.914	0.281	0.294
X2	0.977	−0.014	−0.213
X3	−0.045	0.622	0.782
X4	0.109	−0.405	−0.908
X5	0.279	0.678	0.680
X6	−0.094	−0.268	−0.959
X7	0.055	0.879	0.474
X8	0.136	0.971	0.194
X9	−0.964	−0.035	0.264
X10	0.966	−0.042	0.253
X11	0.718	−0.426	0.551
X12	−0.173	0.956	0.236

Notes: The rotation converges after six iterations; Extraction method: Principal component analysis; Method of rotation: Orthogonal rotation with Kaiser standardization.

$$F2 = 0.061X1 + 0.069X2 + 0.053X3 + 0.061X4 + 0.107X5$$
$$+ 0.120X6 + 0.227X7 + 0.330X8 - 0.100X9 - 0.051X10$$
$$- 0.275X11 + 0.307X12$$

$$F3 = 0.008X1 - 0.139X2 + 0.185X3 - 0.292X4 + 0.112X5$$
$$- 0.335X6 - 0.010X7 - 0.154X8 + 0.171X9 + 0.064X10$$
$$+ 0.293X11 - 0.116X12$$

By substituting the values of the indicators for the four bay areas into the above equation, the scores of each factor can be computed. A comprehensive evaluation model can be constructed by using the proportions of contribution of the variances of the three common factors in the explanatory table of total variance.

$$F = 0.35996 \quad F1 + 0.33129 \quad F2 + 0.30875F3$$

Table 9.   Component score coefficient matrix.

Z score	Components		
	1	2	3
X1	0.209	0.061	0.008
X2	0.244	0.069	−0.139
X3	−0.037	0.053	0.185
X4	0.065	0.061	−0.292
X5	0.047	0.107	0.112
X6	0.023	0.120	−0.335
X7	0.010	0.227	−0.010
X8	0.046	0.330	−0.154
X9	−0.245	−0.100	0.171
X10	0.216	−0.051	0.064
X11	0.131	−0.275	0.293
X12	−0.030	0.307	−0.116

Notes: Extraction method: Principal component analysis.
Method of rotation: Orthogonal rotation with Kaiser
standardization.
Obtained scores.

By substituting the scores of each factor into the above equation, the overall scores of the four bay areas can be obtained, as shown in Table 10.

From Table 10, we can see that the overall score for competitiveness is highest in New York Bay Area. Tokyo Bay Area ranks 2nd, San Francisco Bay Area ranks 3rd and the Guangdong–Hong Kong–Macao Greater Bay Area ranks last. This result is in line with the rankings listed in the Global City Competitiveness Report (2011–2012) on the overall competitiveness of the four cities, the central cities of metropolitan areas and their industries. It shows that there is still a big gap between the competitiveness of the Guangdong–Hong Kong–Macao Greater Bay Area and that of the three international bay areas.

From the three indicators of overall competitiveness, each of the three international bay areas has their own competitive advantages.

Table 10. Comparison of the competitive strengths of the Greater Bay Area of Guangdong, Hong Kong and Macao with the world's 3 major bay areas.

	Competitive Strength	Competitive Potential	Competitive Environment	Overall Score
New York Bay Area	−0.0551	1.4990	−0.0015	0.4763
Tokyo Bay Area	1.3853	−0.4490	0.3597	0.4609
San Francisco Bay Area	−0.9760	−0.5352	1.0055	−0.2182
Greater Bay Area of Guangdong, HK and Macao	−0.3542	−0.5147	−1.3637	−0.7191

Of the four, Tokyo Bay Area has the highest competitive strength, New York Bay Area has the greatest competitive potential and San Francisco Bay Area evidently has more competitive environmental advantages.

Chapter 3

Strengths and Weaknesses of the Guangdong–Hong Kong–Macao Greater Bay Area

Cai Lingnan

Liaoning University

By comparing internationally renowned bay areas with China's domestic city clusters and agglomerations, it can be easily seen that the Greater Bay Area of Guangdong, Hong Kong and Macao is one of the regions with the highest degree of openness and the strongest economic vitality in China. The bay area's basic infrastructure facilities are comparable to those of internationally renowned bay areas, and it has the potential of becoming a world-class bay area and a world-class urban city agglomeration. However, because of the "two political systems and three tariff zones", there are obstacles to surmount in political systems, interconnection (connectivity), cross-border circulation of funds and industrial coordination — factors to be considered in planning for the coordinated development of the Guangdong–Hong Kong–Macao Greater Bay Area.

By comparing internationally renowned bay areas with China's domestic city clusters and agglomerations, it can be easily seen that the Greater Bay Area of Guangdong, Hong Kong and Macao is one of the regions with the highest degree of openness and the strongest economic vitality in China. The bay area's basic infrastructure facilities are comparable to those of internationally renowned bay areas, and it has the potential of becoming a world-class bay area and a world-class urban city agglomeration. However, because of the "two political systems and three tariff zones", there are obstacles to surmount in political systems, interconnection (connectivity), cross-border circulation of funds and industrial coordination — factors to be considered in planning for the coordinated development of the Guangdong–Hong Kong–Macao Greater Bay Area.

I. Strengths of the Greater Bay Area

The Greater Bay Area possesses unique developmental advantages. These advantages are reflected or embodied in the following eight aspects: national and local policies, institutional systems, location and hinterland, economy, industry, innovation, transportation system and international cooperation. The Greater Bay Area of Guangdong, Hong Kong and Macao has what it takes for a first-class international bay area in terms of the economy, industry, innovation and transportation system. Although the international cooperation remains at a very low level, the Greater Bay Area has greater advantages and better prospects in promoting international cooperation than other domestic city clusters such as Beijing, Tianjin and Hebei, as well as those cities of the Yangtze River Delta. Added to these advantages is the policy support at the national level, and this fact means that the conditions for the development of the Guangdong–Hong Kong–Macao Bay Area into an international first-class bay area are ripe and complete.

(A) *Policy advantages*

The Greater Bay Area of Guangdong, Hong Kong and Macao is involved and has been planned for in many national strategies. It is not only the opening gateway to the outside world but also an essential node of the "Belt and Road" Initiative, and it also contains the pilot zones of China's FTZ strategy. At the level of regional cooperation, the signing of the Closer Economic Partnership Arrangement and its supplementary agreements laid the foundation for the cooperation between Guangdong, Hong Kong and Macao. The promulgation of the "Outline of Reform and Development Plan for the Pearl River Delta Region (2008–2020)" bolstered the development of the regional economy in the Pearl River Delta, laying the foundation for the elevation of the Pearl River Delta region into the Greater Bay Area of Guangdong, Hong Kong and Macao. In addition, with the "The Pearl River Delta Framework Agreement for Regional Cooperation", the vast hinterland becomes available for the Guangdong–Hong Kong–Macao Greater Bay Area. This expands the "range" of the Greater Bay Area.

(1) *National strategy*

The Guangdong–Hong Kong–Macao Greater Bay Area strategy

Since 2008, policies on cooperation and development between Guangdong, Hong Kong and Macao have been successively introduced, propelling cooperation and development between Guangdong, Hong Kong and Macao. This is a shift from the strategy of developing the Pearl River Delta regional to that of the Guangdong–Hong Kong–Macao Greater Bay Area, a shift from local strategy to national strategy.

In March 2017, Premier Li Keqiang made the Report on the Work of the Government at the National "Two Sessions" (NPC and CPPCC). When discussing the issues of the Hong Kong and Macao area, he formally put forward the idea of the "Greater Bay Area of Guangdong, Hong Kong and Macao" and asked the Guangdong Provincial Government to study, compile and come up with the "Plans for the Development of City Clusters in the Guangdong–Hong Kong–Macao Greater Bay Area", with the objective of making full use of the unique advantages of the three places, enhancing the role of Guangdong, Hong Kong and Macao in leading China's economic development and strengthening the position and status of the three places in playing an important role in the master plan of China's opening to the outside world. At the same time, the NPC and CPPCC of 2017 formally made the development program of the Guangdong–Hong Kong–Macao Greater Bay Area the top priority of the Central Government, thus elevating it from a regional economic development strategy to a national strategy.

In October 2017, in his report at the 19th National Congress of the CPC, General Secretary Xi Jinping pointed out that "we shall support Hong Kong and Macao in integrating into the overall situation of national development, focus on the construction of the Greater Bay Area of Guangdong, Hong Kong and Macao, the cooperation between Guangdong, Hong Kong and Macao, and the Pan-Pearl River Delta; we need to promote comprehensively the mutually beneficial cooperation between the Mainland, Hong Kong and Macao, and we should also formulate and improve policies to facilitate the business development of Hong Kong and Macao residents in the Mainland." Thus, the development orientation and directions of the Guangdong–Hong Kong–Macao Greater Bay Area were defined. In March 2018, Premier Li Keqiang, in his government work report, incorporated "the implementation of the development plan for the Greater Bay Area of Guangdong, Hong Kong and Macao, and the comprehensive promotion of mutually beneficial cooperation between the Mainland and Hong Kong and Macao" into the work proposals of the government in 2018. This action therefore laid the foundation for the launch of the "Development Plan for the City Clusters of the Greater Bay Area of Guangdong, Hong Kong and Macao".

Currently, the Guangdong Provincial Government is paying close attention to the study of the "Development Plan for the Greater Bay Area of Guangdong, Hong Kong and Macao", which defines the target orientation, development direction and key tasks of the Greater Bay Area. The establishment and development of the Guangdong–Hong Kong–Macao Greater Bay Area will gain support from the Central Government to local governments, as more and more supporting policies for the development of the Greater Bay Area are further introduced.

Strategy of opening to the outside world

Whether it is the 19th National Congress of the CPC or the Report on the Work of the Government in 2018, creating a new landscape in all-around opening-up is the main objective of China's opening-up strategy in the next phase of its development process. Since China's reform and opening-up, special economic zones have been established in Shenzhen, Zhuhai and Shantou of Guangdong Province, Xiamen of Fujian Province and Hainan Province, among which Shenzhen and Zhuhai are the core cities of the Greater Bay Area of Guangdong, Hong Kong and Macao, and these cities are tasked with the mission of opening the windows to the outside world. The Pearl River Delta has always been a "showcase" area of opening-up along the eastern coast of China. The establishment of the Greater Bay of Guangdong, Hong Kong, Macao and the construction of Xiongan New Area are conducive to the formation of a new pattern or situation of regional economic developments whereupon for the North there is the opening up of Xiongan New Area; in the Central region there is the Yangtze River Economic Zone and in the South we have the Guangdong–Hong Kong–Macao Greater Bay Area. This situation would thus drive the accelerated development of South China and provides a strong support for an upgraded "version" of China's economy.

Free trade zone strategy

China's pilot free trade zone (FTZ) is an important strategic measure — adopted in the light of the new economic situations, in its comprehensive and overall opening up to the outside world — and the Central Government has placed high hopes on it, as this strategic measure carries an important historical mission. The establishment of the third group of pilot FTZs will expand the opening-up areas from coastal areas to inland areas, forming a new pattern of all-round and high-level opening up to the outside world within the framework of "1 + 3 + 7" pilot FTZs. The overall coordination of eastern, central and western regions — encompassing land and sea — should bolster the reform and opening-up of the pilot FTZs from "getting in together" to a "flying geese formation". In 2018, the establishment of China's Pilot FTZ in Hainan further stepped up the pace of China's comprehensive opening up.

The Greater Bay Area of Guangdong, Hong Kong and Macao includes Guangdong Pilot FTZ. The national policies introduced to support these pilot FTZs can be gradually replicated and extended to other areas of Guangdong, Hong Kong and Macao. The results of institutional innovation of the Guangdong Pilot FTZ can also be replicated and promoted in the Guangdong–Hong Kong–Macao Greater Bay Area.

The "Belt and Road" Initiative

Since China's economy entered the "new normal" phase, structural problems such as industrial overcapacity need to be resolved. International political and economic situations have also undergone tremendous changes. High-level international economic and trade bodies, such as TISA, TPP (now defunct) and TTIP (with their high standards, strict rules and trade regulations), have hampered China's economic development, and the forces against globalization have reared their ugly heads again. Against this background of political and economic situations at home and abroad, the CPC Central Committee and the State Council have studied the overall situation and formulated the "Silk Road Economic Belt" and the "21st Century Maritime Silk Road" (hereinafter collectively referred to as the "One Belt One Road") strategy, to explore the new pathways of go global.

Fujian and Guangdong are important nodes of the "21st Century Maritime Silk Road" where all three maritime routes are connected. Because of its unique geographical location and shipping advantages, the Guangdong–Hong Kong–Macao Greater Bay Area has become the core node on the "21st Century Maritime Silk Road".

Currently, China is actively promoting the construction of the "Belt and Road" Initiative and has signed strategic agreements with many "Belt and Road" Initiative countries, regions and international organizations, and many major projects are advancing progressively. The "Belt and Road" Initiative brings new opportunities for the development of the Greater Bay Area of Guangdong, Hong Kong and Macao. This "Belt and Road" Initiative introduced by the government will not just bring great benefits to the Greater Bay Area but also bring new trading partners, providing platforms for the export of capital, goods, as well as that of service delivery and standards from the Greater Bay Area.

(2) *The CEPA Agreement*

The "Guangdong–Hong Kong Cooperation Framework Agreement" and the "Guangdong–Macao Cooperation Framework Agreement" were signed in 2010 and 2011, respectively. They are the first regional cooperation agreements signed between the provincial administrative bodies and the special administrative regions in China. Signing the two agreements signifies (not just under the "one country two systems" construct) the practical development and innovation of cross-border cooperation between Guangdong, Hong Kong and Macao, and it represents an important milestone in the process of economic synergy between the Mainland and the two SARs. CEPA clearly defines the respective positions of Guangdong, Hong Kong and Macao, and stipulates the division of labor, cooperation and complementary functions of Guangdong, Hong Kong and Macao. It allows the three places to utilize their own advantages in full to effectively integrate their advantageous resources for the collaborative development of Guangdong, Hong Kong and Macao and to curb the menace of repeated or overlapping construction and the resultant wastage of resources. The CEPA Agreement provides new ideas for the coordination and cooperation between Guangdong, Hong Kong and Macao. It is not only of great significance to the establishment, development and innovation of the institutional mechanism of cooperation between Guangdong, Hong

Kong and Macao but also lays the institutional foundation for the establishment and development of the Greater Bay Area of Guangdong, Hong Kong and Macao.

As a high-level free trade agreement, CEPA and its supplementary agreements are the most open and extensive free trade agreements signed by the Mainland so far. They conform to both WTO regulatory rules and the principle of "one country, two systems". The CEPA Agreement and its supplementary agreements have formulated a number of open measures aimed at gradually reducing and removing the institutional obstacles to economic, trade, industry and technology innovation cooperation between Guangdong, Hong Kong and Macao. CEPA will also help encourage the free flow of various economic factors among the three places, fostering the coordinated economic development of Guangdong, Hong Kong and Macao. Moreover, the CEPA agreement and its supplementary agreements do conform to the actual situation of economic cooperation among Guangdong, Hong Kong and Macao, and they help to explore a feasible path for the establishment of economic communities in the three places. Finally, CEPA and its supplementary agreements lay a cooperative foundation for the development of Guangdong, Hong Kong and Macao at the institutional level.

(3) *Pearl River Delta cooperation policy*

At the end of 2008, nine cities in Guangdong plus Hong Kong and Macao in the Greater Bay Area are slated for close cooperation in the "Outline of Reform and Development Planning for the Pearl River Delta Region (2008–2020)" approved by the State Council. The outline provides support for Guangdong, Hong Kong and Macao to strengthen cooperation in areas such as the modern service industry and others.

The "Outline of the Pearl River Delta Regional Reform and Development Plan (2008–2020)" not only promotes the opening of nine cities in Guangdong Province to Hong Kong and Macao but also fosters the formation of Shenzhen–Dongguan–Huizhou Economic

Sphere, Guangdong–Foshan–Foshan–Zhaoqing Economic Sphere and Pearl River Economic Sphere, providing valuable experience for industrial coordination in the Guangdong–Hong Kong–Macao Greater Bay Area.

The introduction of the Pearl River Delta cooperation policy will promote the establishment of the Guangdong–Hong Kong–Macao Greater Bay Area, whether in the industrial coordination of nine cities or in the opening of service industries to Hong Kong and Macao. The development of the Pearl River Delta cooperation provides valuable experience for the construction of the Guangdong–Hong Kong–Macao Greater Bay Area.

(4) *Pan-Pearl River Delta cooperation agreement*

In March 2004, the "Framework Agreement on Regional Cooperation in the Pan-Pearl River Delta" was signed by the Hong Kong and Macao special administrative regions and nine provinces, including Fujian, Jiangxi, Hunan, Guangdong, Guangxi, Hainan, Sichuan, Guizhou and Yunnan. It is not only the most extensive regional economic cooperation agreement made since the founding of New China but also the largest cross-border cooperation agreement in terms of economic volume so far. On the basis of the framework agreement, the regional governments of the Pan-Pearl River Delta had signed nearly 30 cooperation agreements, such as the "Pan-Pearl River Delta Regions Provincial Cities Cooperation Agreement" and "Pan-Pearl River Delta Regional Industrial and Commercial Administration Cooperation Agreement", further enhancing the sphere of Pan-Pearl River Delta cooperation. In March 2016, the "Guiding Opinions for Enhancing the Pan-Pearl River Delta Regional Cooperation" issued by the State Council confirmed the strategic position of the Pan-Pearl River Delta region — that of a pioneering area of national reform and opening up, that of an important engine driving national economic development and the core area of close cooperation between the Mainland and Hong Kong and Macao. It is strategic in that the Pan-Pearl River Delta region shall be an important construction area along the "Belt and Road" road map and that it is also the pilot zone for the construction of an ecological culture.

The mode of cooperation between the regions of the Pan-Pearl River Delta provides a reference pathway for the Greater Bay Area of Guangdong, Hong Kong and Macao to deal with issues such as economic globalization and regionalization and to solve problems associated with the public in the regions. Being the core region of Guangdong Province, the Greater Bay Area will enjoy the benefits of the Pan-Pearl River Delta regional cooperation and be given access to a broader hinterland in its economic reach, thereby raising the opening-up level of the Greater Bay Area.

(B) *Institutional advantages*

The Greater Bay Area of Guangdong, Hong Kong and Macao includes the special administrative regions of Hong Kong and Macao, which practice the capitalist system. Shenzhen Special Economic Zone is the experimental field for China's reform and opening-up, while we also have China's (Guangdong) pilot FTZ area. These three areas have their own institutional and administrative characteristics and are at the forefront of institutional innovation in China's reform and opening-up.

(1) *Advantages of "one country, two systems"*

Unlike the socialist system in the Mainland, Hong Kong and Macao practice the capitalist system which, at the institutional level, is the same as that of the developed countries in the West. They have retained their original institutional advantages, pursued a free economic policy or market economy, pegged the Hong Kong dollar to the US dollar, opened financial markets, allowed relatively open and easy entry and exit for people, adopted a common law system with both English and Chinese as the official languages and are fully connected to international markets. Over the past 20 years since Hong Kong's return to China, many indicators such as finance, trade, freedom and competitiveness are still at the forefront. Meanwhile, the breadth and depth of economic and trade cooperation with many countries have been strengthened. In addition, Hong Kong's role has somewhat changed from attracting investment and export to promoting capital outgoing and import trade. These are the advantages and outcomes of the successful implementation of the "one country, two systems".

Currently, the Mainland lags behind Hong Kong in many economic indicators such as finance, trade, degree of freedom, competitiveness and so on. The extent of opening up to the outside world is limited, and the commercial trade and investments between the Mainland and developed countries are thereby restricted. With the help of Hong Kong as an international financial and trading center, the Greater Bay Area of Guangdong, Hong Kong and Macao could take the lead in "coupling and docking" or "matching up" with the high standard requirements and regulations in international trade, gradually relaxing access to its markets, elevating the conduciveness of investment and trade and establishing good political and economic relations with the world's major economies, with the goal of promoting the establishment of a community of shared interests with all countries and regions along the "Belt and Road" route.

(2) *Advantages of Shenzhen Special Economic Zone as a resting ground for reform*

Shenzhen was the first to "hitch the free ride" of the reform and opening-up ever since the special economic zones were allowed to be set up in 1980. It took the lead in embracing the market economy, constantly breaking the shackles of the traditional, planned economic system and taking a leading role in exploring the possible establishment of a nationwide socialist market economic system and promoting its implementation throughout the country. Although the Central Government has generally exhausted its policies of reform and opening-up *vis-à-vis* Shenzhen, the legislative powers of Shenzhen Special Economic Zone could still provide legal assurance and protection for Shenzhen to further enhance its reform and opening-up.

The proposed establishment of the Greater Bay Area of Guangdong, Hong Kong and Macao coincides with the time when China is exploring the construction of a new open economic system. It is necessary to explore the establishment of a socialist market economic system adapted to the new open economic circumstances — a socialist market economy in which policy regulations are cut down as institutional coordination is strengthened. The legislative power of Shenzhen Special Economic Zone can provide strong assurance, at the institutional level, that laws and regulations that hinder the development of an open economy will be amended suitably and on a timely basis to capitalize on the advantages of Shenzhen's reform and opening-up, thus providing strong support for the establishment of a new open economy in the Guangdong–Hong Kong–Macao Greater Bay Area.

(3) *Advantages of pilot free trade zone in testing and experimenting*

In the "Overall Plan of China (Guangdong) Pilot Free Trade Zone", it was proposed that the pilot FTZs are to be the engines for the development of the Guangdong–Hong Kong–Macao Greater Bay Area. These pilot FTZs, while "relying on Hong Kong and Macao in serving the Mainland and embracing the world, should be built into a 'demonstration zone' of deepened cooperation between Guangdong, Hong Kong and Macao". This is the important strategic position of the China (Guangdong) Pilot FTZs, which is different from other pilot FTZs. It is also the policy basis upon which China (Guangdong) Pilot FTZs support the construction of the Guangdong–Hong Kong–Macao Greater Bay Area.

Unlike the formerly developed industrial parks, high-tech development zones and national "new zones", where simple preferential policies were applicable, China (Guangdong) Pilot FTZs, are specially planned system experimental zones in which institutional innovations will be the core activities. The setup of the pilot FTZs is aimed at eliminating the obstacles that hindered the free flow of important business and economic factors in Guangdong,

Hong Kong and Macao in the past and exploring new modes of opening to the outside world. Shenzhen's Qianhai Shekou Free Trade Area together with Nansha Free Trade Area in Guangzhou and Hengqin Free Trade Area in Zhuhai will form three essential supports to promoting closer cooperation between Guangdong, Hong Kong and Macao in expanding new channels for opening up, thereby contributing to the construction of the Greater Bay Area of Guangdong, Hong Kong and Macao.

At present, the China (Guangdong) Pilot FTZ has formulated special management measures (the so-called "negative list") for investment access from Hong Kong and Macao in order to foster in-depth cooperation between Guangdong, Hong Kong and Macao. Shenzhen Qianhai Deep Harbor Cooperation Zone of Modern Service Industry has been incorporated into the China (Guangdong) Pilot FTZ, and a system for cooperation with Macao has also been established. China (Guangdong) Pilot FTZ is taking the lead in trying to connect or incorporate the management system and industry standards of Hong Kong and Macao's service industries. In this manner, it has promoted scientific and technological innovation cooperation within Guangdong, Hong Kong and Macao and established a platform for young entrepreneurs in Guangdong, Hong Kong and Macao. Hong Kong and Macao professionals are encouraged to seek employment directly or to offer their professional services in China's (Guangdong) Pilot FTZ. In order to further expand the Mainland markets, entry–exit requirements and pro-residency measures are to be simplified to provide incentives to attract more professionals from Guangdong, Hong Kong and Macao to China's (Guangdong) Pilot FTZ. The aforementioned steps are taken to enhance the level of trading facilities and conduciveness, including creating convenient and efficient flow of various essential factors or economic elements within Guangdong, Hong Kong and Macao. The supervisory and customs inspection system at the entry points or ports should also be improved. This supervision system should be strengthened in coordination with Hong Kong and Macao. The China (Guangdong) Pilot FTZ promotes in-depth cooperation between Guangdong,

Hong Kong and Macao through system innovation and the measures taken can be replicated and extended to the nine cities in Guangdong as well as to other areas.

(C) *Location and Hinterland advantages*

The Greater Bay Area of Guangdong, Hong Kong and Macao is located at the southern tip of China. It is surrounded by mountains on three sides and it is the area of confluence of three rivers. Its geographical position is agreeable for it is endowed with good climate, long coastline, good port groups, vast marine areas and abundant forest vegetation. The Guangdong–Hong Kong–Macao Greater Bay Area has its back facing the inland; it links Hong Kong and Macao while facing ASEAN at the front. It is flanked to the east by the Economic Zone of the Straits and to the west by the Northern Bay Economic Zone. The Greater Bay Area could rapidly connect to China's inland through land transportation such as South Guangzhou Railway. It is the economically developed area that is closest to the South China Sea, and it represents the bridgehead for passage into the South China Sea. Its proximity to the world's first golden navigation waterway — an important maritime route in the Pacific Ocean and Indian Ocean — makes it an important transportation hub in Southeast Asia and even the world. In addition, the Greater Bay Area of Guangdong, Hong Kong and Macao is situated at the intersection of the Silk Road Economic Belt and the 21st Century Maritime Silk Road. It has the world's largest port cluster, airport group as well as one of the most efficient and busiest transportation networks in the world.

Being the hinterland for the Greater Bay Area of Guangdong, Hong Kong and Macao, the Pan-Pearl River Delta region includes nine provinces in South, Southeast and Southwest China plus two special administrative regions: Fujian, Guangdong, Guangxi, Guizhou, Hainan, Hunan, Jiangxi, Sichuan, Yunnan, Hong Kong and Macao SARs. These places are directly or indirectly related to the economic activities and culture of the Pearl River Delta Basin and are also interrelated in terms of resources, industries and markets. There is strong complementarity. The Pan-Pearl River Delta region covers one-fifth of China's territory; its population is one-third of the national total and it is economically strong and robust. In 2016, the GDP reached RMB26443.96 billion, accounting for 38.5% of the national GDP. Not only can the Pan-Pearl River Region undertake industrial transference for the Guangdong–Hong Kong–Macao Greater Bay Area but it can also provide a high-quality labor force and financial support for the Greater Bay Area.

(D) *Economic advantages*

Guangdong Province was the earliest province in China to implement the strategy of opening up to the outside world. Hong Kong is an international financial center with strong economic strengths, and the strengths of the two places provide a solid foundation for the economic development of the Guangdong–Hong Kong–Macao Greater Bay Area.

(1) *Aggregate economic output is comparable to the world's first-class bay areas*

In 2016, the total GDP of the Guangdong–Hong Kong–Macao Greater Bay Area exceeded US$1.3 trillion, and this means that an area less than 1% of the land area of the whole country has created an economic output of 12.5% of the whole country, as shown in Table 1. Compared with the three world-class bay areas, the Guangdong–Hong Kong–Macao Greater Bay Area also has the economic aggregate matching that of the world-class bay areas: the total GDP of Tokyo Bay Area was US$1.8 trillion, the total GDP of New York Bay Area was US$1.4 trillion, and the total GDP of San Francisco Bay Area was only US$0.8 trillion. Thus, San Francisco Bay Area had been overtaken by the Guangdong–Hong Kong–Macao Greater Bay Area.

The Guangdong–Hong Kong–Macao Greater Bay Area ranked 3rd among the four major bay areas in the total economic output. In terms of economic scale and size, the Guangdong–Hong Kong–Macao

Table 1. GDP of cities in the Guangdong–Hong Kong–Macao Greater Bay Area for 2016.

City	GDP (100 million yuan)
Hong Kong	22,129.4
Macao	3,095.3
Guangzhou	19,610.9
Shenzhen	19,492.6
Zhuhai	2,226.4
Dongguan	6,827.7
Foshan	8,003.9
Jiangmen	2,418.8
Zhongshan	3,202.8
Huizhou	3,412.2
Zhaoqing	1,970.0

Source: *Statistical Yearbooks of Guangdong Province,* Hong Kong and Macao (2016).

Greater Bay Area has the possibility and potential of becoming an international bay area.

(2) *Hong Kong is Chinese Mainland's "super-link" or "super-contact" to the world*

As shown in Figure 1, from the top 10 sources of foreign investment in Chinese Mainland for 2015, the sources of foreign investment in China were relatively "concentrated" and fixed. The top 10 sources accounted for 92.3% of the total investment. Japan and the "Four Asian Dragons" were the main sources of foreign investment in China, accounting for 78.3%, of which Hong Kong accounted for 68.4%, far more than other sources of foreign investment. From the history of domestic foreign investment, Hong Kong has always been the main source of investment in Chinese Mainland. After the 2008 financial crisis, more than half of foreign investment came from Hong Kong. A huge amount of international capital using the name of "Hong Kong capital" entered Chinese mainland through Hong Kong. See Figure 2 for details.

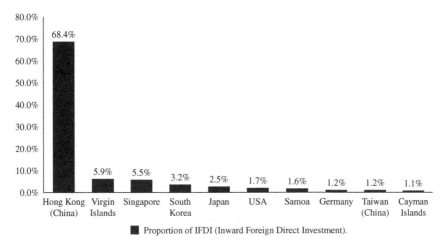

Figure 1.   Major sources of foreign investment in Chinese Mainland in 2015.

Source: National Bureau of Statistics.

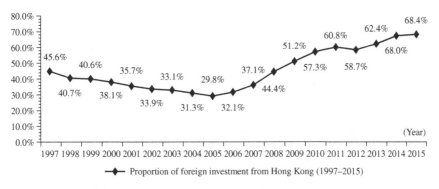

Figure 2.   Proportion of foreign investment from Hong Kong (1997–2015).

Source: National Bureau of Statistics.

Like most foreign investment in Chinese Mainland, for a long time, Chinese Mainland's foreign investment has mainly been poured into Hong Kong, and then through Hong Kong to the world. In recent years, more than half of Chinese Mainland's foreign investment has been invested in Hong Kong. After the 2008 financial crisis, the proportion of Hong Kong's foreign investment in Chinese Mainland has declined, but it has again gradually risen to more than 60%, as detailed in Figures 3 and 4.

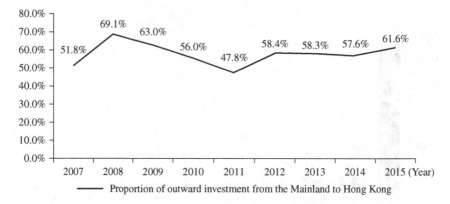

Figure 3. The proportion of outward investment from the Mainland to Hong Kong over the Years.

Source: National Bureau of Statistics.

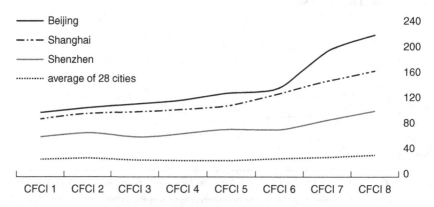

Figure 4. Comprehensive Development Research Institute's Report on the three National Financial Centers' CFCI scores.

Source: China (Shenzhen) Development Research Institute's 8th issue of "China Financial Center Index" Report.

The construction of the Greater Bay Area of Guangdong, Hong Kong and Macao requires not only a large amount of foreign investment but also the enterprises in the Greater Bay Area to go global and participate in international competition via overseas investment. Hong Kong, as Chinese Mainland's super-link or super-contact to the world, is endowed with the conditions for serving the two strategies of "bringing in" and "going out" (of capital) pertaining to the Guangdong–Hong Kong–Macao Greater Bay Area.

(3) *A world-class export base*

Since 1979, governments at various levels in the Chinese Mainland have implemented many reform measures in the Pearl River Delta region that are devoted to the development of merchandise trade, and the said measures had attracted a large number of export-oriented foreign investments. In terms of the volume of foreign merchandise trade in the Guangdong–Hong Kong–Macao Greater Bay Area, by the end of 2012, the total foreign trade in the Greater Bay Area had reached US$1,778.2 billion, which was about US$93.8 billion higher than that of Japan in the same year, making the Greater Bay Area the fourth largest merchandise (goods) trade economy in the world.

As can be seen from Table 2, the export volume of the nine cities in Guangdong had been increasing steadily, with Shenzhen and Dongguan being the two main cities for export. In fact, even without taking into account the contributions of Hong Kong and

Table 2. Total export volume of nine cities of Guangdong from 2010 through 2015. (Unit: US$100 million).

City	2010	2011	2012	2013	2014	2015
Guangzhou	483.79	564.68	589.15	628.07	727.07	811.7
Shenzhen	2,041.80	2,453.99	2,713.56	3,057.02	2,843.62	2,640.40
Zhuhai	208.62	239.77	216.37	265.81	290.15	288.11
Foshan	330.38	390.01	401.50	425.23	467.17	482.05
Huizhou	202.32	231.22	292.04	333.20	363.31	347.75
Dongguan	696.03	783.26	850.53	908.61	970.67	1,036.10
Zhongshan	225.04	245.46	246.44	264.75	278.78	280.07
Jiangmen	104.09	122.52	129.70	139.99	150.87	153.72
Zhaoqing	25.97	33.08	37.81	48.26	46.05	47.66
Total	4,318.02	5,064.89	5,477.09	6,070.93	6,137.68	6,087.57

Source: Annual Year Books of each of the nine cities.

Macao, the export performance of Guangdong's nine cities was enough to be rated as a world-class export base. In 2012, the total merchandise exports of nine cities in Guangdong amounted to US$547.709 billion, which was almost the same as that of South Korea's US$547.9 billion, surpassing Russia's US$529.3 billion and second only to the six foreign economies including the United States, Germany, Japan, the Netherlands, France and South Korea. However, although Hong Kong's export trade remained at a relatively high level, its export volume continued to decline, with its entrepot trade accounting for the vast majority of its merchandise trading, as detailed in Table 3.

Table 3. Volume of Hong Kong's merchandise trade through the years 2000–2016. (Unit: HK$1 million).

Year	Import	Export of HK Products	Trans-Shipment	Total Export Volume
2000	1,657,962	180,967	1,391,722	1,572,689
2001	1,568,194	153,520	1,327,467	1,480,987
2002	1,619,419	130,926	1,429,590	1,560,517
2003	1,805,770	121,687	1,620,749	1,742,436
2004	2,111,123	125,982	1,893,132	2,019,114
2005	2,329,469	136,030	2,114,143	2,250,174
2006	2,599,804	134,527	2,326,500	2,461,027
2007	2,868,011	109,122	2,578,392	2,687,513
2008	3,025,288	90,757	2,733,394	2,824,151
2009	2,692,356	57,742	2,411,347	2,469,089
2010	3,364,840	69,512	2,961,507	3,031,019
2011	3,764,840	65,662	3,271,591	3,337,253
2012	3,912,163	58,830	3,375,516	3,434,346
2013	4,060,717	54,364	3,505,322	3,559,686
2014	4,219,046	55,283	3,617,468	3,672,751
2015	4,046,420	46,861	3,558,418	3,605,279
2016	4,008,384	42,875	3,545,372	3,588,247

Source: Department of Statistics, Hong Kong SAR.

(E) *Industrial advantages*

The Guangdong–Hong Kong–Macao Greater Bay Area possesses a good and comprehensive industrial chain. The industries of the nine cities in Guangdong are vibrant and strong and they form one of the largest high-tech industrial agglomeration areas in China. Hong Kong, Guangzhou and Shenzhen have developed financial industries, while Hong Kong is an international financial center with a sound financial system. In addition, Hong Kong, Guangzhou and Shenzhen are also among the top 10 container ports in the world, with a strong shipping and freight industry. With the geographical advantages of the coastal areas, the maritime economic level of the Greater Bay Area of Guangdong, Hong Kong and Macao is at the forefront of the country and is comparable to the world's first-class bay areas.

(1) *Complete industrial chain*

The nine cities of Guangdong have formed three economic spheres, namely the economic spheres of Shenzhen–Dongguan–Huizhou, Guangdong–Foshan–Zhaoqing and Zuhai–Zhongshan–Jiangmen. They have established good and comprehensive industrial chains. At the same time, the differences in their industrial priorities provide a good foundation for the coordinated economic development of the Greater Bay Area.

The Shenzhen–Dongguan–Huizhou Economic Sphere includes Shenzhen, Dongguan and Huizhou. Shenzhen has four pillar industries represented by its high-tech industry. In terms of industrial developments, Shenzhen focuses on the Internet, new-generation information technology, energy-saving and environmental protection, new materials, cultural and creative industries, biotechnology and new energy industries — industries with strong strategic significance and great value-added capacities. Dongguan's five pillar industries include electronic information manufacturing, electrical machinery and equipment manufacturing, textile, clothing, shoes and millinery (hats manufacturing), food and beverage processing manufacturing, paper and paper products manufacturing and four other specialist industries including toys and sports goods manufacturing, furniture manufacturing, chemical products manufacturing, packaging and printing. The two pillar industries of Huizhou are the electronic information and petrochemical industries.

The Guangzhou–Foshan–Zhaoqing Economic Sphere includes Guangzhou, Foshan and Zhaoqing. In the layout of modern industries, Guangzhou pays particular attention to the integration and coordinated development of the industries, focusing on the development of advanced manufacturing, high-tech and modern service industries. Foshan is situated in the hinterland of the Pearl River Delta, in the middle of the horizontal industrial axis of Guangdong Province. It is adjacent to Zhaoqing in the west and is flanked by Guangzhou to the east. It has its own special industries and is also involved in transference of industries within Guangdong Province. Foshan ranks 3rd in contributing to the total economic volume of Guangdong Province, second only to Guangzhou and Shenzhen, two first-tier cities. It has a good industrial foundation, focusing on developing the manufacturing industry. It also has a large number of industrial parks and specialized townships. The privately operated economy is the main driving force of its development. It is a unique modern manufacturing agglomeration in Guangdong Province. Zhaoqing has abundant tourism resources; hence, its tourism industry is flourishing, but its industrial fundamentals are not inferior either. It mainly develops new industries such as biopharmaceuticals, electronic information, forestry, chemical and automotive accessories industries. New materials industries represented by new building materials and metals are also quite well developed.

Zhuhai, Zhongshan and Jiangmen are located on the west bank of the Pearl River Estuary. As a special economic zone, Zhuhai focuses on the development of emerging strategic industries such as electronic information, precision machinery manufacturing and biopharmaceutical manufacturing industries. Speaking of traditional industries, the Zhuhai–Zhongshan–Jiangmen Economic Sphere has formed an industry chain dominated by electric power supply, the petrochemical industry and household electrical appliances. It has a high overall level of industrialization and contributes a lot to Zhuhai's economy. Zhongshan is the place where traditional industries in Guangdong Province are gathered. It is very strong in traditional industries, and this strength lays a solid foundation for the transformation and upgrading of industries, lending assurance to the development of emerging industries. At present, Zhongshan has formed a traditional industrial cluster with lighting, hardware, home electrical appliances, textiles and clothing as the main component industries. A new industrial cluster specializing in equipment manufacturing, electronic appliances and healthcare medicine is also emerging. It has distinct industrial characteristics and strong industrial competitiveness. However, Jiangmen is short of emerging industries; it has mainly traditional industries. Other than electronic and information industries, Jiangmen focuses on developing heavy industries such as petrochemicals, transportation and marine equipment, as well as light industries such as food, beverage, packaging, printing and paper products. In addition, Jiangmen's modern agriculture is well developed, and it has the potential to become a modern agricultural base in Guangdong Province. On the whole, Jiangmen has a good industrial base and a huge development potential. It can undertake the transfer of industries from the core cities in the Guangdong–Hong Kong–Macao Greater Bay Area as it has a strong advantage of second-mover advantage (Table 4).

In 2015, the value added for industrialization from the nine cities in Guangdong reached RMB2,559.719 billion yuan (while that of the whole country was 28,204.3 billion yuan), accounting for 9.1% of the national total and surpassing most provinces in China and was in the leading position in China.

(2) *A well-developed financial system*

Hong Kong, Shenzhen and Guangzhou are the cities with the most developed financial industries within the Guangdong–Hong Kong–Macao Greater Bay Area. Hong Kong has become the core financial center of the Greater Bay Area since it is already an international financial center. According to the "Global Financial Centers Index

Table 4. The added values (value added) of industries in nine cities of Guangdong for 2015.

City	Added Values of Industrialization (in 100 million yuan)
Guangzhou	5,246.07
Shenzhen	6,785.01
Zhuhai	980.76
Foshan	4,672.53
Huizhou	1,587.97
Dongguan	2,711.09
Zhongshan	1,566.16
Jiangmen	1,078.51
Zhaoqing	969.09
Total	25,597.19

Source: Statistical year books of nine cities of Guangdong (2015).

(GFCI) Report" released in March 2017, Hong Kong ranked 4th among the top 20 financial centers in the world, behind New York, London and Singapore. The financial industries of Shenzhen and Guangzhou occupy the top or first echelon in the whole country, second in position only to Beijing and Shanghai. They possess potential qualifications to become regional financial centers in their own right. The two cities are increasingly more open and their overall strength is also growing steadily.

It is self-evident that Hong Kong has a close relationship with Chinese Mainland, where its interior areas have the fastest economic growth and the biggest potential for development in the world. Owing to the political arrangement of "one country, two systems" and its long history of colonization, Hong Kong has more similarities with the world's "real" financial centers, reflected variously in the freedom of capital flow, the internationalization of regulatory systems and other "soft and flexible restrictions". Hong Kong's financial institutions have their own characteristics, and perform diverse functions. They offer a wide range of activities such as capital lending, securities trading, foreign exchange and bullion trading, forming a complete range of international financial markets. Hong Kong's foreign exchange market, gold market and interbank lending market are relatively developed, and the stock exchange has been developing rapidly. The proportion of Hong Kong's financial industries in Hong Kong's GDP is increasing year-by-year. By 2015, the proportion of finance reached 17.6% of Hong Kong's GDP, while the employed population for financial industries accounted for only 6.5% of Hong Kong's total employed. The per capita contribution rate of financial industries is much higher than that of the other pillar industries, as shown in Table 5.

Table 5. Proportions of Hong Kong's financial industries in its GDP from 1997 to 2015.

Year	Proportion of GDP (%)	Proportion of Population Employed (%)
1997	10.4	5.4
1998	9.8	5.4
1999	11.3	5.5
2000	12.8	5.3
2001	12.1	5.5
2002	12.3	5.5
2003	13.3	5.2
2004	13.1	5.2
2005	13.8	5.4
2006	16.7	5.4
2007	20.1	5.5
2008	17.1	5.9
2009	16.2	6.1
2010	16.3	6.2
2011	16.1	6.3
2012	15.9	6.3
2013	16.5	6.2
2014	16.7	6.3
2015	17.6	6.5

Source: Data from Hong Kong Monetary Authority.

In 2016, Shenzhen's total financial industry assets exceeded 12 trillion yuan, slightly less than those for Beijing and Shanghai, thus leading Shenzhen to rank 3rd among all cities in the country, with 1% of the population producing 15% of Shenzhen's GDP and contributing more than 20% of its tax revenue.

According to the 8th issue of the "China's Financial Center Index", Shanghai, Beijing and Shenzhen are the three major national financial centers, and Shenzhen ranks 3rd in overall competitiveness. Among the three, Shenzhen's financial market ranks 2nd in size, while in the performance of its financial industries, the strength of financial institutions and the financial ecological environment, Shenzhen ranks 3rd. Capitalizing on the vitality and strength of Shenzhen Stock Exchange, Shenzhen has accelerated the development of a multi-level capital market system consisting of the main board, small and medium-sized boards and start-up boards. The bullion night market has also continued to maintain its momentum of rapid development. The strength of securities institutions is excellent, and the total assets of securities companies rank 1st in China.

Although differences and gaps exist between Guangzhou's financial industry and the financial industries of Hong Kong and Shenzhen, Guangzhou does have the basic requirements to become an international financial center. After many years of development, Guangzhou's financial industry has made a qualitative leap and its position in the world has been constantly improving. In March 2017, Guangzhou ranked 37th among the world's financial centers. Not only was this the first time that Guangzhou was included in the ranking system of global financial centers but it was also an important milestone in its development from a regional financial center to an international financial center. For historical reasons, Guangzhou was one of the earliest cities to a financial market in China, and many areas of its development are in the forefront of China. For example, in 2016, the growth rate for listing of its "New Three Boards" ranked 1st in China. In the same year, Guangzhou also ranked 1st in the country in the growth rate of insurance premium income and in the proportion of direct financing. To date,

Guangzhou ranks 3rd in the country in insurance premium income, with the total premium exceeding 100 billion yuan, and ranks 4th in the country in total direct financing. Of these, the volume of loan balance exceeds 3 trillion yuan, and the balance of local and foreign currency deposits was close to 5 trillion yuan.

(3) Leader in international shipping and freight

Over the past 40 years, the economic transformation of the Pearl River Delta and the development of the regional manufacturing system have produced a comprehensive port system. Within the Greater Bay Area of Guangdong, Hong Kong and Macao, there is now a hub port, and there are also "trunk" ports and feeder ports.

From the description of "location and hinterland advantages" in this chapter, we can see that the Greater Bay Area of Guangdong, Hong Kong and Macao has abundant natural resources, superior geographical location and a vast hinterland to provide support for the industrial development of the Greater Bay Area. With the economic advantages of the Greater Bay Area and the Pan-Pearl River Delta region, the shipping industry of the Greater Bay Area is bound to flourish. At present, there are nearly 200 large and small ports and harbors in Guangdong, Hong Kong and Macao, and a port group system with good facilities and other amenities has been established. Hong Kong, Guangzhou and Shenzhen are undoubtedly the pillars of the port group system in the Greater Bay Area. All three cities are international shipping centers, with container throughput ranking among the top 10 in the world. In recent years, the Western Guangdong Port Group on the flank of the Guangdong–Hong Kong–Macao Greater Bay Area has developed rapidly, especially the port of Zhanjiang whose rise has catalyzed the overall development of the western Guangdong area and which supported the development of the Greater Bay Area, helping to establish the supporting auxiliary port cluster from Jiangmen Port to Huizhou Port — westward to eastward.

Container throughput in the Guangdong–Hong Kong–Macao Greater Bay Area is mainly from Hong Kong, Shenzhen

Table 6.   Throughput capacities of the World's 10 largest container ports in 2016.

Ranking	Port	Throughput Capacity (in 10,000 TEUs)
1	Shanghai, China	3,654
2	Singapore	3,092
3	Shenzhen, China	2,420
4	Ningbo-Zhoushan, China	2,063
5	Hong Kong, China	2,007
6	Busan, South Korea	1,945
7	Qingdao, China	1,747
8	Guangzhou, China	1,722
9	Jebel Ali Port, Dubai UAE	1,560
10	Tianjin, China	1,411

Source: Report on World Shipping Council's Ranking of Container Ports.

and Guangzhou. According to the statistics released by the World Shipping Council in March 2017, the world's 10 largest container ports are in Asian countries, with China accounting for 7 of the world's 10 largest container ports. Shanghai leads in China's container ports, handling 36.54 million TEUs (Twenty-foot Equivalent Unit) in 2016. Among other Chinese ports, the ports in the Guangdong–Hong Kong–Macao Greater Bay Area occupy three places, with Shenzhen, Hong Kong and Guangzhou ranking 3rd, 5th and 8th, respectively, as detailed in Table 6. In 2016, the total container-handling capacity of Shenzhen, Hong Kong and Guangzhou reached 61.49 million TEUs, which ranked 1st in the world. The Guangdong–Hong Kong–Macao Greater Bay Area is becoming one bay area with the largest port groups in the world.

From the overall layout scheme of the port clusters of the Guangdong–Hong Kong–Macao Greater Bay Area, these port clusters exist to serve the shipping requirements of the Greater Bay itself. In addition to that, they also provide convenient shipping transit services for cities outside the Greater Bay Area as well as other provinces in the Pan-Pearl River Delta region. According to the targeted destination classification of shipping services, the shipping services in the Greater Bay Area of Guangdong, Hong Kong and Macao can be divided into foreign trade shipping services and domestic trade shipping services. Of the ports within the Greater Bay Area, Hong Kong and Shenzhen chiefly provide services for overseas trade, particularly for foreign trade shipping services, while the ports of Guangzhou focus on external trade, particularly domestic trade shipping services.

Looking from the west to the east, we note that Zhanjiang Port drives the western Guangdong Port Cluster to provide support for the development of the Guangdong–Hong Kong–Macao Greater Bay Area. The port focuses on the distribution of oil and dry goods. It is the core for shipping-related services in South China and the coastal hub port in the Greater Bay Area. The port cluster in eastern Guangdong is represented by Shantou Port, which fronts eastern Guangdong, Fujian, Jiangxi and other provinces to offer transit services for import and export goods in these areas. Whether handling internal or external shipping, the division of labor of the port clusters in the Greater Bay Area of Guangdong, Hong Kong and Macao is clear-cut. The shipping industry chain is quite complete, and it meets the future needs of the shipping industry of the Greater Bay Area.

(4) *Strong maritime economy*

In recent years, China's maritime economy has developed rapidly; its contribution to the economy has been rising, and the overall size of the maritime economy has also been rising. According to the "China Maritime Economic Development Report" issued in 2015, China's maritime economy accounted for 9.4% of China's GDP in 2015, and the value of its total output was close to RMB6.5 trillion yuan. Compared to 2014, China's maritime economy grew by 7 percentage points, and its growth rate was basically the same as that of the previous year. The growth rate of China's maritime economy is slightly higher compared with China's GDP growth, indicating that China's maritime economy plays a significant role in promoting national GDP growth and that its influence on the economy is increasing.

Since Hong Kong and Macao do not have relevant statistics on maritime economy, the report describes and analyzes only the present situation of maritime economy in nine cities of Guangdong. In 2015, the total output value of the maritime economy of nine cities in Guangdong reached 1.38 trillion yuan, not only accounting for 18.9% of the total GDP of Guangdong but also contributing more than one-fifth of the total maritime economic output of the whole country in the same period. This maritime economy occupied the 1st position in the country for 21 successive years.

Generally speaking, it can be said that the maritime economy of the Greater Bay Area of Guangdong, Hong Kong and Macao has been developing steadily, and there is good synergy among maritime economy industries within the Greater Bay Area as well as efficient and orderly regional economic cooperation. New maritime and associated service industries are emerging rapidly, and the overall industrial structure has been optimized. The general development trend is positive, and the maritime economy of the Greater Bay Area will continue to grow steadily.

(F) *Advantages of innovation*

The Guangdong–Hong Kong–Macao Greater Bay Area is strong in innovation and not inferior to other first-class international bay areas in this regard. In terms of investment, the proportion of R&D investment in GDP in nine cities of the Pearl River Delta alone is 2.7%, which is at the same level as that in the United States (2.8%) and Germany (2.83%). In terms of high-tech industries, the Guangdong–Hong Kong–Macao Greater Bay Area is also as strong as the three major bay areas of the world. Taking Shenzhen as an illustration, it is noteworthy that the four pillar industries of Shenzhen contributed to 33.4% of Shenzhen's GDP in 2015, and the value added on GDP created by high-tech industries reached 584.791 billion yuan. In addition, Shenzhen has 13,300 patent collaboration agreements, figures which are comparable to the three major bay areas in the world. The total contribution made by high-tech industries to the GDP during the same period was 4.05%,

Table 7. Total number of (invention) patents from the Greater Bay Area of Guangdong, Hong Kong and Macao through the years 2012–2016.

Year	Total Number of Invention Patents	Rate of Increase (%)
2012	61,764	—
2013	71,037	15.01
2014	103,610	45.85
2015	155,074	49.67
2016	193,712	24.92

Source: Statistics from the Ministry of Science and Technology.

and this figure placed Shenzhen in the forefront of the high-tech industrial city agglomeration in the country. In addition, Shenzhen has witnessed the emergence of many internationally renowned and leading high-tech enterprises, such as Huawei Communications Technology, whose products are widely used in the world, and DJI's innovative drones or UAVs for civilian use. DJI's drones and other products are hugely popular abroad (Table 7).

In terms of invention patents, the total number of invention patents in the Greater Bay Area of Guangdong, Hong Kong and Macao has been increasing steadily from 2012 to 2016, with the largest increase in 2014 and 2015, close to an increase of 50%. In those 5 years, the total number of invention patents in the Greater Bay Area increased rapidly, with a cumulative increase of 213.6% — doubling in 5 years.

Compared to other international bay areas, it is found that the number of invention patents in the Guangdong–Hong Kong–Macao Greater Bay Area has overtaken that in San Francisco Bay Area in the past 5 years, and the gap is widening. In 2012, the Greater Bay Area of Guangdong, Hong Kong and Macao surpassed San Francisco Bay Area by 27,600 invention patents, and by 2016, the number will be 138,200. We could also see that the number of invention patents in San Francisco Bay Area has not increased since 2014; in fact, it has begun to show negative growth. In 2015, the growth rate has dropped by 17.96%, while the number of invention patents in the Guangdong–Hong Kong–Macao Greater Bay Area has increased, with an average annual growth rate of 33.86%, of which the largest growth rate occurred in 2015, an increase of 49.67% over 2014.

In 2017, the Global Innovation Index (GII) Report ranked 100 science and technology innovation centers of the world, and the Guangdong–Hong Kong–Macao Greater Bay Area had two places listed. Shenzhen–Hong Kong ranked 2nd in the world — surpassing San Francisco Bay Area (Silicon Valley) which ranked 3rd — and was behind Tokyo Bay Area only. Tokyo Bay Area and San Francisco Bay Area led the world in high-tech industries during the era of consumer electronics and PC Internet. However, in recent years — in the new era of mobile Internet — China and the Guangdong–Hong Kong–Macao Greater Bay Area has begun to catch up, and in certain areas, has even surpassed Tokyo Bay Area.

(G) *Transportation advantages*

In recent years, in order to boost the economic development of the Pearl River Delta region, the local governments of the Guangdong Province and the Pearl River Delta have completed a number of traffic and transport planning projects tasked during the 12th Five-Year Plan period, and a number of such projects have been planned and formulated in the 13th Five-Year Plan with a view of strengthening the interconnection or connectivity with Hong Kong and Macao.

In rail transportation, the Pearl River Delta region has planned and constructed an intercity rail transport network with a total length of 1,890 km during the "12th Five-Year Plan" period to meet the anticipated passenger demands brought about by city–county integration in the Pearl River Delta region. The Guangdong Provincial Government has also constructed a "three-ring and eight-radiating" rapid rail transit network proposed in the "Pearl River Delta Intercity Rail Transit Network Planning (Revised in 2009)". The network connects nine cities in Guangdong, Hong Kong and Macao in the Greater Bay Area to Hong Kong, Macao and other areas in Guangdong Province.

By 2020, 23 railway lines with trains traveling at maximum speeds of 140 kilometers/hour or 200 kilometers/hour will have Guangzhou as the nucleus (or center), making the Guangdong–Hong Kong–Macao Greater Bay Area reachable within an hour's commuting time in a circle spanning a total length of 1,480 kilometers.

During the 12th Five-Year Plan period, the Guangdong Provincial Government built 1,661 kilometers of (high-speed) expressways, which markedly improved the internal connectivity between the Guangdong–Hong Kong–Macao Greater Bay Area with other cities in Guangdong Province as well as between the Greater Bay Area and the Pan-Pearl River Delta region. The construction of the expressways enhances the level of interconnectivity and communication between the eastern and western sides of the Pearl River estuary, strengthens the coordinated development between them, provides infrastructure support for the "radiated" areas of the Pearl River estuary and serves to strengthen the radiation-driven effect of the eastern and western sides of the Pearl River estuary *vis-à-vis* the Guangdong–Hong Kong–Macao Greater Bay Area.

In the 13th Five-Year Plan, the Guangdong Provincial Government has planned 33 provincial expressway corridors or passageways, including four links to Hong Kong and two links to Macao which will tremendously improve the network of "external passage and internal links".

There are four international airports in the Guangdong–Hong Kong–Macao Greater Bay Area: Hong Kong International Airport, Macao International Airport, Guangzhou Baiyun International Airport, Shenzhen Bao'an International Airport as well as (non-international or "feeder" airports) Zhuhai Airport and Huizhou Airport, etc. In the future, the Guangdong–Hong Kong–Macao Greater Bay Area will form a "three-core and three-auxiliary" airport system with Hong Kong International Airport, Guangzhou Baiyun Airport and Shenzhen Bao'an Airport as the core, and Macao Airport, Huizhou Airport and Lianxi Airport as the auxiliary or supporting airports to meet the aviation needs of China and those of international air transport.

In the area of bridge construction, the first cross-sea bridge in China, the Hong Kong–Zhuhai–Macao Bridge, which was completed in February 2018, and the cross-border commuting policy of the Hong Kong–Zhuhai–Macao Bridge is being formulated. The Hong Kong–Zuhai–Macao Bridge flyovers across the Pearl River estuary are important links between Hong Kong and the cities on the western coast of the Pearl River Delta, while Humen Bridge's flyovers spanning across the Pearl River estuary connect the eastern and western wings of the Greater Bay Area, such that traffic from Dongguan, Shenzhen and Eastern Guangdong to Zhuhai, and to Zhongshan, Jiangmen and Western Guangdong do not need to detour to reach their destinations, thus greatly shortening the travel time and actual distances travelled between the two places.

The spatial or three-dimensional transportation system (involving land, sea and air transport) within the Guangdong–Hong Kong–Macao Greater Bay Area has been initially established. In the future, the infrastructures for interconnection with Hong Kong and Macao will be further strengthened to support, maintain and enhance the coordinated development of Guangdong, Hong Kong and Macao.

(H) *Advantages of international cooperation*

The Greater Bay Area of Guangdong, Hong Kong and Macao leads the nation in internationalization. In addition, most of the overseas Chinese residing in Southeast Asian countries have their ancestral roots in Guangdong, Hong Kong and Macao, with cultural ties to English-speaking and Portuguese-speaking countries. These special characteristics will make it easier for the Guangdong–Hong Kong–Macao Greater Bay Area to integrate into the international environment and to participate in international cooperation than for other domestic urban areas or city clusters.

(1) *High level of internationalization*

Compared with the other city clusters in China, Guangdong–Hong Kong–Macao Greater Bay Area ranks 1st in the country in the extent and level of internationalization, creating advantages and opportunities for the Greater Bay Area to participate in international cooperation. Of the 11 cities in the Greater Bay Area, Hong Kong is the most internationalized city and the most open free port in the world. Not only is its international trade at the forefront of the world, its financial services are highly influential in the world too. Hong Kong Container Port Terminal is one of the busiest in the world and Hong Kong Airport is also the busiest and the most efficient international airport in the world. Hong Kong holds thousands of exhibitions and conferences every year and is aptly known as the "Capital of Exhibitions and Conferences". More than half a million foreigners live in Hong Kong, giving it a pluralistic atmosphere.

Shenzhen was among the first batch of cities in China to carry out reforms and opening-up. It was the first city in the country to explore the path to internationalization. Its level of internationalization is on par with the first-tier cities like Beijing, Shanghai and Guangzhou. In recent years, Shenzhen has been promoting cooperation with Hong Kong. It is always working closely with Hong Kong to become more compatible with Hong Kong's market economy environment, and in many areas and sectors, Shenzhen is expanding constantly, forming a unique system of opening-up to the outside world for a Chinese city.

In addition, the establishment of China (Guangdong) Pilot FTZ provides institutional support for the exploration of internationalization of the Guangdong–Hong Kong–Macao Greater Bay Area. The core or main objective for the setting up of the pilot FTZ is to encourage institutional innovation. This is done via six "dimensions": prompt and convenient facilitation of investment, trading, financial innovation, interim and post-event supervision, establishment of a system of laws and building a mechanism for institutional innovation. The facilitation of investment and trade is aimed at exploring the possible "docking, coupling" or connecting to the high specification and high standards of international economic and trade rules and regulations. The aforementioned facilitative measures are taken to further enhance the level of internationalization of the Greater Bay Area.

(2) *A wide Influence of the overseas Cantonese Chinese*

Southeast Asia has the largest number of overseas Chinese. Over 85% of overseas Chinese have settled in Southeast Asian countries and regions. Thailand, Malaysia and Indonesia are the three Southeast Asian countries with the most overseas Chinese. The numbers of overseas Chinese in the three countries are 4.65 million, 5.9 million and 6 million, respectively. The total number of overseas Chinese in these three countries is 15.74 million, which is close to two-thirds of the total number of overseas Chinese in the whole world. By their ancestral origins, most overseas Chinese originated from Guangdong, accounting for about 54% of the total number of overseas Chinese in the world. These people are the Cantonese.

In recent years, the issue of the low sociopolitical status of overseas Chinese in Southeast Asian nations has gradually improved. This state of affairs is a result of influence of overseas Chinese on the economy of Southeast Asia. Another reason could be because of the active integration of Southeast Asian overseas Chinese into the life of the peoples of Southeast Asian countries and regions. Overseas Chinese in Southeast Asia have slowly abandoned their "ethnocentric ideas and bias" against people of different social classes. They have been stepping up commerce and trade with local people, and some have intermarriage relationship with them, integrating into the daily lives of the people of Southeast Asian countries and regions. At present, overseas Chinese have maintained good cooperative relations with the people of Singapore, Thailand, Indonesia, Malaysia and other countries with a large number of overseas Chinese. Not only has business and trade flourished but the degree of integration with the local residents is also at a high level. In addition, Singapore, Thailand, Indonesia and Malaysia and other Southeast Asian countries and regions have institutionalized and legislated on the political rights of overseas Chinese — they are allowed to enter politics.

The good relations between overseas Chinese in Southeast Asia and the local people not only reduces the unfavorable public opinions of Southeast Asian countries and regions against the Greater

Bay Area of Guangdong, Hong Kong and Macao but also alleviates trade disputes between the Greater Bay Area of Guangdong, Hong Kong and Macao and Southeast Asian countries and regions. Real benefits will accrue, and even preferential treatment for the Greater Bay Area may materialize to help it achieve the goal of "going or moving out" to Southeast Asian countries and regions effectively in support of the "Belt and Road" Initiative.

(3) English and Portuguese languages as bonds for cultural interactions

Owing to the historical colonization of Hong Kong and Macao, the development of Hong Kong and Macao, respectively, embodied the cultures of the English-speaking and Portuguese-speaking world. Hong Kong therefore maintains a good relationship with English-speaking countries. Similarly, Macao also has the cultural foundation to develop hand-in-hand with the Portuguese-speaking countries. Since the reform and opening-up, Hong Kong has always been the "gateway hub" for China to communicate with the English-speaking countries of the West. For one, Hong Kong is an international financial center and one of the most developed cities in the world. Second, Hong Kong and English-speaking countries do share the same culture, administrative system and philosophy.

Likewise, Macao's advantages in Portuguese culture are conducive to Macao's establishment of a platform for cooperation between China and Portuguese-speaking countries. China and Portuguese-speaking countries are highly complementary in terms of factors of production and commodity and merchandise markets. In addition, Portuguese-speaking countries constitute huge markets and have established good economic cooperation with many countries and regions. The range of their influence includes not only countries and regions with strong Portuguese cultural influences such as some countries in the European Union and Latin America but also countries and regions whose residents speak Portuguese because of Portuguese colonization in history. On the prospects of collaboration, Portuguese-speaking countries have the necessary conditions for China to explore new markets and create new platforms, commensurate with China's "moving or going out" strategy in areas influenced by Portuguese culture.

The cultural ties between Hong Kong, Macao and English-speaking and Portuguese-speaking countries are favorable to the strengthening of ties with English-speaking and Portuguese-speaking countries for the Greater Bay Area of Guangdong, Hong Kong and Macao. Upon such strengthening, the investment and trade cooperation between the Greater Bay Area and the English-speaking and Portuguese-speaking countries through the collaboration platform of the Greater Bay Area in promoting its "go global" into English-speaking and Portuguese-speaking countries are thereby enhanced. The entry or inflow of capital, personnel and technology from English-speaking and Portuguese-speaking countries into the Greater Bay Area is thus made possible.

II. Weaknesses of the Guangdong–Hong Kong–Macao Greater Bay Area

There exist "two systems and three tariff zones" within the Greater Bay Area of Guangdong, Hong Kong and Macao. As a result, there arise conflicts not only in administrative systems but also in the different standards applied in the economic systems. Coordinated development of the Guangdong–Hong Kong–Macao Greater Bay Area requires the unimpeded flow of various essential elements and factors. However, owing to security concerns, Chinese Mainland's opening to Hong Kong and Macao is limited, and this situation hinders the integration and development of Guangdong, Hong Kong and Macao. The lack of uniform planning and regulations results in overly stiff competition in industries among the three places, which causes internal attrition of their energies.

(A) *Problem of the compatibility of "One Country, Two Systems"*

"One Country, Two Systems" is a unique advantage of the Guangdong–Hong Kong–Macao Greater Bay Area, but it also constitutes an institutional obstacle to the coordinated development of the Greater Bay Area. The differences between capitalist and socialist systems not only manifest themselves as obstacles in administration but also produce different market economic systems and different legal systems.

(1) *Administrative system*

The cooperation between Guangdong, Hong Kong and Macao under the "one country, two systems" principle is facing insurmountable administrative barriers, especially the problems of "pan-politicization" and "legislative chaos" within Hong Kong, causing many areas of cooperation aimed at "testing and trying out" or experimenting institutional innovations to become blocked or put on hold. For example, the "one place, two inspections" system of the Guangzhou–Shenzhen–Hong Kong high-speed railway took 7 years to break the ice. The reason lies in the procrastination and disputes in the Hong Kong Legislative Council.

When Hong Kong was a British colony, Hong Kong's political system was one of authoritarian dictatorship. There was no election of the Legislative Council nor election of the Chief Executive. The Governor of Hong Kong was appointed directly by the British Government. The management and legal systems of the Hong Kong Government also copied that of the British. With the introduction of the "electoral system" just before Hong Kong's return to Chinese mainland, different interest groups fought among themselves and they tried to sway the electorate to their sides. These internal scuffles seriously affected the cooperation between Guangdong, Hong Kong and Macao. As an example, the Guangzhou–Shenzhen–Hong Kong high-speed railway was originally scheduled to be completed and opened in 2015. However, owing to the involvement of different interest groups, the target completion date was revised from the end of November, 2015 to the third quarter of 2018, and an additional HK$19.6 billion was budgeted. The Shenzhen section across the river had already been completed and was awaiting the opening for passage of rail traffic for a long time. The problem of the Hong

Kong section of the Guangzhou–Shenzhen–Hong Kong high-speed railway is just the tip of the iceberg of the situations in which the cooperation projects between Guangdong, Hong Kong and Macao have been frequently blocked. In recent years, Hong Kong is experiencing serious over-expenditure or delays in several collaborative infrastructure projects between Guangdong, Hong Kong and Macao. For another example, the Hong Kong section of the Hong Kong–Zhuhai–Macao Bridge was delayed from the end of 2016 to 2018. The cost of building the Hong Kong entry point or entry port of the Bridge has also increased from HK$30.4 billion to HK$35.89 billion.

In view of the fact that the establishment of the Guangdong–Hong Kong–Macao Greater Bay Area has been elevated to a national-level strategy, there are now calls for institutional breakthroughs and innovations in Guangdong, Hong Kong and Macao. However, institutional innovations involving unfamiliar territories pose difficulties for traditionalist government departments and civil servants. Currently, the institutional innovations of the Greater Bay Area of Guangdong, Hong Kong and Macao are mainly to be found in China (Guangdong) Pilot FTZ. Many institutional innovations in China (Guangdong) Pilot FTZ concern new areas, new issues and new breakthroughs, which pose greater challenges to the traditional government structure and functions, as well as to the comprehensive quality and ability of civil servants. Because of the "risks" of reforms and the imperfections of the government's mechanism of exemption from accountability, system reforms in many fields are not carried out or at best are not carried to conclusion. At the same time, Hong Kong's civil service system follows the structure and management model of the colonial period, and the system may be good at execution but is not good at creativity and innovation. Moreover, the Hong Kong government has been pursuing the non-interventionist (*laissez faire*) policy of "small government, big market", but the government lacks awareness and foresight of the importance of system and policy design, and these shortcomings have seriously hampered the innovation of the model of cooperation between Guangdong, Hong Kong and Macao.

The China (Guangdong) Pilot FTZ has been promoting the development of the Guangdong–Hong Kong–Macao Greater Bay Area, taking the lead in exploring new systems and models of enhanced cooperation between Guangdong, Hong Kong and Macao. However, even this most active body of system innovation — i.e. China (Guangdong) Pilot FTZ within the Guangdong–Hong Kong–Macao Greater Bay Area — does not have the strength and capacity to push for the comprehensive innovation model of cooperation between Guangdong, Hong Kong and Macao. Shenzhen's Qianhai Shekou Free Trade Zone Management Committee has brought in a number of professionals to engage in institutional innovation research and to set up a Hong Kong Cooperation Office, but it is still in the initial stage of development. Guangzhou's Nansha FTZ follows the previous district-level government management structure, but the assessment and knowledge reserve of civil servants do not match the institutional innovation requirements of the Guangdong–Hong Kong–Macao Greater Bay Area.

Generally speaking, the emergence of new problems and issues in the international financial areas and that of new industries do not have simple solutions for the general functioning departments and staff of Guangdong, Hong Kong and Macao. To further promote the in-depth cooperation between Guangdong, Hong Kong and Macao, we need to make innovative breakthroughs in the administrative systems of the three places of Guangdong, Hong Kong and Macao.

(2) *Legal systems*

Owing to the different status quo of the three places (Guangdong, Hong Kong and Macao) of "one country, two systems, three jurisdictions and three legal systems" encompassing differences in political system, economic conditions and social environment, there are great differences in legal concepts, legal system, interpretation of laws, sources of law, legislation and administration of justice among the three places.

Speaking of legal systems, in the Guangdong–Hong Kong–Macao Greater Bay Area, there is currently a socialist legal system in the Chinese mainland, which are mainly based on the Chinese constitution, plus the legal system of the Hong Kong Special Administrative Region, which is based on the common law system and the British legal model for overseas territories, as well as the Macao Special Administrative Region, which is based on the continental legal system and the Portuguese legal model for overseas territories. There are therefore three legal systems within the Greater Bay Area.

In terms of specific contents of the law, there are not only differences in the emphasis on regulatory laws but also differences in the application of general law, as well as differences in the applicability of international treaties. For example, Hong Kong has always emphasized the use of economic legislation to regulate the market economy. There are more than 200 economic laws and regulations alone, accounting for almost half of the current 500 statutes.

The laws of Guangdong, Hong Kong and Macao also differ greatly in terms of jurisdiction. In terms of administrative authority, the governments of the Hong Kong and Macao special administrative regions have the power to handle administrative affairs each on their own according to the provisions of the Basic Law, while Guangdong has no such power. In terms of legislative authority, the Hong Kong and Macao special administrative regions enjoy a high degree of legislative power. Chinese national laws are generally not implemented in the special administrative regions, and Guangdong has no right to make new legislation. In terms of jurisdiction, Hong Kong and Macao enjoy independent legislative power and rights of final adjudication. They have jurisdiction (i.e. they could adjudicate) over all cases in the special administrative regions except in areas involving national defense and diplomacy. However, in Guangdong, the situation is different.

The crux of the legal differences between Guangdong, Hong Kong and Macao is that these differences are caused by different sources or founts of legislative power, there being a single sovereign state with regional jurisdictions. This situation also reflects the differences between the national laws and the "inland laws" of a special administrative region with a high degree of autonomy in a specific period. Nevertheless, these differences will not thwart the ability of the three "jurisdictions" to seek cooperation amidst the differences and to solve them through "legal" coordination. In line with the paramount principle of safeguarding the sovereignty and dignity of the state and maintaining the legal independence of Hong Kong and Macao under "one country, two systems", all problems and issues can be amicably solved by means of consultations, negotiations and execution of regional legal agreements on the basis of equality.

(3) *Economic systems*

Because of the conflict of interests between the three places, Guangdong, Hong Kong and Macao have set up institutional barriers in their respective economic systems, hindering the free flow of "internal factors" for the Guangdong–Hong Kong–Macao Greater Bay Area. On financial openness, no one dares to dabble in certain financial areas that require macroprudential considerations, and ideas for reforms have been rather conservative. On the entry and exit of people, Hong Kong's efforts to attract high-quality talents from the Mainland are also very limited. Protecting local people from the "influx" of "outsiders" will do Hong Kong more harm than good in the long run. In the construction of cooperative (industrial) parks, the consideration for Hong Kong and Macao is their right to develop and use land, while for the Mainland the priority is to develop the economy. The differences of interest between Guangdong, Hong Kong and Macao render the system setup rigid and inflexible while the speed of cooperation is hindered.

In addition, in order to protect local industries and professions, some of Hong Kong's traditional service industries have long been closed to the Mainland, purportedly to maintain their professional authority and economic status. For example, professionals in services such as in medical and legal professions, Hong Kong's efforts are insufficient. This in effect limits the supply of local medical and legal professionals in Hong Kong, while it also restricts the export of professional services from Hong Kong to the Chinese mainland.

On the contrary, although the nine cities of Guangdong and China (Guangdong) Pilot FTZ have collectively planned a special regional scheme to connect or be in sync or to connect or "couple" with Guangdong, Hong Kong and Macao cooperation, in efforts to break down the economic and institutional barriers between them, if the industries of Hong Kong and Macao negatively impact on the nine cities of Guangdong and China (Guangdong) Pilot FTZ, restrictive policy counter-measures will also be adopted to protect the development of key industries within the nine cities and that of the Pilot FTZ.

(4) *Supervisory systems*

In two high-security risks and difficult supervision areas of customs and finance, China (Guangdong) Pilot FTZ implements the "first-line liberalization, second-line high-efficiency supervision" model of macroprudential supervision. In these two areas, emphasis is placed on carrying out "stress testing" experimentally to accumulate supervisory experience. The China (Guangdong) Pilot FTZ and Hong Kong still have much room for reforms in terms of inspection of goods and quarantine, mutual recognition and two-way opening up of their financial industries. In contrast to the continuous opening up of the China (Guangdong) Pilot FTZ to financial and customs supervision *vis-à-vis* Hong Kong's, the financial and customs supervision of Hong Kong is more stringent and conservative.

Many of Hong Kong's control and regulatory measures follow the policies and laws promulgated by the British colonial government, and the said laws and regulations have failed to keep pace with the times and they have not been revised or amended accordingly. Apart from being outdated and hindering the economic development, the regulatory system also indirectly leads to political and social problems. For example, the development of country parks and wasteland and barren beaches could help solve the problem of social antagonism caused by acute shortage of land and housing in Hong Kong. However, due to the fact that land development in Hong Kong has always followed the "statutory plan" devised during Hong Kong's colonial days, it takes 5–11 years for a piece of land to become legally usable. Such a situation adversely affects the progress of people's housing constructions. Because of the rigid regulations pertaining to land use and construction development in Hong Kong, it took 7 years to clear up and level the land and complete the Lok Ma Chau Loop area project, despite going through many steps of approval and formalities. This area was in fact among the easiest areas to develop in Hong Kong. Such low efficiency will have a very negative impact on the cooperation of projects and economic exchanges between Guangdong, Hong Kong and Macao.

(B) *Lack of a mechanism for legislative alliance*

Though the work and arrangements related to promoting the deepened cooperation between the three places for the establishment of the Greater Bay Area of Guangdong, Hong Kong and Macao have been continuing for many years — such as the "Joint Guangdong–Hong Kong Cooperation Meeting" in 1998 and the "Pan-Pearl River Delta Cooperation Framework Agreement" signed in Guangdong in 2004 — and even after the formation of the Greater Bay Area was elevated to the level of national strategy, there has been no major breakthroughs in the establishment of a mechanism for the legal alliance between the governments of Guangdong, Hong Kong and Macao. The reality of "one country, two systems" affects the coordinated development of the three places. Moreover, the three places involve the administration of provincial and SAR governments and departments, and as there is so far no distinction made as to which body or bodies are the superior ones and which are the subordinate ones, leadership (in the sense of having been given powers to lead) in coordinating the project of the Greater Bay Area has not been properly determined. As it is, there is no unified, coordinated effort to allocate the resources of the three places and no legal mechanism for an alliance to coordinate industrial development has been put in place. It is apparent that if negotiations and consultations continue to separate bilateral discussions between the governments of the three places, the usual obstacles due to the different systems will remain.

At present, the cooperation between Guangdong, Hong Kong and Macao mainly involves the areas of self-starting or "spontaneous" industries, investment and trade. For the Hong Kong government, the issue of cooperation with the Mainland and the topic of "Belt and Road" Initiative have attracted much attention. However, the topic of Hong Kong and the China (Guangdong) Pilot FTZ has been given scant attention and is not really given much thought and consideration. As for Macao, the government focuses more on customs clearance and investment cooperation with Zhuhai, and there is little research conducted on the mechanism and plan for integrating resources in the Great Bay Area of Guangdong, Hong Kong and Macao.

In terms of the state of cooperation between Guangdong, Hong Kong and Macao, Shenzhen and Hong Kong have closer market cooperation, Macao and Zhuhai have closer government-led cooperation, while Guangzhou's cooperation with Hong Kong and Macao is relatively loose. It is precisely because of the lack of a mechanism of legal–statutory alliance in the Greater Bay Area of Guangdong, Hong Kong and Macao that the cooperation between Guangdong, Hong Kong and Macao has not received or given an integrated and unified approach and thinking, nor given the top-level planning, design and consideration, resulting in insufficient planning and relatively loose cooperation between Guangdong, Hong Kong and Macao.

(C) *Limited flow of important factors of production*

Owing to the different regulatory and supervisory systems and policies in different industries in Guangdong, Hong Kong and Macao, the factors of production in the Greater Bay Area of Guangdong, Hong Kong and Macao could not enter and exit freely in the three regions. One reason is that the infrastructures at the three places have not "docked" or made connections in the sense of commensuration and compatibility. Another reason is that the access thresholds for industries and professions are distinctly different in the three places, and inspection and quarantine standards and tariff systems differ as well.

(1) Infrastructure interconnectivity is low

The financial market in the Mainland and Hong Kong's financial market are two separate markets, lacking a unified interacting platform. Although the "Shenzhen–Hong Kong Stock Connect" of the stock market has already been implemented and the Qianhai Joint Trading Center of the Hong Kong Stock Exchange has also settled in the Qianhai–Shenzhen–Hong Kong Modern Services Cooperation Zone, the bond, gold, and interbank markets of the Guangdong–Hong Kong–Macao Greater Bay Area have not yet realized the connection with the corresponding financial market of Hong Kong; a unified trading (transaction) platform is thus lacking.

Due to information security considerations, Chinese Mainland is open to Hong Kong and Macao — subject to conditions — in the field of telecommunications and the Internet. It is difficult for residents of Hong Kong and Macao to access accurate information from important webpages in Chinese mainland; likewise, the information residents of Chinese Mainland obtain about Hong Kong and Macao is also incomplete and limited. The data transmission system between Guangdong, Hong Kong and Macao is not good enough, with low efficiency in transmission. Telecommunications to Hong Kong and Macao leave much to be desired, and the channels of international communication "docking" or connecting and joining Hong Kong and Macao are limited in effect. Such a situation is not conducive to the information exchange between Guangdong, Hong Kong and Macao.

The transport systems of Guangdong, Hong Kong and Macao are not yet fully linked and interconnected, and the infrastructure needs to be further improved. Problems due to the management systems of the Hong Kong and Macao governments have delayed a number of major projects that are supposed to enhance cooperation between Guangdong, Hong Kong and Macao. Some were even put on hold. The Hong Kong section of the Guangzhou–Shenzhen–Hong Kong high-speed railway was a striking example. At the same time, the limited number of motor vehicles that can freely travel to and from Guangdong, Hong Kong and Macao has resulted in big crowds at various ports of entry and exit connected to the subways and long customs clearance time, situations which are not condu-cive to the free movement of people in Guangdong, Hong Kong and Macao.

(2) *Residents of the three places are not allowed to move freely in and out of the three places*

Residents of the Greater Bay Area of Guangdong, Hong Kong and Macao cannot travel freely in the three places of Guangdong, Hong Kong and Macao. They need to apply for visas to travel between the three places, and the number of entries is limited. Residents of the nine cities in Guangdong can only travel to Hong Kong once a week and Macao twice a month, even if they go on a self-arranged tour in Hong Kong and Macao.

Second, Hong Kong and Macao practice the measures of entry requirements for professionals and personnel. Some professional service industries are not open to people from the Mainland, so professional service providers with Mainland licenses are not allowed to provide professional services directly in Hong Kong and Macao. Although the protective measures of Hong Kong and Macao have reduced the possibility of their industries being impacted by the Mainland, they have also hindered the growth and agglomera-tion of outstanding professionals in Hong Kong.

(3) *Issue of the customs clearance of goods*

Hong Kong has the highest degree of openness, but it also has the strictest "interim and post-event" regulations. It has inspection and quarantine standards and tax arrangements that are compatible with internationally assessed high standards of economic and trade rules and regulations. At present, many goods and commodities in the Chinese Mainland still fail to meet the inspection and quaran-tine requirements of Hong Kong; this situation is not conducive to the smooth customs clearance of goods in Guangdong, Hong Kong and Macao. Another negative factor is that there are three complete tariff zones within the Greater Bay Area of Guangdong, Hong Kong and Macao. The three tariff systems are quite different, leading to different taxation standards or criteria for goods in circulation within Guangdong, Hong Kong and Macao.

(D) *Limitation of capital inflow and outflow*

Although Hong Kong is a "super-contact" for the Mainland in both foreign and overseas investments, free exchange of funds between Guangdong, Hong Kong and Macao is restricted because of the stricter foreign exchange controls in the Mainland and the low level of RMB internationalization.

(1) *Foreign exchange control*

Compared to Hong Kong and Macao, which allow the free flow of domestic and foreign currencies, the Mainland strictly prohibits the free flow of foreign currencies and has strict regulations regarding foreign exchange. In the management of foreign exchanges, the Mainland requires enterprises to sell all foreign exchange earned from export trade to designated banks within a specified period of time in accordance with the official closing and selling exchange rate. In the case of imports, an enterprise must obtain the approval of the Administration of Foreign Exchange before it can exchange the amount of foreign currencies specified by the banks designated by the Administration for the purchase of imported goods. As for non-trade foreign exchange earnings, the controls are very similar to those for export foreign exchange management. The relevant rules stipulate that enterprises or individuals should sell all or part of the foreign exchange to the designated banks in accordance with the relevant regulations of the Administration of Foreign Exchange and following the official closing and selling exchange rates. At the same time, individuals and enterprises are proscribed from carrying, carrying on behalf, or sending by mail gold, platinum or silver out of the country.

As a result of the Mainland's strict prohibitions and control measures, foreign exchange (currencies) could not be used or circulated freely in Guangdong, Hong Kong and Macao. From the perspective of capital movements, the aforesaid controls and measures add on to the steps required for capital to move around. Therefore, the best solution is to convert all foreign currencies into RMB in order to render free circulation and flow of capital within the nine cities of the Guangdong–Hong Kong–Macao Greater Bay Area.

(2) *Hong Kong's offshore RMB status has weakened*

For a long time, Hong Kong had been the largest offshore market of RMB for the Mainland and one of the main centers for international RMB settlement. It has made great and indelible contributions toward the internationalization of RMB. However, Hong Kong's status as an offshore RMB center has declined in recent years, negatively impacting the cross-border RMB flows in the Guangdong–Hong Kong–Macao Greater Bay Area.

The total amount of RMB deposits and certificates of deposit in Hong Kong has been declining steadily since 2014 — from over 1 trillion yuan to nearly 600 billion yuan, as shown in Figure 5. At the end of 2016, the total amount of RMB deposits and certificates of deposit in Hong Kong fell by 21.5% to 625.1 billion yuan, compared with the figures 6 months ago. Of the figures, customer RMB deposits fell by 23.2%, while corporate or enterprise customer deposits fell individual customer deposits. But the decline in deposit certificate balances narrowed from 46.8% in the first half of 2016 to 7.5% in the second half.

Despite the contraction of the RMB liquidity (or amount of current assets or capital) pool, the banks' RMB liquidity management is still healthy and fine, and the pool is large enough to support a large number of RMB payments and financial transactions. The average daily turnover of the RMB instant/real-time payment and settlement systems rose to 863.6 billion yuan in 2016. After adjustment in the first half of 2016, the balance of RMB loans recovered by 2.6% in the second half of the year. On the contrary, the amount

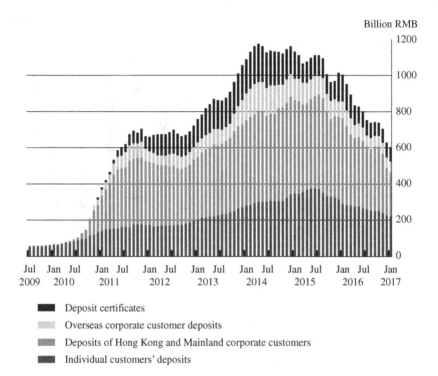

Billion RMB

Deposit certificates

Overseas corporate customer deposits

Deposits of Hong Kong and Mainland corporate customers

Individual customers' deposits

Figure 5. Total amount of RMB deposits and certificates of deposits in Hong Kong.

Source: "Report on Financial & Monetary Stability", Hong Kong Monetary Authority (2016).

of RMB trade settlement handled by the banks of Hong Kong fell to 2176.9 billion yuan in the second half of 2016, down 8% from the first half. Although remittances from Hong Kong to the Mainland continued to decline, other trade remittances, including remittances from the Mainland to Hong Kong and remittances from offshore markets via Hong Kong, recovered moderately, as shown in Figure 6.

It is expected that the RMB liquidity situation in Hong Kong will still be affected by the uncertain trend of RMB exchange rates and that such uncertainties will hamper the cross-border use of RMB in the Guangdong–Hong Kong–Macao Greater Bay Area.

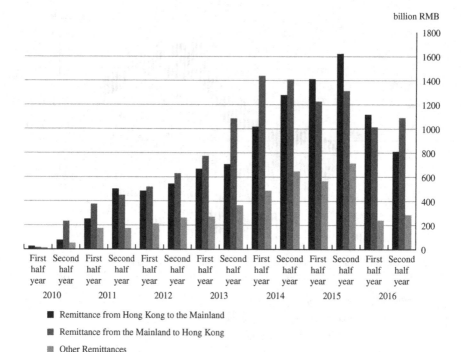

billion RMB

■ Remittance from Hong Kong to the Mainland
■ Remittance from the Mainland to Hong Kong
■ Other Remittances

Figure 6.   RMB remittance in Hong Kong.

(E) *Imbalance in collaboration and cooperation of industries*

We recognize that industrial cooperation between Guangdong, Hong Kong and Macao is steadily advancing. However, due to the lack of top-level design and planning and the lack of strategic cooperation between Guangdong, Hong Kong and Macao, cooperation in industries among the three cities remains uncoordinated.

After two financial crises and the trauma of SARS, the trend of the industrial differentiation, consolidation, simplification and hollowing-out phenomenon in Hong Kong is evident. On the one hand, we have the financial, real estate and professional services industries with high values added and low employment figures. On the other hand, there are the traditional services such as tourism, catering, accommodation and retail industries with low values added and high employment figures. The "intelligent" manufacturing industry with high knowledge and technology content has been lacking for a long time. For a long time, the "siphoning effect" produced by Hong Kong's financial, trade, accountant, legal and medical services has weighed in considerably among the development elements of the science and technology industry, making it less vibrant and quite sluggish, and the atmosphere of innovation and technology development in Hong Kong is simply lacking.

Influenced by the dichotomy of "small government, big market" that connotes inaction and onerousness in action, the supporting role of the Hong Kong government is very limited. While other economies have begun to develop the knowledge economy, Hong Kong has missed the "open-window period" of transition to the knowledge economy. At present, the closest and most effective cooperation between Guangdong, Hong Kong, Macao and Hong Kong is the Qianhai–Shenzhen–Hong Kong Modern Service Industry Cooperation Zone, but most of the industries involved are still in finance, trade and logistics.

On industrial cooperation with Macao, the dominance of the gambling tourism industry is still a serious drawback or weakness in Macao's industrial structure. Many people from all circles have paid close attention to Macao's economic diversification for a long time, and many valuable suggestions have been put forth. However, the inherent constraints of a small economy and limited land have reduced Macao's vision of diversified economic development to a "much talked but little realized" situation. One comforting piece of information is that the industrial cooperation between Macao and Zhuhai is relatively close, but it is limited to one-way investment in the tourism industry. There is still much room for mutually interacting, diversified investments between the two sides.

Chapter 4

Economic Spatial Structure of the Guangdong–Hong Kong–Macao Greater Bay Area

Zhao Genhong

Shenzhen Institute of Information Technology

A region is a concept of space that exists objectively, but for specific connotation and in physical terms, different scholars have given it slightly different definitions. From a geographical point of view, a region is an abstract concept of space that exists objectively. Any part of the earth's surface, an area of space, a country or several countries may be called a region.

In regional economic development, the changes of economic spatial structure and the economic development are mutually reinforcing and complementary, and the relationship between them is one of mutual feedback and promotion. As Clark Edwards, an

American regional economist, puts it, in "Spatial Aspects of Rural Development"[1], "Economic growth occurs in a given space, and it is influenced by the spatial economy and is reflected as feedbacks to economic growth". With the development of human spatial economic activities both in breadth and depth, the study on the formation and development of spatial economic structures becomes more and more significant.[2] In the study of the economy of the Greater Bay Area, its spatial economic structure naturally becomes an unavoidable issue.

With nine cities in the Pearl River Delta area acting as the pilot "epicenter" or core, internationalized Hong Kong and Macao special administrative regions acting as bridges and with the backing of the Pan-Pearl River Delta city clusters, the Greater Bay Area has made remarkable achievements and attracted worldwide attention as part of China's reform and opening-up. Today, the regional division of labor and industrial structures of cities in the Greater Bay Area have undergone tremendous changes. Hong Kong and Macao's status as international metropolises has been further consolidated, while Shenzhen and Guangzhou have become two of the world's first-class cities. Zhuhai, Foshan and Dongguan have developed into sub-centric cities. The road to industrial upgrading in other regions is also rapidly progressing. However, there are still disparities in economic development within the Greater Bay Area, and the goal of the coordinated regional development has not been fully real-

---

[1] Clark Edwards: "Spatial Aspects of Rural Development", *Agricultural Economics Research*, Vol. 33, No. 3, 1981, pp. 11–12.

[2] In fact, traditional Western economic theories have long ignored the issue of economic behavioral space, as economists Walter Isard *et al.* (1981) believe: "Those theories concerning development, growth, evolution, transition and change — generally contain shortcomings *vis-à-vis* the theory of social dynamics." To us, the shortcomings arise because these theories fail to take into account spatial factors. Therefore, "exogenous variables such as space, distance and location should be introduced into the economic model".

ized. Although the differences among regions are shrinking, one cannot deny or conceal the fact that differences still exist. Therefore, it is imperative that the main content of the analysis of the economic spatial structure of the Guangdong–Hong Kong–Macao Greater Bay Area should include predicting the extent, progress and trends in the disparities of regional economic development, exploring the reasons for the disparities and reflecting on the influencing factors. The following is a theoretical introduction, analysis of disparities, exploration of causes and progressive optimization of the spatial economic structures in the Greater Bay Area, which we hope will provide theoretical support for further strengthening the interaction between economic development and spatial structure in the Greater Bay Area.

I. Regional and Spatial Effects and Spatial Structure of the Regional Economy

(A) *Regional and spatial effects*

(1) *Region*

A region (or an area) is a concept of space that exists objectively, but for specific connotations and in physical terms, different scholars have given it slightly different definitions. From a geographical point of view, a region is an abstract concept of space that exists objectively. Any part of the earth's surface, an area of space, a country or several countries may be called a region.

On the surface of the earth, any country, region, territory, part or several countries can be called a region.[3] From the perspective of economics, a region can be understood as a regional economic entity with its own complete jurisdiction, clear functions and

---

[3] An Husen: *General Theory of Regional Economics*, Beijing, China: Economic Science Press, 2004.

strong cohesion within it.[4] To become a region, an area should possess five elements: internal cohesion, structure, function, size and boundary. Of these five elements, internal cohesion brings about the formation and evolution of the region, determines the formation and functional division of the internal structure and further affects the realization of the size and boundaries, ultimately forming an interdependent economic unit with common regional interests.[5] Within the economic region, its existence is of two forms, namely: homogenization and polarization. The former refers to the phenomenon of homogenizing, pertaining to the similarity that is obtained when the region is divided by a specific sign, hallmark or marker; the latter refers to the polarizing phenomenon, attributable to the interaction between essential factors shaping the regional division of the strong internal cohesion.

This book attempts to study the Greater Bay Area — a region that mainly includes the nine cities of Guangdong Province including Guangzhou, Shenzhen, Dongguan, Foshan, Zhuhai, Zhongshan, Zhaoqing, Jiangmen and Huizhou, plus the two special administrative regions of Hong Kong and Macao, collectively known as "9 + 2" region.

(2) *Spatial effects*

Generally speaking, spatial effects include the following two aspects: spatial correlation and spatial heterogeneity.[6] Spatial correlation (or dependence) refers to the correlation characteristics of different spatial regions manifested in economic growth; that is, spatial location as a factor joins the associated factors that

---

[4] Sun Jiuwen: *Regional Economics*, Beijing, China: Capital University of Economics and Business Publishing House, 2007.
[5] Wei Houkai: *Modern Regional Economics*, Beijing, China: Economic Management Publishing House, 2006.
[6] Zhang Keyun: "Review, Progress and Commentary of Spatial Econometrics Studies Abroad", *Industrial Economic Review*, Vol. 1, 2016, pp. 5–21.

determine regional economic development. The correlation between different spatial locations can be divided into positive correlation and negative correlation from two perspectives. Positive spatial correlation means a situation in which the economic developments of adjacent regions display convergence or similarity, while negative spatial correlation indicates that there is no similarity between economic growths in different spatial locations. Spatial heterogeneity is manifested by spatial differences in real economic activities, meaning that economic activities show heterogeneous characteristics in different regions. Spatial heterogeneity and correlations together determine the regional spatial structure, producing spatial economic effects.

Spatial correlation is a cross-sectional correlation formed by the spatial interaction between the subject entities or units in different regions. Because of the flow of various economic factors, the diffusion of innovation and technology spillovers, the shape or pattern of spatial structures of regional economic development and innovation differences will evolve among different regions. For example, labor force and capital flow will result in regional economic development differences and R&D investment will produce demonstrable effects in different regions.[7]

(B) *Regional economic spatial structure*

(1) *Concept of regional economic spatial structure*

At present, there are different definitions for regional spatial structure in academic circles. For example, some academics consider that the spatial structure of the regional economy refers to the interaction and mutual relationship between social and economic objects in space and the spatial scale or size and

---

[7] Sun Jiuwen and Yao Peng: "Research Paradigms and Latest Developments of Spatial Econometrics", *Economist*, Vol. 7, 2014, pp. 27–35.

form of agglomeration of objects and phenomena reflecting this relationship.[8] Others think that it refers to the relative location of the key economic elements *vis-à-vis* the region and the form of the distribution thereof.[9] There are also others who think that it is the spatially combined relationship of human economic activities in a certain region and the sum total of the regional economic center, periphery and network relations[10] or the form of existence and objective entity of economic phenomena and economic variables within a certain geographical range characterized by distribution and location, shape, size and interaction[11] or the organizational structure formed by the action of human economic activities in a certain geographical area[12] or the structure formed by the interaction of the forces of agglomeration and the dispersal of economic spatial phenomena within a certain region.[13]

(2) *Theory of regional spatial structure*

The theory of the regional spatial structure covers both the evolutionary theory of regional spatial structure and the model theory of regional spatial structure. Friedman, a well-known American economist, and Lu Dadao, a domestic Chinese scholar, are good advocates of this theory (Tables 1 and 2).

---

[8] Lu Dadao: *Regional Development and Its Spatial Structure*, Beijing, China: Science Press, 1998.

[9] Cui Gonghao, Wei Qingquan, and Liu Kewei: *Regional Analysis and Regional Planning*, Beijing, China: Higher Education Press, 2006.

[10] Chen Cai: *Regional Economic Geography*, Beijing, China: Science Press, 2009.

[11] Zeng Juxin: *Spatial Economy: Systems and Consequences*, Wuhan, China: Wuhan Publishing House, 1996.

[12] Lu Yuqi: *Research on Spatial Structure in Regional Development*, Nanjing, China: Nanjing Normal University Press, 1998.

[13] Nie Hualin and Zhao Chao: *Probability of Regional Spatial Structure*, Beijing, China: China Social Science Press, 2008.

Table 1. Friedman's evolutionary theory of regional spatial structure.

Development Stage	Spatial Characteristics	Composition	Regional Links	Economic Characteristics
Pre-industrialization stage	The regional space is homogeneous and without order, and there is no hierarchical structural differentiation.	There are several local centers + vast rural areas.	Relatively closed, with fewer links with each other.	Low productivity, with an extremely underdeveloped economy, in a low equilibrium state.
Early industrialization stage	Conspicuous spatial polarization; the regional spatial structure is becoming increasingly unbalanced.	A certain regional economic center + backward peripheral areas.	The center attracts the concentration of key economic elements from peripheral areas.	A particular place has gained some momentum for development, and its economy grows rapidly, while the peripheral areas are becoming more backward.
Industrialization stage	The regional spatial structure tends to be more complex and orderly.	Several regional economic centers + peripheral areas.	Closer and more frequent interactions between the different centers (of varying levels) and the periphery.	New economic centers are founded and a system of regional economic centers is established; the established regional spatial structure has a positive impact on regional economic growth.
Post-industrialization stage	The unity or integration of functions of the spatial structure system will eventually lead to the unity or integration of space.	The boundaries between the centers and the peripheries gradually disappear leading to the unity and integration of the regional space.	Closer and wider economic interactions among different areas of the region, and closer ties between the different economic centers and the peripheral areas.	The economic development has reached a more advanced level and the difference in regional economic development levels is narrowing (between different areas within the region).

Table 2. Lu Dadao's evolutionary theory of regional spatial structure.

Development Stage	Spatial Characteristics	Composition	Regional Links	Economic Characteristics
Stage of absolute dominance of agriculture	Low-level equilibrium state, relatively stable.	Inhabitants are widely scattered.	There is very little interaction and exchange between the urban and rural areas in terms of people, logistics, information and other aspects.	Towns/cities gradually appear, but there is little or poor regional infrastructure.
Transitional period	There is regional spatial imbalance, with extremely underdeveloped peripheral areas.	A single center–periphery structure.	The links between towns and villages are now stronger, and a large number of the rural population has moved into towns/cities.	A more rapid regional economic growth accompanied with continuous growth in production and exchange of goods within the region.
Stage of industrialization and economic takeoff	The urban hierarchy system begins to take shape, and the remote and backward areas are being developed.	Multi-core or multi-nucleus structure.	The exchanges between urban and rural areas and between cities become more and more active.	The regional economy enters a period of strong and dynamic growth.
Stage of technology and high consumption	Higher-level equilibrium state.	Great extent of integration.	Urban settlements, service facilities and the areas of their influence each have formed their own hierarchical system.	High level of social productivity and modern transportation and communication networks have been formed, and regional differences have gradually disappeared.

II. Spatial–Temporal Analysis of Economic Disparities in the Greater Bay Area

(A) *Methods of testing and calculation*

There are many indicators to measure regional economic disparities, such as Gini and range coefficients and Theil index. In this book, we choose to use the Theil index to quantitatively measure regional economic disparities. The main reason for choosing this index is so as to analyze in depth the differences or disparities between regions. The bigger value of Theil index, the greater economic disparities between regional units. The formula for calculating the Theil index is as follows:

$$T_d = \sum_{i=1}^{n_i} \sum_{j=1}^{n_i} \left(\frac{y_{ij}}{Y} \right) \log \left(\frac{y_{ij}/Y}{p_{ij}/P} \right) \tag{4.1}$$

In the above formula, $N(n_1, n_2)$ is the number of regions, y_{ij} is the GDP of city j of region i with characteristics, p_{ij} is the population of city j of region i, and Y and P refer to the region's total GDP and population, respectively.

It is necessary to "decompose" the Theil Index in order to determine whether the cause of the disparities is more due to intra-regional or inter-regional disparities

Define

$$T_{di} = \sum_{j}^{n_2} = 1 \left[\left(\frac{y_{ij}}{Y_i} \right) \log \left(\frac{y_{ij}/Y_i}{p_{ij}/P_i} \right) \right]$$

we then obtain

$$T_d = \sum_{i=1}^{n_i} \left[\left(\frac{Y_i}{Y} \right) T_{di} \right] + \sum_{i=1}^{n_i} \left[\left(\frac{y_{ij}}{Y} \right) \log \left(\frac{y_{ij}/Y}{p_{ij}/p} \right) \right] = T_{wr} + T_{br} \tag{4.2}$$

where

$$T_{wr} = \sum_{i=1}^{n_1} \left[\left(\frac{Y_i}{Y} \right) T_{di} \right]$$

indicates the difference between the regions with characteristics (i.e. the intra-regional difference); and

$$T_{br} = \sum_{i=1}^{n_1} \left[\left(\frac{y_{ij}}{Y} \right) \log \left(\frac{y_{ij}/Y}{p_i/P} \right) \right]$$

denotes the difference between the regions with different characteristics, i.e. inter-regional differences (disparities).

(B) *Evolution process of economic disparities in the Greater Bay Area*

In this chapter, the GDP per capita of the 11 cities of the Guangdong, Hong Kong, Macao Greater Bay Area from 2001 to 2016 is taken as the indicator of regional economic disparities. The Theil indices are calculated and plotted to analyze the changing trend of economic disparities within the Greater Bay Area in the past 15 years or so.

From Figure 1, we can see that in the past 15 years from 2001 to 2016, the economic disparities have gradually narrowed down between the cities of Guangdong, Hong Kong and Macao. The Theil indices dropped from 0.599 in 2001 to 0.129 in 2016, with a decrease of 78.46%. There are two stages of development in this decline of economic disparities.

From 2001 to 2009, the economic disparities in the Greater Bay Area of Guangdong–Hong Kong–Macao shrank rapidly, showing an almost unilateral downward trend. The Theil index declined rapidly from 0.599 in 2001 to 0.179 in 2009, with a decrease of 89.5% in the overall economic disparities over the past 15 years, with an annual average composite disparity decline of 8.31%.

From 2009 to 2016, regional economic disparities were still gradually narrowing, but the rate of contraction was obviously decreasing. The Theil index gradually declined from 0.179 in

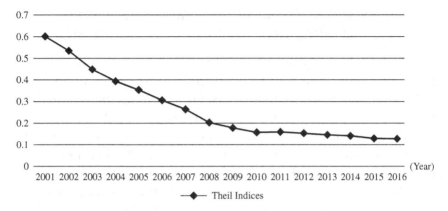

Figure 1. Plot of relative differential variation of per capita GDP in the Greater Bay Area, 2001–2016.

2009 to 0.129 in 2016, and the absolute index declined by 0.05, accounting for 10.5% of the total economic disparities in the past 15 years, while the annual composite disparity decreased by only 1.26%.

Overall, during 2001–2016, the economic disparities in the Guangdong–Hong Kong–Macao Greater Bay Area declined rapidly. Especially before 2009, the domestic economic development experienced a period of upsurge. With the rapid development of the Mainland economy, the overall regional economic disparities narrowed significantly. After 2009, with the global economy entering a "post-financial crisis era" and the Chinese economy gradually entering an era of "new normal", the decline slowed down evidently. However, in the context of supply-side structural reform, with the establishment of Nansha, Qianhai and Hengqin Free Trade Zones in Guangzhou and Shenzhen and with a series of regional cooperation mechanisms such as CEPA involving Guangdong, Hong Kong and Macao, the economic factors in the region began to flow and integrate effectively. Therefore, even in the new stage of macroeconomic growth from "high speed" to "medium high speed", the overall economic disparities within the region continue to maintain the gradually narrowing trend.

(C) *Decomposition of economic disparities between regions of the Guangdong–Hong Kong–Macao Greater Bay Area*

The "9 + 2" economic units within the Greater Bay Area include different economic units at different degrees of development. In order to further analyze the economic disparities among the regions, the 11 units corresponding to the 11 places are divided into three groups. By the criterion of the economic system, Hong Kong and Macao are grouped into one. In the nine inland urban unit areas, Guangzhou and Shenzhen are placed under another group, and the remaining seven urban units are put together to form one last group. Using the formulas provided above, the Theil index analysis of the Guangdong–Hong Kong–Macao Greater Bay Area is carried out, based on the said city units.

From Figures 2 and 3, it can be seen that the economic disparities between Guangdong, Hong Kong and Macao in the Greater Bay Area narrowed rapidly from 2001 to 2010, but the disparities showed a weak trend of expansion in 2011, and then has gradually narrowed once again — but the speed of narrowing disparities has slowed down markedly. The economic disparities between Guangdong and Shenzhen regions maintained a gradually narrow-

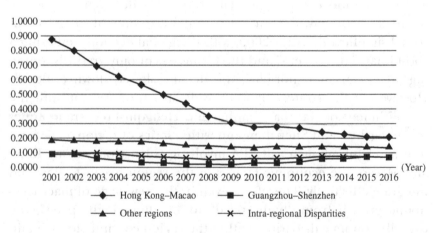

Figure 2. Intra-regional decomposition of the disparities of per capita GDP of regions within the Greater Bay Area.

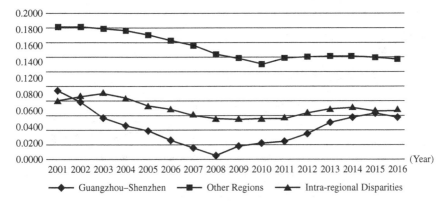

Figure 3. Intra-regional decomposition of the disparities of per capita GDP of regions (excluding Hong Kong and Macao) within the Greater Bay Area.

ing trend in 2001–2008, but after 2009 there has been an increasing trend in the disparities between the two places. The economic disparities gradually increased until 2016, when they showed a slight decrease, displaying a U-shape structure overall. The economic disparities within the other regions gradually decreased from 2001 to 2010 and then mostly remained stable from 2011 to 2016. From the positions of the three regions in the curves on the figures, it can be seen that Hong Kong and Macao have always been above Guangdong–Shenzhen and other regions, indicating that the economic disparities between Hong Kong and Macao were relatively large. However, the level of disparities in the other economic units in the region is always greater than that of Guangzhou–Shenzhen, showing that the development of Guangzhou and Shenzhen go hand-in-hand, which in reality is commensurate with the status of the two cities as the economic leaders of Guangdong.

From Figure 4, we can see that after the Theil indices have been decomposed for inter-regional (area) and intra-regional disparities, the movement of inter-regional Theil indices correlates closely with the Theil index for total disparities, and the values are much higher than those for intra-regional (area) Theil indices. Through the intra-regional Theil indices, we can see that the intra-regional eco-

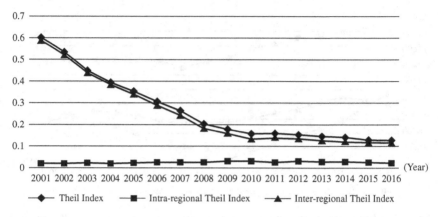

Figure 4.   Decomposition of the Theil indices for per capita GDP of the Greater Bay Area.

nomic disparities show a weak inverted "U" structure, that is, the disparities increase and then decrease, but the overall value (of the disparities) is relatively small. The economic disparities in the Greater Bay Area in the past 15 years are mainly caused by inter-regional disparities, and the overall economic disparities are gradually narrowing. This shows that since the beginning of this century, the economic disparities between Hong Kong–Macao, Guangzhou–Shenzhen and other regions are gradually narrowing because of the strengthened regional cooperation and the close economic ties.

III. Economic Spatial Structure and Its Changes in the Guangdong–Hong Kong–Macao Greater Bay Area

Under the combined actions of spatial agglomeration and disper-sal, a regional economic spatial pattern will inevitably emerge as a result of various correlations and interactions between regions. Premised on this, the economic agglomeration and polarization of the regional spatial structure will be the main manifestation of regional economic spatial disparities. Following is an empirical study using the per capita GDP and its growth rate as indicators to carry out an analysis of the change or evolution of the spatial pattern of the economic development level of "9 + 2" cities in the Greater Bay Area.

(A) *Measuring and calculating indicators*

To measure the economic spatial structure of the Greater Bay Area from the perspective of spatial correlation, generally two indicators are required: one is the spatial structural index, including the spatial autocorrelation Moran index (Moran's I) and the local (or partial) spatial autocorrelation Moran index (local Moran's I); the other is the indicator for the evolution trend of spatial structures, including the Getis–Ord statistical values.

(1) *Moran's Index (Moran's I)*

Moran's I is generally used to investigate the overall or total spatial correlation. The specific formula is as follows:

$$I = \frac{n}{S_0} \cdot \frac{\sum_i^n \sum_{j=1}^n w_{ij}(x_i - \overline{x})(x_j - \overline{x})}{\sum_i^n (x_i - \overline{x})^2} \tag{4.3}$$

where x_i is the observed value on the ith spatial unit, w_{ij} is the spatial weighted matrix, S_0 is the sum of all elements in the spatial weighted matrix and

$$\overline{x} = \frac{1}{n}\sum_{i=1}^n x_i \circ I \in (-1,1)$$

where a value nearer to 1 indicates greater positive correlation, whereas a value nearer to -1 indicates greater negative correlation.

(2) *Local or Partial Moran Index (local Moran's I)*

$$I_i = \frac{n(x_i - \overline{x})\sum_i w_{ij}(x_j - \overline{x})}{\sum_i (x_i - \overline{x})} = z_i \sum_j w_{ij} z_j \tag{4.4}$$

In the above equation, z_i, z_j are the standardized forms of the investigated variable for regions i and j, representing how much the variable for each region deviates from the mean; w_{ij} is the spatial weighted matrix and $\sum_j w_{ij} z_j$ is the weighted mean of the deviation of the investigated variable for the adjacent regions. Local spatial structure pattern of the region are divided into four distinct categories of regions depending on the values of I_i and z_i: high–high (H–H), low–low (L–L), high–low (H–L) and low–high (L–H) agglomeration regions.

(B) *Evolution in the spatial structure of economic development level in the Greater Bay Area*

In order to prompt or intuitively "discover" the spatial pattern distribution of regional economic development levels in the Greater Bay Area, the ratios (λ) of per capita GDP to its regional average in "9 + 2" cities are divided into four categories: backward areas with $\lambda < 0.75$, underdeveloped areas with $\lambda \in [0.75, 1]$, developing (or mid-level developed) areas with $\lambda \in [1, 1.5]$ and (fully) developed areas with $\lambda > 1.5$. In addition, this chapter chooses 2004, 2008, 2012 and 2016 as cutoff points to analyze the spatial–temporal changes of economic development levels in the Greater Bay Area for the past years.

From Table 3, it can be seen that: (i) at the four cutoff years, the number of economic entities or units of low-level economy in the Greater Bay Area has gradually decreased, from the five cities to the three cities, but Jiangmen, Huizhou and Zhaoqing have always been in an economically backward cities in the region; (ii) the number of economically developed regions gradually increased, except for Hong Kong and Macao, which have always been in developed cities all along. Through years of development, Shenzhen and Guangzhou have gradually entered the ranks of the developed regions; (iii) the economically underdeveloped regions have successfully become the cities of the developing regions, or in other words, the positions of the underdeveloped regions have been replaced by undeveloped areas. When Shenzhen and Guangzhou

Table 3. Table showing the distribution of development categories of economic entities (Units) of the Greater Bay Area over 4 cutoff points (Years).

Region	2004	2008	2012	2016
Developed areas	Hong Kong, Macao	Hong Kong, Macao, Shenzhen	Hong Kong, Macao, Shenzhen	Hong Kong, Macao, Guangzhou, Shenzhen
Developing areas	Guangzhou, Shenzhen	Guangzhou	Guangzhou	Foshan, Zhuhai
Underdeveloped areas	Foshan, Zhuhai	Dongguan, Foshan, Zhuhai	Foshan, Zhuhai, Zhongshan	Dongguan, Zhongshan
Undeveloped areas	Dongguan, Zhongshan, Jiangmen, Huizhou, Zhaoqing	Zhongshan, Jiangmen, Huizhou, Zhaoqing	Dongguan, Jiangmen, Huizhou, Zhaoqing	Jiangmen, Huizhou, Zhaoqing

morphed into the developed areas, Foshan and Zhuhai, formerly less developed regions, entered the ranks of the developing regions; (iv) great changes have taken place in the economic units of the underdeveloped regions and the transformation of the backward regions into underdeveloped regions also occurred. After Foshan and Zhuhai in the former underdeveloped areas entered the mid-level developed category (i.e. still developing category), Dongguan and Zhongshan in the backward areas becomed the underdeveloped areas. In this process, it is noteworthy that Dongguan, after becoming the underdeveloped areas in 2008, retreated into the backward category in 2012 due to the adverse influence of the global economic climate. Through development and transformation efforts under "new normal" conditions, Dongguan is now re-entering the less developed category.

From the relevant data obtained from the year 2000 onward, we can see that the developed and mid-level developing regions are expanding, and the less developed regions are mainly the surrounding areas of the neighboring developed regions, while the underdeveloped and backward regions are mainly the surrounding areas of the neighboring developing regions. It can be concluded that growth polarization does exist in the Greater Bay Area, and the radiating or diffusion effect in the core or central Greater Bay Area is very obvious. The success of the developed regions within the Greater Bay Area positively impacts the economic development level of the adjacent areas. This has effectively promoted the balanced development of regional economies, significantly narrowing the regional economic disparities between regions of the Greater Bay and bringing about regional economic integration. However, one notes that the backward areas in the region occupy a very large area which is widely distributed. First, the economic foundation is weak in these backward areas, and hence, their development momentum is insufficient. Second, they do not experience the economic impact of the growth pole. The economic development is still at a low level.

(C) *Specific feature changes in the economic spatial structure of the Greater Bay Area*

(1) *Correlation analysis of the economic spatial structures of the Guangdong–Hong Kong–Macao Greater Bay Area*

Based on the statistical indicators of GDP per capita of the "9 + 2" economic units in the Guangdong–Hong Kong–Macao Greater Bay Area from 2001 to 2016, the global Moran's I index values of each economic unit are calculated according to the above formulas, and the spatial correlation and spatial structure agglomeration of the Guangdong–Hong Kong–Macao Greater Bay Area are analyzed.

From Table 4, we can see that the Z scores of Moran's I in the Greater Bay Area satisfy the significance test, with a p value less than 0.05, indicating that all the test results satisfy the significance level of 5%, which means we can reject the null hypothesis at the 5% significance level. First, Moran's I values are all positive from 2001 to 2016, showing that GDP per capita in the region exhibits the characteristics of concentration/agglomeration, and there is a significant

Table 4. Moran's I estimates of the per capita GDP index in the Greater Bay Area, 2001–2016.

Year	Moran's I	Z score	P score
2001	0.4077	3.03	0.02
2002	0.4353	3.59	0.01
2003	0.4645	3.13	0.01
2004	0.4789	2.67	0.02
2005	0.4684	3.39	0.01
2006	0.4583	2.84	0.04
2007	0.4451	2.73	0.01
2008	0.4156	3.02	0.02
2009	0.3837	2.37	0.02
2010	0.3582	2.96	0.02
2011	0.3083	2.60	0.02
2012	0.2769	2.56	0.04
2013	0.2430	2.47	0.03
2014	0.2526	2.34	0.02
2015	0.3462	2.29	0.02
2016	0.3692	2.14	0.05

positive spatial correlation between economic units. This shows that spatial agglomeration occurs in the economic development of the Guangdong–Hong Kong–Macao Greater Bay Area. The regions with relatively good economic development in the Greater Bay Area still have peripheral regions which are economically better off, and the regional economies display polarization. Similarly, those economic units with relatively backward economy are often surrounded by the economically backward regions. Second, from 2001 to 2016, the Moran's I index first increased, then decreased and then increased again. This signifies that the "9 + 2" economic units in Guangdong, Hong Kong and Macao have experienced increasing, shrinking and increasing spatial correlations. From 2001 to 2004, the values of Moran's I gradually increased, and the degree of economic spatial concentration/agglomeration in the region gradually increased. This shows that the "attracting" or "pulling" effect of the core economic regions plays a more important role, and this is closely related to the weakness of domestic economic development at the beginning of the century, the primary roles of the core areas of Hong Kong and Macao in opening up and their vibrant economic development. From 2005 to 2013, the domestic economy experienced a period of great economic expansion, with a sharp rise in the size and scale of the economy, a substantial optimization of the development structure, a considerable improvement in the quality of development and a significant reduction in spatial differences — the Moran's *I* values declined for 9 consecutive years. During this period, the diffusion effect of the core economic regions played a greater role, and the extent and degree of spatial agglomeration in the region contracted. From 2014 to 2016, under the "post-financial crisis" influence and "new normal" situation, the absolute speed of economic development slowed down markedly. Although the economic structure was optimized, the optimization effect was felt after experiencing sluggishness. At the same time, the economically well-off regions showed their relative advantages again, and the pulling effect was strong again, improving the degree of spatial agglomeration. By 2016, the global or overall Moran's *I* index reached a high of 0.3692, indicating that although the spatial correlation between regions had decreased, the spatial autocorrelation in the region was still high: exclusive spatial "clubs" still existed in the Greater Bay Area, and the economic disparities between polarized and non-polarized regions were still substantial.

The spatial analysis method takes into consideration the influence of the geographical location on regional economic growth, while the Theil index, which measures relative disparities, does not take into account the influencing factors of the geographical location. By comparing the Theil indices and the global Moran's *I* values of the "9 + 2" economic units in Guangdong, Hong Kong and Macao, we discover that there is a great difference between the two in their variation trends between 2001 and 2013. Although the regional economic disparities generally showed a gradual downward trend, the values of the Moran index maintained a positive correlation (synchronous decline) with the Theil index in 2004–2013, while the values of the Moran index had a negative correlation with the Theil index in 2001–2003, 2014–2015 (the Moran indices rose and the Theil indices fell). Since 2003, the Moran indices were higher than the Theil indices, indicating that the spatial factors significantly increased the impact of economic disparities. After considering the spatial location, the economic disparities were not as small as the Theil indices indicated. This shows that the growth poles within the region had played a diffusive or dispersal role, but the polarization phenomenon and the spatial "clubs" existed nonetheless. This reflects the fact that in the Greater Bay Area, after more than 10 years of development, of strengthening of economic ties and the construction of transportation network, the factors of labor force, capital, technology and information have been transferred spatially between the growth poles and the surrounding areas in the region, resulting in the gradual economic development of low-level economic regions and reducing the economic disparities between the "9 + 2" economic units (Figure 5).

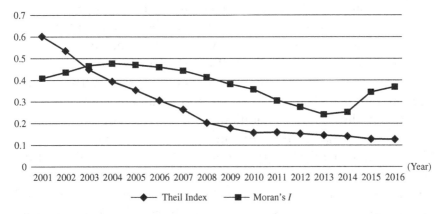

Figure 5. Comparison of Moran's *I* Values and Theil indices of (Economic) per capita GDP in the Greater Bay Area.

(2) *Economic spatial agglomeration pattern of the Guangdong–Hong Kong–Macao Greater Bay Area*

The global Moran index performs statistical testing on the overall correlation from a holistic perspective. The goal is to show the average degree of spatial disparities between a particular economic unit in the region and its adjacent areas. It makes the assumption that the region is homogeneous, and it does not analyze the specific conditions of spatial disparities between an area and its surrounding areas. It is difficult to represent the spatial aggregation characteristics of each region on the whole using the global Moran indices. Therefore, it becomes necessary to introduce local Moran indices to study the spatial agglomeration characteristics of each economic unit.

The local Moran's *I* values at the four cutoff points of 2004, 2008, 2012 and 2016 are 0.4789, 0.4156, 0.2769 and 0.3692, respectively. It can be seen that there are H–H agglomeration phenomena in the Greater Bay Area. From 2001 to 2013, Hong Kong was the H–H agglomeration area in the region. Unfortunately, the H–H agglomeration area did not show an expanding trend, reflecting the reality of the single polarization of Hong Kong in the Greater Bay Area and the large gaps between Hong Kong and other economic units. From the four cutoff points of the local Moran's *I*, we can see that the index declined continuously in 2012, which shows that Hong Kong's economic diffusion (dispersal) effect on other economic units became more conspicuous, effectively narrowing its economic disparities with other economic units. In 2016, the local Moran's *I* increased gradually to 0.3692 again, indicating that the economic diffusion effect of high-agglomeration areas has diminished, and it has a negative impact on the surrounding areas. In addition, from the relevant Moran scatter-plot, there is a spatial binary structure in the whole Guangdong–Hong Kong–Macao Greater Bay Area, and the data of the members of the "backward" club with low levels of economic development are much larger than for those of the "developed economy" club. Because of the large economic disparities between regions with low economic levels and those with high economic levels, the overall economic disparities within the Guangdong–Hong Kong–Macao Greater Bay Area are still relatively large.

IV. Empirical Analysis of the Factors Influencing the Spatial–Temporal Differences in the Economy of the Greater Bay Area

Previously, we have analyzed the economic disparities and the agglomeration of the spatial structure among the regions of the Greater Bay Area, but the factors affecting the spatial–temporal differences and each factor's role in the formation of the spatial–temporal differences need to be further analyzed through empirical tests. Generally speaking, the factors influencing the spatial and temporal differences of regional economies include natural endowments, capital labor, industrial structure, transportation conditions and regional policies. We shall next use spatial econometric empirical methods to test the economic convergence and influencing factors of the Guangdong–Hong Kong–Macao Greater Bay Area.

(A) *Selection of the models and their variables*

(1) *Spatial regression model*

With the development of spatial economics, the development of spatial econometric models is changing with each passing day. On the basis of the normal regression model, two basic models, including the Spatial Lag Model (SLM) and the Spatial Error Model (SEM), have been formulated to investigate the spatial and temporal differences of regional economies. For the specific choice of the two models, we can refer to the specific test results for selection.

(2) *Spatial lag model*

The SLM is used mostly to test whether spillover (diffusion) effects occur in regional economic units. Its model may be described as follows:

$$Y = \rho W_y + X\beta + \varepsilon \tag{4.5}$$

where Y is the dependent variable, X is the exogenous explanatory variable matrix of $n \times k$; ρ is the spatial regression coefficient, W is the spatial weighted matrix of order $n \times n$ and the adjoint matrix is generally chosen, Wy is the spatial lag-dependent variable, ε is the random error term and parameter β reflects the influence of independent variable X on the dependent variable y.

(3) *Spatial error model*

The SEM can be expressed by the following formulas:

$$y = \beta X + \varepsilon \qquad (4.6)$$

$$\varepsilon = \lambda W_\varepsilon + \mu \qquad (4.7)$$

where λ the spatial error coefficients of the $n \times 1$ cross-sectional dependent variable vectors and μ is the random error vectors of the normal distribution. The parameter λ measures the spatial dependence effect in the observed values of samples, that is, the direction and degree of the influence of the observed values y of adjacent regions on the observed values of this region. The spatial dependence of SEM exists in the perturbation error term, which measures the influence of the errors of dependent variables in the adjacent region on the observed values in the region. Because the SEM model is similar to the sequential correlation problem in the practical sequence, it is also called the spatial autocorrelation model.

(4) *Estimation and selection of spatial econometric models*

In the estimation of models, generally the ordinary least squares (OLS) method is often used to obtain the empirical results. However, the shortcomings of the Least Squares Method are that it may produce biased or invalid coefficients, so using other methods to replace or improve it may be an alternative. Generally, the maximum likelihood method can be used to estimate the parameters of SLM and SEM. In the further specific selection of SLM or SEM, it is necessary to distinguish the two Lagrange multipliers by LMERR, LMLAG tests and robust LMRR, LMLAG tests. Anselin and Flores (1995) give the following general judgment criteria: if LMLAG is statistically more significant than LMERR, and R-LMLAG is significant while R-LMERR is not significant, then the SLM is chosen to fit; if LMERR is statistically significant, R-LMERR is significant and R-LMLAG is not significant, then it would be more appropriate that the selection of SLM should be abandoned. If both of them are not significant statistically, it would be necessary to retreat to OLS for analysis and investigation. In fact, the Spatial Dubin Model (SDB) is the result of the revision and development of this method.

(B) *Selection of variables*

(1) *Capital and labor elements/factors*

In classical economic growth theory, economic development is chiefly driven by capital and labor. Although the economic development theory is undergoing constant revision and improvement, the basic role of these two factors in economic development has always been unanimously recognized. In a broader sense, capital can include human capital and material capital, but one needs to distinguish these two kinds of capital at different stages of economic development — the part played by each and the importance of each are different. In the early stage of economic development, economic growth is mainly determined by the amount of material capital investment, and the overall economy shows more extensive and large-scale development scenarios. With the economic development entering the "mature" stage, material capital investment is no longer the only determinant of economic development, but human capital — taking the form of people in charge of scientific and technological progress and regional innovation — replaces material capital. Capital investment has become an important source of power for economic growth. In quantitative analysis, capital elements are usually expressed by the per capita investment in fixed assets of each economic unit and labor elements are expressed by the number of employees at the end of the year, represented by $X1$ and $X2$, respectively.

(2) *Elements of the industrial structure*

The difference in industrial structure is also the main cause of regional economic disparity. For economic units of the Greater Bay Area of Guangdong, Hong Kong and Macao, the elements of the industrial structure are expressed by the proportions of the added values of the secondary and tertiary industries in the total GDP of each economic unit: the secondary industry is represented by $X3$, while the tertiary industry is represented by $X4$.

(3) *Degree of openness*

Considering that the Greater Bay Area is the earliest open "core" area in China and that open development is the key factor for the regional economy to take off, it is an inevitable choice to incorporate the degree of openness into the spatial model. In the specific quantitative analysis, the total import and export of each economic unit in the region in its current GDP ratio are taken as the proxy variable of the degree of opening-up, represented by $X5$.

(4) *Level of urbanization*

Although Hong Kong and Macao are fully urbanized regions in the Greater Bay Area, and Shenzhen is in fact urbanized too, we also need to consider economically backward areas such as Zhaoqing, Jiangmen and Huizhou. This indicator of urbanization is therefore of practical significance. The degree of openness is expressed by the total urban population/resident population of each economic unit, represented by $X6$.

(5) *Transportation*

Transportation is an element of economic development. It is important to strengthen the inter-regional flow of important factors, strengthen regional ties, reduce regional economic disparities and achieve regional economic integration. With the gradual construction of the transportation network, regional economic disparities will gradually narrow, and the extent of regional economic integration and coordination will improve substantially. The measure for this transportation element is expressed in terms of mileage per 100 square kilometers (i.e. road density) of each economic unit and is represented by $X7$.

(6) *Livelihood/standard of living of residents*

The standard of living of residents is the direct result of regional economic development, and it also provides driving and support capacity for regional economic development. Evidently, the living standards of residents in the region will have direct and indirect effects on regional economic disparities, so we need to consider introducing the spatial regression model. In this quantitative analysis, the disposable income of the residents in each economic unit/jurisdiction is used as the proxy variable to measure the standard of living, represented by $X8$.

Source of Data: Guangdong Statistical Yearbook (2001–2016), China Economic Net Database, Hong Kong Statistical Yearbook and some public data reports.

(C) *Selection and estimation of the spatial regression model*

According to relevant literature, the model is initially set as follows:

$$\ln Y = \beta_0 + \beta_1 \ln X_1 + \beta_2 \ln X_2 + \beta_3 X_3 + \beta_4 X_4$$
$$+ \beta_5 X_5 + \beta_6 \ln X_6 + \beta_7 \ln X_7 + \beta_8 \ln X_8 + \mu \qquad (4.8)$$

where Y is the explained variable and GDP per capita is chosen as the proxy variable to express the difference in the economic growth level of each economic unit. $\beta 0$ is an intercept constant term, $\beta 1$, $\beta 2$, ... , $\beta 7$ are coefficients of variables and $X1$, $X2$, ... , $X8$, are explanatory variables, as defined above.

Using GEODA software, the GDP per capita in 2016 is selected as a dependent variable. The independent variable is composed of the investment in fixed assets per capita, the logarithm of the number of employees at the end of the year, the proportion of secondary industry, the proportion of tertiary industry, the degree of dependence on foreign trade, the level of urbanization and the density of highway and the geographic weight matrix is loaded (this chapter chooses the first-order Rook geographic weight matrix). In other words, the main consideration is using the geographic boundary adjacency to construct the spatial regression model. Before investigating spatial regression, the general regression test should be conducted with the OLS method. The non-significant variables $X1$ and $X6$ in the model are neglected to form a new model as follows:

$$\ln Y = \beta 0 + \beta 1 \ln X2 + \beta 2 X3 + \beta 3 X4 + \beta 4 X5 \\ + \beta 5 \ln X7 + \beta 6 \ln X8 + \mu \qquad (4.9)$$

The results of least squares estimation are as follows:

From the test results in Table 5, it can be seen that the fit estimated by the least squares method reaches a good 0.985889, which shows that the model is a remarkable fit on the whole. The normality test of the least square estimation error of economic growth in regional economic cities shows that Jarque–Bera cannot satisfy the test at the 10% significant level, signifying that the random variable in the fitting estimation does not obey a normal distribution. Both Breusch–Pagan and Koenker–Bassett statistics fail to pass the test at the 10% significance level, which shows that the regression model constructed has a heteroscedasticity problem. The existence of heteroscedasticity indicates that the random error factor in least squares estimation may have a spatial autocorrelation issue. So, the simple classical linear regression model cannot explain the problem of skew in model design. Therefore, the spatial location factor is to be included in the regression model.

After loading the spatial weighted matrix, the diagnostic results of spatial dependence of OLS regression are obtained (Table 6). It can be seen from the above Lagrange multiplier test that LMLAG is statistically more significant than LMERR, and robust or stable R-LMLAG is more significant than R-LMERR model. Therefore, the choice of spatial lag is more appropriate.

After loading the spatial weight matrix, the SLM regression is used again in Eq. (4.9), and the results are as follows (Table 7).

Table 5. OLS Estimation of Factors Affecting Economic Growth Agglomeration and Disparities in Urban Areas (2016).

Model	Coefficient	t-Statistic	P score (value)
Constant	1.52043	0.811289	0.46271
$\ln X2$	1.15216	3.89675	0.01759
$X3$	2.75235	1.87674	0.13379
$X4$	2.26449	1.23916	0.28303
$X5$	−0.335769	−3.57068	0.02336
$\ln X7$	−0.323966	−2.73857	0.05198
$\ln X8$	0.874644	3.33342	0.02901
R^2	0.985889		
F	46.5785		0.00117233
Test for error from normality (normal distribution, n)	Degrees of freedom (DF)	Statistic score (value)	P
Jarque–Bera	2	0.4453	0.80038
Heteroscedasticity test	Degrees of freedom (DF)	Statistic score (value)	P
Breusch–Pagan	6	3.0986	0.79637
Koenker–Bassett	6	2.9707	0.81252
$\mathrm{Log}L$	12.6532		
AIC	−11.3064		
SC	−8.52116		

Table 6. Diagnostic Test Results of Spatial Dependence.

Test Statistic	MI/DF	Statistical Value	p Value
Lagrange multiplier (SLM)	1	3.2442	0.07168
Robust Lagrange multiplier (SLM)	1	4.9376	0.02628
Lagrange multiplier (error model)	1	0.2668	0.60549
Robust Lagrange multiplier (error model)	1	1.9602	0.16149
Lagrange multiplier (Thelma method)	2	5.2044	0.07411

It can be found that the lag term of the SLM, considering spatial correlation, is highly significant at the 1% level, with the coefficients of other variables being very significant at the level of 1%, and the goodness of fit has improved, and the logarithmic likelihood function value $\mathrm{Log}L$ has also increased. At the same time, Akai

Table 7.   SLM Estimation of Factors of Economic Agglomeration and Disparities Thereof.

Model	Coefficient	Z Statistic	P Score (Value)
Lny (−1)	0.301694	2.6346	0.00842
Constant	−1.721	−1.15241	0.24915
ln$X2$	1.22819	8.43207	0.00000
$X3$	4.44043	3.46874	0.00052
$X4$	3.71223	3.46874	0.00052
$X5$	−0.422706	−7.89057	0.00000
ln$X7$	0.356746	−6.14499	0.00000
ln$X8$	0.725684	5.08503	0.00000
R^2	0.990965		
Heteroscedasticity test	Degrees of freedom (DF)	Statistic score (value)	P
Breusch–Pagan	6	7.2159	0.30134
Spatial dependence test	Statistical value	P	
Log$L$	14.9215		
AIC	−13.8431		
SC	−10.6599		
LR	4.5366	0.03318	

Information Criteria (AIC) and Schwarz Criteria (SC) have been reduced. Therefore, overall, the SLM is a better fit.

(D) *Analysis of the empirical results*

Through regression analysis of the SLM, the following regression equation can be obtained:

$$\ln Y = 0.301694 \ln y(-1) - 1.721 + 1.22819 \ln X2 + 4.44043 X3$$
$$+ 3.71223 X4 - 0.422706 \, X5 + 0.356746 \ln X7$$
$$+ 0.725684 \ln X8 + \mu$$

It can be found that the spatial lag regression coefficient based on the first-order ROOK spatial weighted matrix is 0.301694, and the significance level is 1%. This shows that during the process of economic growth in the Guangdong–Hong Kong–Macao Greater Bay Area, the impact of lagging on the adjacent regions is very significant: there is a positive interaction between the change of economic growth of a region and the surrounding regions, and the overall economic growth displays a continuous agglomeration in the region.

(a) In the SLM, the regression coefficient of labor force at the level of economic growth is 1.22819, satisfying the test at 1% significance level. This shows that the labor population still plays a greater role in promoting the economic growth of the Greater Bay Area and is closely related to the large influx of people into the Greater Bay Area (except into Hong Kong and Macao). As one of the core areas of China's economic development, the Pearl River Delta region — especially the first-tier cities like Guangzhou and Shenzhen — still has a huge attraction for outside labor force, resulting in an increasing number of those employed. As the industrial structure of the Pearl River Delta region is generally more developed than the labor sourcing regions, with the increase of the labor force, the work or labor efficiency has significantly improved, thus boosting economic development. At the same time, after China's economy entered the "new normal" stage, the "9 + 2" cities in the Greater Bay Area launched various industrial upgrading measures, with the intention of changing the structural pattern or situation whereby economic growth relies too much on labor input. Of course, it still takes time for the effects of policy to become visible. Nevertheless, the increase in labor force is still one of the effective ways in driving regional economic growth.

(b) The regression coefficients of the industrial structure for regional economic growth are positive: the "influence" coefficients of the proportions of the secondary and tertiary industries in the spatial lag regression equation are 4.44043 and 3.71223, respectively, and they are significant at the 1% level. These figures indicate that both industrialization and the development of tertiary industries have effectively promoted the growth of the Greater Bay Area, and optimization of industrial structure has become the main path leading to regional economic growth. They also provide empirical support for the governments of the regions of the Greater Bay Area to come out with policies for industrial upgrading, optimizing planning and adjusting the economic structure.

(c) In fact, by 2016, the proportions of the secondary and tertiary industries in the core cities of Hong Kong, Macao, Guangzhou and Shenzhen generally reached or exceeded 99%. But in terms of the impact of the secondary and tertiary industries on regional economic growth, industrialization seems to be a more effective adjustment orientation than tertiary industries. This seems to be at odds with the general policy direction of increasing the proportion of tertiary industries. The reason for this situation is that there are great differences in the rate of tertiary industry growth within the Greater Bay Area. For example, the percentage or proportion of tertiary industries in Hong Kong and Macao is more than 90% and that of Guangzhou and Shenzhen is more than 60%, but in other regions of the "9 + 2" economic units, the proportion is only more than 50%. This affair is still closely related to the reality that the Pearl River Delta is a traditional manufacturing base for China.

(d) The regression coefficient for the influence of foreign trade dependence on economic growth is negative, and it satisfies the significance test at the 1% level. This shows that economic growth in the Greater Bay Area does not depend on the development of foreign trade, an empirical result contrary to intuitive understanding. The reason for this diagnostic result is that the core cities in the region generally have a high degree of dependence on foreign trade, which is quite different from other cities in the Greater Bay Area. Specifically, as the pioneering region of China's reform and opening-up, the high degree of dependence on foreign trade is directly related to the policy orientation of vigorously developing an export-oriented economy in the early stage of the region's development. After years of economic development, the absolute level of foreign trade dependence on regional economic units has reached a high level. Of course, the degrees of external dependence also vary within the region. For example, Dongguan, a typical manufacturing city, has 167% dependence on foreign trade, while Zhaoqing, a relatively backward region, has only 22% dependence on foreign trade. Among the main forces driving China's economic growth, the role of imports, exports and investment in the economy has gradually fallen behind, and domestic consumption has become a major factor in China's economic growth. During this period, especially after the impact of the subprime crisis in 2008, it is understandable that the economic growth of the former regions with high dependence on foreign trade has relatively slowed down, causing a negative regression coefficient.

(e) The regression coefficient for transportation in influencing regional economic growth is positive, and it satisfies the significance test at the 1% level. The development of transportation plays a significant role in the coordination of regional economies. Transportation significantly affects the extent of economic disparities between regions and promotes the process of regional synergy and integration. From the perspective of location, transportation not only promotes regional economic and social developments but also offers opportunities for economic development in underdeveloped areas. In theory, it fits François Perroux's growth pole theory: regional economic development is an unbalanced development process, with high or low standards of economic development and some successful economic developments preceding others. In the area first developed, because the cost of each factor in the region increases, the endogenous requirements of economic diffusion develop, resulting in the diffusion effect. In this diffusion process, transportation is an important factor. The development of transportation effectively promotes the flow of labor, materials, capital and information within the region, especially if this involves the transfer of these factors to less developed areas in bids to promote the economic development of relatively backward areas. Ultimately, the goal of coordinated regional economic development is attained.

(f) The regression coefficient for the influence of residents' living standards on regional economic growth is 0.725684, which also satisfies the test at the 1% significance level. Consumption is becoming the main driving force of economic growth, and consumption growth is based on the growth of the residents' income level. Particularly, in the Greater Bay Area environment of rigid or fixed expenditure with higher demands for housing, education and medical treatment, the improvement of living standards of residents will directly affect consumption expenditure and lead to significant changes in economic development.

V. Optimizing the Economic Spatial Structure of the Guangdong–Hong Kong–Macao Greater Bay Area

The goals of regional economic development not only require the general direction of optimum and rational allocation of resources but also include more specifically an imperative to reduce the disparities in economic development among regions. With the development of the Guangdong–Hong Kong–Macao Greater Bay Area labeled and recognized officially as a "national strategy", the regional economic cooperation between "9 + 2" cities will take on a new level of development. Hence, in order to boost the economic cooperation and create synergy within the Greater Bay Area, enhance the overall level of regional economy, narrow down regional economic disparities, and to promote regional integration, the following aspects are to be examined — from the perspective of optimization of economic spatial structure.

(A) *Overcoming the obstacles of administrative divisions and strengthening regional cooperation and development*

Administrative classifications are a form of regional division for our nation. Through demarcations of administrative boundaries, different administrative regions are formed, distinctly different management methods will be practiced and even different management thinking modes or "mind-sets" will permeate. Economically, the administrative divisions involve a high cost of maintaining formal and informal systems, which could hinder the development of regional economic cooperation. The commonly known phenomenon of "local protectionism and localism" has emerged. In the Greater Bay Area, the administrative division is even more complex. There are not only different administrative divisions in the "9 + 2" cities but also different social, legal and even cultural differences between the Hong Kong and Macao Special Administrative Regions. Under the current administrative system, local administrative organs are still guided by local interests and achievements, and under the guise of adhering to "rules" of different administrative regions, they establish trade barriers, thus hampering the flow of resources and economic "elements" in the market. This kind of administrative models poses great obstacles to the expansion of regional economic space, adversely affecting the diffusion effects of "growth pole" cities and regions and eventually slowing down or negating the effects of regional economic cooperation concomitant with the rising cost of administration and running of enterprises. In fact, after Hong Kong and Macao joined the Greater Bay Area, this problem has become even more serious. Owing to the impact of different socioeconomic systems and cultural conflicts, how to overcome the "barriers and obstructions" contingent on talent flow, logistics, capital flow and information flow will become the major crux of the coordinated efforts to integrate the development of regional economies. Briefly speaking, the breakthroughs in administrative divisions include on the one hand ways to break the administrative barriers between the nine cities in the Mainland and on the other hand steps and measures to resolve the administrative "obstructions" between Hong Kong, Macao and the nine cities in the Mainland. The development plan of the Guangdong–Hong Kong–Macao Greater Bay Area, which has been elevated to the national strategy level, is being formulated and implemented. Under the proposed plan, the main organs of different social systems, legal environments and entities with different economic development levels of each regional unit shall be "aggregated" into one entity for macro or overall consideration. In this way, effective internalization of externalities will provide a strong institutional assurance or guarantee for regional economic cooperation.

(B) *Facilitating the diffusion effect of growth poles and strengthening the radiating effect of core cities*

Based on the analysis of the spatial pattern changes in the Greater Bay Area, we can see that the regional economic disparities have been greatly reduced, but the status of growth poles for Hong Kong and Macao is still maintained. From the perspective of the whole region, Guangzhou and Shenzhen still have some room for development, but the two cities have not really entered the development stage of being growth poles. Nevertheless, from the perspective of the nine cities in the Mainland, Guangzhou and Shenzhen have begun to play their role as growth poles. With the gradual economic slowdown of Hong Kong and Macao, this trend will become more noticeable. In the light of the emergence of Qianhai, Nansha and Hengqin Special Zones in the region, the focus on economic development of Hong Kong and Macao will be inclined or "skewed" spatially toward the Mainland. Guangzhou and Shenzhen will gradually move into the rank of growth poles whereupon they shall take on the role of diffusing and radiating their influence, in effect narrowing regional disparities. Therefore, on the one hand, the nine cities in the Mainland should try to further accelerate regional agglomeration, taking full advantage of the radiation diffusion function of the growth poles. Their emergence serves to promote the common development of the marginal areas and prevent the further aggravation of regional disparities. On the other hand, the leading roles of the core cities in the Guangdong–Hong Kong–Macao Greater Bay Area should be further strengthened. The core cities in the region are divided into three tiers. The first-tier cities are Hong Kong and Macao, which have international influence. The second-tier cities include Guangzhou and Shenzhen, which are the administrative centers of the inland regions. They should make efforts to strengthen contacts and develop concurrently with other cities in the province. The third-tier cities cover some other regions with relatively good economic foundation and a relatively high level of economic development such as Zhuhai, Foshan, Dongguan.

For the future, the Guangdong, Hong Kong and Macao regions should strengthen the diffusion effect of the first-tier growth poles of Hong Kong and Macao and the diffusion effect of Hong Kong and Macao on the inland areas of the Mainland. Focus should be placed on building the second-level or second-tier growth poles of Guangzhou and Shenzhen to make them become new growth poles of the regional economy. The core spaces must be continuously expanded, and the region should move from the non-equilibrium stage of polarized nuclear development to a non-equilibrium stage of diffusion development, to ultimately obtain a multi-core equilibrium stage. In the process, we should pay attention to the intermediary role of Guangzhou and Shenzhen in bridging the gap between Hong Kong and Macao and other regional economic units. The goal is to promote some cooperation between Hong Kong and Macao and other regions within the Greater Bay Area, to encourage them to connect directly with other regions, in order to promote the narrowing of regional economic disparities and strengthen the coordinated development within the Greater Bay Area.

(C) *Optimizing the industrial structure and accelerating the construction and improvement of the common market system*

With regards to the optimization of the industrial structure, each regional unit possesses different development directions or orientations. First, Hong Kong and Macao should fully utilize their advantages of a high-level, highly optimized industrial structure, strong capital strength, mature and excellent management experience and integration with the world markets. The two cities should strengthen cooperation with inland regions, open up markets in the interior and take the lead in promoting the development of industrial cooperation in the Greater Bay Area. Second, Shenzhen and Guangzhou should aggressively develop technology-intensive industries and transfer their low value added, labor-intensive and resource-based industries to the peripheral areas through industrial upgrading. Meanwhile, each of the other economic units in the Greater Bay Area should make use of their own resource advantages to take over labor-intensive industries which have been transferred from Guangdong and Shenzhen, and at the same time improve their own scientific and technological knowhow and capacities to promote the level of industrialization in their region. In addition, the Greater Bay Area should attempt to knock off market barriers, improve the institutional environment of the common market, coordinate the overall layout plan and the construction of the regional market system — taking cognizance of local conditions and advantages. The Greater Bay Area must realize the flow of regional factors and accelerate the construction of the market networks in the Pan-Pearl Region.

(D) *Continuing to promote the construction of transportation networks*

Transportation is the bond providing regional economic links and the fundamental requirement for regional economic development. The division and inter-connection of different levels of space in a regional space chiefly depend on the radiating passages or channels from the core area to the peripheral areas. The presence of good and efficient transportation infrastructure is the basis of radiating channels in the region. An "unreasonable" or deficient traffic layout may lead to redundant construction and could also lead to stunted growth of regional economy. After undergoing regional integration, a unified and rational traffic layout for the Guangdong–Hong Kong–Macao Greater Bay Area will have to avoid duplication of construction, eliminating regional differences and promoting regional integration. According to the current situation of economic development of the "9 + 2" economic units, this book holds that the "axial belt" development model (or the "axial fan" development model) should remain the main development idea to adhere to. By strengthening the corridor effect of the main axes of Hong Kong–Macao–Shenzhen, Hong Kong–Macao–Zhuhai and Shenzhen–Guangzhou, several "auxiliary axes" and "growth axes" could then be built to achieve rapid regional economic growth. In the selection of auxiliary axes, we should stick to the strategy of "relying on the axes while strengthening the centers" and choose cities such as Foshan, Dongguan and Zhongshan for further development.

Chapter 5

Developing Guangdong– Hong Kong–Macao Greater Bay Area into China's Economic Growth Pole

Guo Ji

Shenzhen Institute of Information Technology

The concept of "growth pole" was first put forward by Francois Perroux, a French economist. He believes that the economic growth rates are unbalanced among different regions, industries or sectors. Economic growth first appears in innovative industries, which are concentrated at some points in space, forming a growth center or growth pole. A growth pole is a group of vibrant and closely associated industries organized around a leading industrial sector. Not only does it grow rapidly but also it promotes the growth of the other sectors through the multiplier effect. When the output of a growth pole increases, it drives the growth of the output or input of other industries as well. In addition, it produces a strong chain effect and a "bolstering" effect, finally forming "industrial clusters".

The Greater Bay Economic "Belt" of Guangdong, Hong Kong and Macao will become the development area with the most potential for growth in China and will also become the growth pole of China in driving the national economy.

I. The Mechanism for the Formation of the Growth Pole

(A) *The concept and essence of growth poles*

The concept of "growth pole" was first put forward by Francois Perroux, a French economist. He believes that the economic growth rates are unbalanced among different regions, industries or sectors. Economic growth first appears in innovative industries, which are concentrated at some points in space, forming a growth center or growth pole. A growth pole is a group of vibrant and closely associated industries organized around a leading industrial sector. Not only does it grow rapidly but also it promotes the growth of other sectors through the multiplier effect. When the output of a growth pole increases, it drives the growth of the output or input of the other industries as well. In addition, it produces a strong chain effect and a "bolstering" effect, finally forming "industrial clusters".

The concept of the "growth pole" has been revised and periodically improved in economic research and application. It embodies the double meanings of economic and geographical spaces. The economic space of a growth pole refers to the leading enterprises or industries in the region. Leading enterprise refers to a single enterprise or a combination of several core enterprises with a very strong influence in a sector or industry. A leading industry is an industry with a strong driving force in a region. There are many enterprises in the upstream and downstream industries for the leading industry. They have a big demand for the products of this industry, and the industry has wide and good market prospects. The leading industry possesses the ability to drive the development of related industries. Spatially or geographically, a growth pole refers to the core city cluster in a certain region, bringing about the agglomeration effect of industries within these cities, giving rise to core city cluster and leading industries, thus driving the rapid growth of the regional economy. To some extent, the growth pole can also be regarded as a geographically developed urban agglomeration or city cluster with economic "driving" capacity. The regional economic development starts with a single city as the regional center. With the rapid economic development, this single city gradually expands its influence and becomes the core city driving the industries in the region. The industries spread or become dispersed to the surrounding or peripheral cities, finally forming the urban agglomeration or city clusters which promote, assist, complement and mutually constrain one another.

(B) *The dynamic system of regional growth pole development*

A regional growth pole is the result of the interaction between market and government mechanisms and also the result of the interplay of multiple factors in mutually promoting and restricting each other. The favorable factors promote the rapid growth of the regional economy, while the unfavorable factors restrict or limit the growth of the regional economy. When the effects of key favorable factors outweigh those of unfavorable factors, a growth pole gradually takes shape in the region. These key factors contributing to the formation of growth poles constitute a dynamic system of regional growth poles, and they also "promote and check" each other. The capabilities for innovation, industrial upgrading, the health of market mechanism and government policies are usually the most important driving forces contributing to the formation of growth poles.

(1) *Innovative ability*

Innovation is the source of the formation and development of growth poles. Schumpeter believes that there are five facets of innovation: new products, new processes, new markets, new materials and new organizational structures. Innovation means the establishment of a new production function, which is the reassembly of factors and conditions of production. Innovation involves higher risks, including high costs and the possibility of failure. And the spirit of entrepreneurship is an important driving force for innovation. The entrepreneur's courage of innovate and meet challenges form the basis of his or her continuous innovation activities. When the external environment is suitable for entrepreneurs to express their innovative spirit, it would be easy for the whole economy to create an innovative atmosphere. However, not every industry's innovations could result in the formation of growth poles. Innovation needs to occur in combination with leading industries in order to become the engine of regional economic growth. Leading industrial innovations not only promote the development of the industry itself but also possess a strong ability for external "diffusion" or dispersal, in which diffusion fosters the development of upstream and downstream industries, thus stimulating the economic development of the whole region and forming a regional economic growth pole. Enterprises in leading industries rely on the long-term accumulation of technologies and experience to enhance efficiency, cut costs or improve product quality through innovation and to enhance their competitiveness, so as to procure a higher market share and achieve higher profits. Positive income growth also strengthens the enterprise's ability to withstand risks resulting in the enterprise's greater willingness and improved ability to innovate. In order to maintain the competitive edge of the enterprise, innovation activities should and must continue to promote the sustainable development of growth poles. The spillover effect of the leading industries in turn drives the development of the upstream and downstream industries. With the continuous technological innovation of the leading industries, the enterprises of the upstream industry (in order to procure orders) and the downstream industry (in order to improve competitiveness) will have to carry out innovations commensurate with the technological level of the leading industries. In this way, the development of the whole industrial chain is fostered. This cooperative innovation mechanism becomes very important for the development of regional growth poles. In summary, the combination of innovation and leading industries has become the most fundamental driving force for the formation and development of growth poles.

(2) *Industrial upgrading*

Industrial upgrading plays a bridging role in the dynamic system of the growth pole. The essence of industrial upgrading is the further differentiation or "division" of industries. Industrial differentiation makes the industry focus more on innovation in subdivided areas, and more new products and services will be introduced into the market. At the microlevel, the pulling or drawing effect of demands would be able to drive enterprises to innovate independently. Industrial upgrading can cause enterprises to produce more innovative products, and this in turn helps promote the expansion and segmentation of markets. As more enterprises enter the market, the competition gets more intensified, and the enterprises need to continue their technological innovation to reduce production costs, improve product quality and grab a good market share. In the medium term, industrial synergy has the effect of fostering independent innovation at the relevant industrial level. With the upgrading of an industry, the production technology and technical expertise will also progress accordingly; the requirements for raw materials and other supporting facilities will be higher and higher and this situation necessitates higher requirements for the technology and technical expertise of upstream and downstream industries as well. In order to survive, upstream and downstream industries will have to continue to innovate to meet the development needs of the propulsive, forward-looking industries.

(3) *A sound market mechanism*

A sound and "perfected" market mechanism enables the subject body in the market to make the best choice based on its own interests. In such a market, both enterprises and families could accurately measure their own costs and benefits and make optimal decisions. Enterprises pursue maximum profits while consumers pursue maximum utility. Driven by interests, enterprises are motivated to improve and upgrade their technological levels in order to reduce costs, improve product quality, better meet the needs of consumers, expand market share and achieve economies of scale and increase revenue. They would also be able to foster aggregation of industries in the region, thus stimulating regional economic growth. Being on the demand side of products, families could choose the best products according to their own needs: their actions facilitate "the survival of the fittest" among enterprises in the market. In order to enhance their competitiveness, enterprises — being on the demand side of production factors — require more support from high-quality resources. They are willing to pay more for high-quality production factors. Now, for families — who are on the supply side of the production factors of production — high-quality labor gravitates more toward economically developed areas, because there are more job opportunities and higher wages and remuneration involved. Therefore, households with a high net worth are more willing to invest in economically developed areas, because there are more stable investment opportunities with higher rates of return. Additionally, the good infrastructure and cultural atmosphere in the economically developed areas attract more families with high net worth and high quality: they wish to pursue a life of high quality in the region. These families bring resources as well as highly efficient labor to the region, thereby promoting local economic growth. A sound market mechanism can promote the optimal allocation of the factors of production, and it provides a driving force for the formation of growth poles. In conclusion, it is evident that a sound market is an important prerequisite for the formation and development of growth poles.

(4) Government policy

Government policy is yet another important force driving the formation and development of the growth poles. A good system of government policy (with good governance) provides a healthy external environment for the growth pole. A policy that is effective reduces the transaction costs of economic activities, thus helping regional enterprises to save costs and enhance their competitiveness. For example, an efficient and clean government provides better administrative services for enterprises, thereby reducing the expenses incurred by enterprises when applying for administrative approvals (e.g. licenses, approval for investment plans) and improving their operational efficiency. In addition, when the market mechanism does not produce effective results, expedient government interventions may be necessary to regulate and improve the effectiveness and reduce the shortcomings of the market. Two important criteria for making a market more effective are sufficient and effective information and the free flow of key factors. The government could facilitate improvements in the market by trying to fulfill these two criteria. Generally, at the initial stage of a growth pole, policy support by the government is necessary; in other words, an external environment conducive to the development of a growth pole is required. At the beginning of its development, the growth pole will experience constraints and restrictions attributed to the old system. Hence, it is necessary to establish a new and more effective system to regulate its development. New technologies such as Internet or online payment emerge when many restrictions and constraints of the old financial system are still in existence. Additionally, there are deficiencies in regulating the development of growth poles. Therefore, it is necessary for the government to revamp and update the relevant system in a timely manner and to make arrangements to steer the healthy development of growth poles. Effective government policies could guide the healthy development of the market, promoting orderly development of innovative products of enterprises. These policies also help produce rational consumption and investments, foster economies of scale, realize efficient industrial agglomeration and ultimately promote the formation of new growth poles.

II. Experiences in Cultivating and Developing World Economic Growth Poles

(A) *Growth pole of scientific and technological innovation: Silicon Valley*

(1) *Origin of the name "Silicon Valley"*

"Science Park" is a contemporary, science and technology innovation-oriented, economic growth pole. The typical representative is Silicon Valley located in Northern California in the south of the San Francisco Bay. In this area, there are first-class research universities and scientific research institutions that provide scientific and technological professionals and cutting-edge technologies for the development of the local high-tech enterprises. High-tech enterprises aggregate to form clusters that produce spillover effects, fostering collaborative innovation among enterprises and facilitating close integration of the industry, education and research. These high-tech enterprises constitute a powerful engine for global technological innovation. On January 11, 1971, *Business Weekly* published a series of articles on "Silicon Valley". The reason why it was called "Silicon Valley" was that the products of local semiconductor and computer industries were mostly made of high-purity silicon, while "Valley" refers to the Santa Clara Valley. Silicon Valley at that time straddled Highway 101 from the southern end of the San Francisco Bay, stretching from Monroe Park, Palo Alto through Mountain View, Sunnyvale to the heart of Silicon Valley — Santa Clara — passing through Campbell to the narrow strip of San Jose.

(2) *Development of Silicon Valley*

Purchasing orders from army played an important part in the early development of the Silicon Valley. Originally, a US Navy workstation was set up in Silicon Valley, including a Naval Flight Research Base. Later, many technology companies were established around the Naval Research Base. At the end of the Second World War and with the outbreak of the Korean War, the US Army had a large demand for sophisticated military technologies, and Silicon Valley enterprises naturally became the recipients and beneficiaries of these military orders. In terms of product innovation capabilities, Silicon Valley enterprises were able to meet the requirements of the military. The military orders generally adopted the cost-added pricing model, where cost constraints on enterprises are smaller than those for private enterprises. Hence, corporations producing military technologies were highly motivated to develop advanced but relatively expensive military technologies. At the same time, Silicon Valley enterprises could obtain federal subsidized R&D funds, rendering the leading edge of Silicon Valley enterprises more conspicuous.

At the beginning of 1960, because of the expenditure cuts of the US Defense Department, the development of local military enterprises lost the army's strong support, resulting in a short recession in Silicon Valley. As corporations and enterprises producing military technologies needed to find new customers, the application of military technologies to civilian areas became a new direction for these so-called military enterprises. Semiconductor-led industries developed rapidly and formed industrial clusters. Later, revolutionary technologies and emerging industries such as semiconductors, personal computers, the Internet and green technologies developed alternately or successively, and these new industries became the important and sustained source of innovation in the world. In the 1970s, the invention of microcomputers led to the rapid rise of the semiconductor manufacturing industry. Every 2 weeks, a new company was born in Silicon Valley, and most of them showed great tenacity and vitality. Around 75% of them survived for more than 6 years, a survival rate that was much higher than the average life span of most American companies, making Silicon Valley one of the highest income regions in the United States. In the 1980s, the invention of personal computers further bolstered the development of high-tech enterprises in Silicon Valley, and the internationalization of high-tech enterprises accelerated. In 1981, IBM took the lead in inventing personal computers, which attracted good market response. This situation led to the development of software and hardware companies whose products were compatible with personal computers. Computer maintenance services also sprang up. By then, the PC industry had become a new engine that was driving the development of the Silicon Valley. Silicon Valley had about 3,000 electronics manufacturing companies alone — mainly small companies employing about 50 workers. In addition, there were about 3,000 companies providing services to producers/manufacturers and 2,000 companies engaged in high-tech activities. During this period, accelerated growth was observed in technological innovation, and venture capital emerged to provide strong financial support for technological progress and became the main source of financing for Silicon Valley entrepreneurs. Silicon Valley not only has a large number of high-tech enterprises but also generates a self-supporting financial system developmental pathway. Silicon Valley creates wealth and nurtures new entrepreneurs via the mode of venture capital. Since the late 1990s, technological innovation in Silicon Valley has continued unabated, but the main thrust of technological innovation has undergone significant changes: start-ups are no longer the main bodies of technological innovation. Some giant companies have established research centers, such as IBM's Almaden Research Center, which has become the main driving force of innovation in Silicon Valley. But in recent years, large companies' technological investments have declined in the United States and Silicon Valley. For example, the federal government's investment in research and development of cutting-edge computer science and electronic engineering has declined sharply. Some large high-tech enterprises are paying more attention to projects that can make quick profits, and their investment in science and technology research has also suffered a reduction.

In the development of Silicon Valley, colleges, universities and financial industry have provided strong support for technological innovation. One good example is Stanford University which plays a pivotal role in the development of Silicon Valley — by integrating research results with technological applications. The university employs science and technology leaders from emerging industries to promote the development of related disciplines in schools, while producing a large number of graduates with practical knowledge and skills for the enterprises of Silicon Valley. Stanford University has also promoted the development of science and technology industrial parks. It has abundant land resources to provide cheap rentals for a large number of science and technology companies. This helps reduce the cost of start-ups and encourages and promotes an innovative atmosphere. Another aspect is of course the financial industries. Innovative financing not only provides the necessary financial support for technology companies but has also become a means by which enterprises improve their efficiency. Angel investment has become the main source of funds for innovative enterprises in Silicon Valley. In this regard, equity financing is the main financing method for innovative enterprises. A number of world-renowned venture capital institutions, such as Sequoia Capital, were born in Silicon Valley, and some innovative incentives were introduced. In order to retain the key talented, professional staff of the enterprise, the enterprises and companies allow and encourage important employees to participate in profit sharing. Equity incentives are widely used in Silicon Valley enterprises. These financial innovations add to the already strong support for the development of high-tech enterprises in Silicon Valley.

(3) *Problems in the development of Silicon Valley*

After more than a century of rapid development, Silicon Valley has incubated many well-known high-tech enterprises and new technologies and has become the growth pole of global technological innovation. However, with the rapid development of Silicon Valley, some constraints and negative factors affecting the development of this growth pole have emerged and are becoming increasingly evident as detailed below.

The first constraint is the rising living costs. This not only exerts higher pressure of cost on enterprises but also affects the local residents' life quality. With high income and remuneration, there are more employment opportunities and prospects for personal development in Silicon Valley; more talented people have been attracted by the Silicon Valley, resulting in inadequate infrastructure, congested traffic conditions and the lack or reduction of school education resources, all of which have failed to keep pace with the population growth. The cost of living and the cost of office space and housing in Silicon Valley all have risen sharply. Another problem is that the income gap in Silicon Valley is widening. Apart from a small proportion of high-income people, the quality of life of most people has gone down. High-intensity and high-pressure work occupies most of the time and energy of the individuals. The time and energy that should be spent on self-care as well as caring for family members are shortened and more family conflicts ensue. This directly leads to an increasing divorce rate in Silicon Valley, while the birth rate is declining. The attractiveness of high income and quality living environment in Silicon Valley is diminishing relative to the pressure of work and family conflicts.

Second, there is insufficient motivation for innovation. When the market share of products of large enterprises reaches a certain point, these large enterprises are often reluctant to develop new technologies that "subvert" existing products, while emerging enterprises are often impetuous in their innovation, and they lack good technical support and long-term market prospects. Gimmicks and speculative concepts have become the financing methods for many of these innovative enterprises. It is very rare for them to really sink down, think hard and work hard to become viable and valuable enterprises. Selling equity arbitrage has become the ultimate goal of some of these enterprises. Some within industry circles believe (e.g. Grove) that today's newly emerged companies simply can't be compared (or can't hold a candle for) with the Silicon Valley giants; they won't become the next Intel, Cisco, Oracle, HP, Apple or Google. Today, some business operators and companies in Silicon Valley are short-sighted and unambitious.

Third, technology start-ups face the teething problem of financing. After the outbreak of the financial crisis, many companies in Silicon Valley went bust and the number of enterprises worth investing in or with investment value decreased, and venture capitalists no longer have the courage they had more than a decade ago. Investors' choice of investment targets and the amount of investment have become more cautious. The Angel investments of venture capital companies which used to invest in start-up companies continued to decrease. The venture capital experts in Silicon Valley are beginning to slash down the future prospects for growth of innovative companies in the future. Even some leading companies in the Internet industry, such as Facebook, are not spared from slashing down. Not only has the environment for entrepreneurship and venture capital changed dramatically, but government support for Silicon Valley has also declined in terms of government policy. In Silicon Valley, it is now becoming very difficult for innovative companies to get federal funding. Many companies have moved out of Silicon Valley because of the changing business environment.

Fourth, environmental pollution is serious. High and new technology does not equal to zero pollution. Most people associate high-tech products with little pollution; they think the worst pollution is found in traditional heavy industries. The truth is that Silicon Valley, as a high-tech production region, is nevertheless facing the threat of pollution as well. Pollution comes from a variety of sources: (1) leakage of highly dangerous solvent wastes and other chemical substances; (2) toxic waste generated in the production of high-tech products and (3) the discharge of heavy metals (including cadmium and nickel) into the sewage system. The consequence of the production and discharge of pollutants is that about 100 chemicals have been found in the groundwater, causing serious environmental hazards to nearby wetlands. Air quality has become poor and heavy haze appears in the sky.

Silicon Valley is the most important growth pole of technological innovation in the United States. It brings a strong spillover effect to the economic development of the United States and is an important engine driving its economic growth. And when the development of Silicon Valley encounters bottlenecks, the consequent dampening of the overall technological innovation capabilities of the United States will adversely affect not only the regional economy but also the overall economic development of the United States because of the spillover effect. Although these unfavorable factors have existed for many years and are "concealed" by the rapid economic growth, when the economic growth slows, the ill effects and negative impacts on the development of Silicon Valley will become increasingly conspicuous.

(B) *Growth pole of the industrial complex: Lac region, Southwest France*

In April 1957, a large natural gas field was discovered in southwestern France, in the Lac region of the Lower Pyrenees. At the beginning, production of the gas field reached 1 million cubic meters per day. Since then, the production had risen rapidly, reaching 20 million cubic meters per day 4 years later. A total of 13 wells, each with an average depth of more than 4,000 meters, had been drilled in this area. The plant processing the natural gas was built on the natural gas layers, covering an area of 2,200 hectares, and the entire transportation network from the wells to the processing plant was underground. There was only one plant of this type in the whole Europe, and the plant's desulfurization unit occupied the most important position in the world. In 1961, the Lac Industrial Complex was formally established, with a thermoelectric center and three power-generating units, producing 125,000 kWh of electricity. Meanwhile, chemical plants related to natural gas, such as acetylene, ammonia, methanol, polyethylene and nitrate fertilizer, were established in succession. In 1961, Lac natural gas was used in thermal power plants and energy industries and distributed to the public, Lac's integrated enterprises and other chemical industries and used to fuel internal combustion in the proportion of 31.5%, 25.5%, 23.5%, 16.8%, 1.2% and 1.5%, respectively. It is clearly seen here that 82% of natural gas was mainly used as energy, while the other 18% was utilized as input products. The sale of natural gas by France's geographical regions was 38% in the southwest, 28% in Paris, 23% in the middle and the east, with 11% in the west and mid-west.

When Lac's natural gas was first discovered, France had hoped that it could help to promote the development of regional industries, in turn boosting the economic development of southwestern France.

By Perroux's definition of the type of industries that are capable of propelling development, the Lac Industrial Complex possesses features that satisfy the definition, such as the asymmetric effect and growth rates that are higher than the national average. However, its driving effect on the economic development of southwestern France is just the opposite of what was initially expected. Although it has also led to the development of some "resultant or induced" industries, the expansion of the Lac Industrial Complex has been limited to neighboring areas, with little impact on regional employment. In other words, the Lac Industrial Complex is basically a regional phenomenon and has little influence in improving the economic situation in the southwestern part of France. According to a survey carried out by relevant departments, the total output value of the Lac Industrial Complex reached 1.190 billion francs in 1964, of which 337 million francs were mainly purchases made from outside the region for goods and services rendered. Consequently, 75% of the added values of the complex might have in fact exited the region and were distributed as income elsewhere. None of the raw materials produced in Lac are further processed locally (sulfur, aluminum, industrial chemicals and raw materials etc.); most undergo processing in other parts of France or even abroad. As far as natural gas is concerned, when not used in the industries of the local complexes, most of natural gas needs to be transported over long distances, while a large part of the natural gas produced in the region is also transported to large cities such as Bordeaux and Toulouse, 200 kilometers away. Low-priced concessions for local users failed to attract the desired new industries because the natural gas produced by Lac could be easily exported without local processing or any local marketing measures, resulting in a very small impact on regional economic growth. The number employed in the integrated complex itself was not very large, with 10,000 people in 1959 and 7,500 in 1964. After the completion of the natural gas development project, 3,500 more people were to be recruited locally. All or almost all of the decisions were made in Paris. The huge profits from the development and utilization of natural gas were all used for reinvestment in petroleum or chemical research in other parts of France or abroad. In 1964, the total added value of the industrial complex was 857 million francs, with only 112 million francs paid for wages (including employer contributions to social security), and 626 million francs for profits and taxes. The development of the modern industry initiated by the complex has not achieved the desired results, and the economic structure has not been improved. In fact, it has had a negative impact on agriculture and has become a typical dual economic development model.

The government's policy is also one of the reasons why the Lac Industrial Complex has failed to foster the economic development of the wider regions. Because natural gas has been distributed to many areas, and the southwest region only accounts for a small part of its own utilization, thus a good opportunity to create a growth pole to have a positive impact on the entire southwest region was lost. It seems reasonable to fault government policy on this count. However, government policy is not the decisive factor. Whether to utilize Lac's natural gas in the southwestern region or not depends more on the market mechanism. Whether natural gas can lead to the local development of the industry depends on the extent of expansion of other sectors. Natural gas has two industrial uses: as industrial energy and as the main input material of chemical industries. When natural gas is used as energy, the prospects or possibility of industrialization depend on two fundamental factors: how important are energy costs in the output values of different industries and the extent of growth of these industries. In 1956, energy consumption varied among different industries. The following were the sectors with a relatively high demand for energy as part of the final product value: aluminum (16.3%), electricity (15.3%), steel products (14.7%), mineral chemicals (11.6%), glass (10.0%), building materials (9.7%), organic chemicals (9.3%) and synthetic fibers (6.4%). These data suggest the possibility of attracting major energy-consuming industries to Lac. However, even in these sectors, their non-energy expenditure accounted for 84–93% of total expenditure. The establishment of factories for these industries in other areas may be determined by non-energy expenses. Some of the factors to consider included distances from the origin of raw materials, small size of the market, the characteristics of the labor force, the nature of industries and even the weight of products — all of which may hinder the establishment of factories in energy areas.

The case of the Lac Industrial Complex shows that the development of an industrial complex growth pole must fulfill certain conditions. A noted French scholar summarized these conditions as follows. First, the growth pole must be supported by related industries and production factors. If economic activities are too complex as not to be able to provide for local subcontracting industries and necessary technicians, then most of the investment will have to be completed through extra-regional resources; underdeveloped areas are typical examples. In the development of the natural gas industry in Lac, the necessary equipment and technology had to be purchased and brought in from outside. The actual impact of this "pseudo-growth" on the local economy was negligible, and experience has proved that the growth incentive generated by small manufacturing industry multipliers is greater than that generated by large but non-integrated mobile industries. Second, localization of industries is an important driving force for the formation of growth poles. The more localized the processing of products, the greater the impact on economic development. An illustration: once raw materials are exported outside the region, resultant or "induced" compensatory industries could not develop. The proportion of industry-related costs of these resultant industries determines whether or not raw materials are to be produced in the country of origin. Where transportation costs are not a decisive factor, plants for processing and finished products are situated close to the market rather than near the origin of raw materials (as is the case in the Lac region). It is much more economical to deliver natural gas to customers than to establish new industries in energy sources. Third, the impact of the growth pole on local employment and income distribution determines the drawing power of the growth pole to the economy. Another important way for the growth pole to foster economic growth is the income multiplier effect. The industrial expenditure of the growth pole is converted into incomes of local residents. The increase of residents' income generates more consumption demand, which in turn stimulates the demand for local enterprises. The more local people the industries employ, the higher the skill level of the local labor, the higher the labor's technology skills, the more wages the local residents get and thus the greater the effect of consumer demand. But we must also realize that the cost of labor for petroleum industry-based natural gas and electric power industries accounts for only a small proportion in the overall cost structure.

(C) *Prerequisites for growth pole development*

Growth poles foster the development of upstream and downstream industries through industrial linkages, and their multiplier effect is manifested in quantitatively promoting regional economic growth, thus driving the rapid growth of regional economy. Through the case studies of the development of natural gas in Lac, southwestern France, and Silicon Valley, which is the US technology-based growth pole, we can easily conclude that the cultivation and development of growth poles require certain preconditions or prerequisites. Whether we can make good use of these basic conditions is the key for the sustainable development of the growth pole: (1) *Policy guidance*: Government policies do play an important part in shaping a growth pole, but too much government intervention could deter fair competition and lower efficiencies. A long-term efficacious policy is particularly important in the formation of growth poles; (2) *A good market environment*: fair and orderly competition could improve the efficiency of market operation and effectively protect the legitimate rights and interests of enterprises, which are indispensable requirements for sustainable innovation; (3) *Geographical and resource advantages*: in the initial stage of growth pole, geographical location and resource conditions are particularly important. In areas with abundant resources and convenient transportation, low cost of resource use and transportation help enterprises reduce costs, achieve economies of scale more easily, and create fundamental conditions for the formation of new growth poles; (4) *Good infrastructure*: convenient and efficient transportation system within and between cities in the region, a transportation network system comprising expressways and railways, inland river and ocean transportation and air transportation all contribute to the integration of regional industries, promote the agglomeration and diffusion of industries in the region. These are indispensable for the formation of economic growth poles; (5) The industrial and technological base is the key factor for growth pole development: the formation of any growth pole is dependent on industrial backgrounds and on the technological level. The level of industrial division and agglomeration determines the prospects of technological innovation. The level of existing technology and the industrial advantages also determine the ability of innovation and development. The higher the industrial level and the stronger the innovation ability, the more suitable it is for the creation and development of a growth pole.

III. Growth Models for the Guangdong–Hong Kong–Macao Greater Bay Area during Different Periods

The Greater Bay Area of Guangdong, Hong Kong and Macao accounts for less than 1% of the national land area and less than 5% of the population, but it comprises about 13% of the total national economy. As far as international bay areas are concerned, the total economic volume of the Guangdong–Hong Kong–Macao Greater Bay Area ranks 3rd only after New York Bay Area and Tokyo Bay Area. The forces driving economic growth in Guangdong, Hong Kong and Macao change over time. In the process of regional economic development in Guangdong, Hong Kong and Macao, the forces of growth in different periods and for different regions come from focusing on certain different leading sectors or innovative industries responsible for the economic growth of each of the regions within the Greater Bay Area.

(A) *The "front store and rear factory" model*

After China's reform and opening-up in 1978, the advantageous geographical proximity to Hong Kong and Taiwan brought opportunities to Guangdong's economic development. At the beginning of the reform and opening-up, Guangdong's economy was backward; its industrial base was weak, its capital scarce and its idle labor force was large. In 1978, Guangdong's GDP was only 19.114 billion yuan, and its per capita GDP was less than 400 yuan, more than 20 yuan lower than that of the whole country. During this time, Hong Kong industries adjacent to Guangdong were in the stage of upgrading and adjustment. The rising prices of land, raw materials and labor force led to the rising cost of traditional labor-intensive manufacturing industries in Hong Kong, resulting in Hong Kong's gradual loss of competitiveness. Spurred by the policy of reform and opening-up, Guangdong became the preferred area for industrial transfer from Hong Kong by virtue of its similar "congenital advantages" such as geographical location, language and culture. Guangdong was instrumental in reducing costs for Hong Kong's manufacturing industries by providing cheap labor. Through the injection of Hong Kong capital, Guangdong began to develop labor-intensive industries. It took over Hong Kong's light industries and attained the initial stage of industrialization.

For a period of time, Guangdong, Hong Kong and Macao complemented each other in economic development, and the "processing" trade mode of "front shop and rear factory" gradually took shape. Guangdong was the "factory" and Hong Kong the "shop". Hong Kong and Macao became the window for Guangdong's overseas trade. The various processes involved taking overseas orders, marketing, foreign sales, raw material supply, new products and new process development were all completed by Hong Kong. Hong Kong played the role of "shop" in direct contact with customers. Guangdong, on the contrary, undertook the production and manufacturing processes, taking advantage of the low cost of land and labor to process and assemble products, thus playing the role of "factory". In the 1980s, the main industries in Guangdong were food, clothing, textiles and other consumer goods. Food and textiles and clothing developed rapidly and became the pillar industries. From the end of 1980s to the beginning of 1990s, durable consumer goods, such as color TVs, air conditioners and refrigerators, were produced. Guangdong enterprises adopted the model of "processing materials, assembly of components, further processing and compensatory trading".

At the same time, Hong Kong took advantage of its financial prowess to provide financial support for Guangdong's economic takeoff. At that time, the financial market in the Mainland was not developed and inefficient; development of manufacturing industries which stimulated the economic development of Guangdong required a lot of funds and it was difficult to obtain financing in Guangdong. Hong Kong played the role of financing for the economic development of Guangdong, and the financial demand of Guangdong also promoted the further prosperity of Hong Kong's financial market. Since 1978, Hong Kong's capital have accounted for the majority of Guangdong's foreign direct investment. By introducing direct investment from Hong Kong and Macao, Guangdong fostered the initial cooperation between Guangdong, Hong Kong and Macao in the areas of product division and finance. At this stage, the economic cooperation between Guangdong, Hong Kong and Macao was mainly manifested in the direct investment to Guangdong by Hong Kong and Macao whereupon Hong Kong and Macao transferred their industries to Guangdong, spilling over and in turn boosting the economic development of Guangdong. Thus, Guangdong Province became the main area of economic spillover from Hong Kong and Macao into the Mainland.

(B) *The "export-oriented" (exogenous) model*

Since the 1990s, with the deepening of China's reform and opening-up, Guangdong gradually developed a good investment environment. During this time, Guangdong's foreign investment sources were getting more extensive, and it had become an important area for attracting foreign investment in China. This was especially so in 1992 after Deng Xiaoping delivered his speech during his visit to the South, making Guangdong a window for the opening up of the whole country. Guangdong made great efforts to attract foreign investment by introducing a series of policies. Although traditional manufacturing industries were still the main areas of FDI inflows during this stage, new changes were also taking place in the sources of FDI and the industries of these FDI influx. In terms of sources of foreign investment, the proportion of foreign investment in Hong Kong and Macao declined, and the structure of foreign investment became more diversified. Industrial transfer from East Asian countries and regions added new impetus to the growth of Guangdong's economy. In the industry structure of foreign investments, foreign investment in electronic information industry had surged. Taking Taiwanese investments as an example, Chinese Mainland began to become the base for Taiwan's computer production. Taiwanese investors in related industries chose Shenzhen, Dongguan and Huizhou in Guangdong as their main locations of investment. After the middle and late 1990s, industries producing everyday items and necessities continued to develop. With the growth of foreign direct investment in electronic information and electrical machinery industries, Guangdong Province leapt to the stage of high-precision processing manufacturing industry. Convenient and hassle-free customs and clearance at entry ports plus developed urban transportation networks have promoted industrial agglomeration in Guangdong Province, and a great variety of industries have formed a relatively complete industrial chain in Guangdong Province. Driven by industrial agglomeration, specialist towns (or "counties") with their own industrial characteristics have become an important feature of Guangdong's industrial development. These towns possess their own strong characteristics of specialization, concentrating on a certain industry or a particular product, and with these advantages, they form an "effect of scale" for certain types of products in each town. The development of industrial agglomeration not only promotes the formation of a system of matching manufacturing enterprises in Guangdong but also bolsters the development of upstream and downstream industries and auxiliary industries. In this way, Guangdong has successfully "established" three major industrial entities or bodies concentrated in the Pearl River Delta. Zhuhai, Shunde, Zhongshan and Jiangmen industries in the western regions of the Pearl River are mainly involved in manufacturing durable and non-durable household consumer goods and hardware products and have well-known brands such as Kelong and Galanz. Shenzhen, Dongguan and Huizhou industries in the eastern regions of the Pearl River are mainly electronic communication equipment manufacturing industries, which are the largest agglomeration of electronics industries in the country. In the central part of Guangzhou, Foshan and Zhaoqing form an industrial belt with electrical machinery, steel, shipping and textile-building materials as their main industries. During this period, Guangdong's development was export oriented with its total export volume ranking 1st in the country for more than 10 years in a row. The Pearl River Delta region alone has established trade relations with all countries and regions in the world.

(C) *The "endogenous" growth model*

After 2008, consequent to the sub-prime mortgage crisis, the global economy slowed down, and the development of foreign trade in all countries faced a tremendous pressure, and Guangdong was no exception. With the constraints of labor costs, land resources, environment and other factors, Guangdong's economic growth model faces big challenges. Behind the rapid economic development, the industrial restructuring has become increasingly urgent. The pressure of rising costs and the remarkable improvement of people's living standards in China result in the rising domestic demand in the economy. The export-oriented growth mode of utilizing foreign capital and cheap domestic labor has become untenable, and a new growth driving power needs to be explored urgently. Stimulating and increasing the domestic demands has become an important means to promote economic growth in Guangdong Province. The Guangdong provincial government has to implement measures such as expanding domestic demands, maintaining foreign trade and undertaking environmental protection to cope with the impact of the financial crisis. The transformation of industrial structure and change in the mode of economic development are high on the agenda at present.

While making efforts to improve the relevant supporting facilities, Guangdong must also try to improve the investment environment and pay attention to domestic demand. At the same time, the province should enhance the capacity for innovation and service, strengthening the abilities to draw quality foreign investments. The post-2008 period is a new adjustment phase for Guangdong in utilizing foreign capital. While improving the investment environment, Guangdong has been strictly adhering to the principle of controlling the quality of foreign investment and actively striving for high-quality foreign investment. The new round of international industrial transfer involving service and high-tech industries helps to bring about the elevation of economic development and upgrading of industrial structure of Guangdong. Since 2008, Guangdong has been aggressively promoting independent industrial innovation, has formulated policies as documented in the "Guangdong Independent Innovation Plan" and has implemented "Ten Innovation Projects". The driving forces of technological innovation, capital investment and human resources investment in facilitating Guangdong's industrial transformation and upgrading are undergoing positive changes. There has been an increase in the number of larger enterprises with high added values in new high-tech industries. In 2015, the number of high-tech manufacturing enterprises in Guangdong reached 6,194, an increase of 365 compared with 2010, and the proportion of industries above the average normal size increased to 14.7%, an increase of 3.8% over 2010. The added values of the industries reached 753.734 billion yuan, accounting for 25.6% of industries above the average and normal, an increase of 4.5% over 2010. The total assets reached 2,688.261 billion yuan, an increase of 64.8% over 2010; and the total profits attained 203.414 billion yuan. The total amount of taxes paid was 91.964 billion yuan, doubling that of 2020. Since 2008, the proportion of the secondary industries has begun to decline, while that of the value added of the tertiary industries in GDP has been rising, and the role played by the industries in driving the economy has become increasingly significant. From 2008 to 2013, the proportion of tertiary industries in Guangdong increased from 44.4% to 48.8%, an increase of 4.4%.

IV. Cultivation and Development of the Growth Poles in Guangdong, Hong Kong and Macao in the New Era

The growth pole of Guangdong, Hong Kong and Macao is changing from an extensive, export-oriented growth mode to one of "endogenous", scientific and technological growth mode. The advantages of traditional factors such as land, labor and capital, factors that used to support the early economic takeoff of Guangdong, Hong Kong and Macao, are no longer available. Economic growth achieved by input (i.e. growth by exogenous extension) and produced by the effects of structural transformation is no longer sustainable or tenable. When simple injection of more capital and increase of labor does not beget higher returns, high costs and low output will lead to unsustainable economic growth. Therefore, at the stage of "endogenous" growth mode of science and technology, industrial upgrading relying on technological progress has become the main pathway to promote economic growth. The mode of economic growth must be transformed into one of intensive development. In order to achieve this transformation, Guangdong, Hong Kong and Macao must make good use of their advantages and overcome the unfavorable factors.

(A) *Favorable conditions for the development of Guangdong, Hong Kong and Macao growth poles*

After years of exploration and cooperation, Guangdong, Hong Kong and Macao have gradually established a mechanism for cooperation and they have made considerable progress in science, technology and infrastructure, thus laying a solid foundation for the cultivation of growth poles in Guangdong, Hong Kong and Macao in the new era.

(1) *Institutional support at the national level*

The principle of "one country, two systems" provides a solid institutional basis for the coordinated development of Guangdong,

Hong Kong and Macao. Although "one country, two systems" seems to be the political arrangement for realizing national unification, in essence, it provides a new development model for the economic development of the three places. Allowing Hong Kong and Macao to keep their original capitalist system unchanged over a long period of time not only safeguards the economic stability of Hong Kong and Macao but also enables the two places to make use of and rely on their respective economic advantages. The "one country, two systems" imperative provides institutional assurance and basis for the cooperation between Guangdong, Hong Kong and Macao — three places with different economic systems. The CEPA agreement is a free trade agreement signed between our national, main geopolitical body and the separate tariff zones of Hong Kong and Macao. The signing and implementation of CEPA agreement promotes the free and full flow of factors of production between Guangdong, Hong Kong and Macao, reduces the cost of cooperation between enterprises in different regions of Guangdong, Hong Kong and Macao and facilitates the optimal allocation of regional resources. Under the framework of "one country, two systems" and CEPA agreement, Guangdong, Hong Kong and Macao will be able to fully utilize their respective advantages and integrate into the economic globalization and regional economic integration.

(2) *The government's relevant policies and institutional support*

The Shenzhen National Independent Innovation Demonstration Zone, approved in 2014, is China's first independent innovation demonstration zone with cities as its basic economic units. In September 2015, the State Council approved the establishment of the National Independent Innovation Demonstration Zone in the Pearl River Delta, covering eight cities above the "Prefecture" level, namely, Guangzhou, Zhuhai, Foshan, Huizhou, Dongguan, Zhongshan, Jiangmen and Zhaoqing. This is the largest Independent Innovation Demonstration Zone in the whole country. In April 2016, the Guangdong Provincial Government formulated the "Plan for the Implementation of the Construction of Pearl River

Delta National Independent Innovation Demonstration Zone (2016–2020)". In September 2015, the "General Plan Relating to the Promotion of Comprehensive Innovation Reform Experiments in Some Regional Systems" was issued, which listed Guangdong as one of the eight comprehensive innovation reform areas in China. In June 2016, the State Council approved the Guangdong Provincial Innovation Reform Experimental Program. In principle, it agreed with the "Guangdong Provincial Comprehensive Innovation Reform Experimental Program", requiring serious organization and implementation thereof. Upon the approval of the State Council, in November 2016, Guangdong Province swiftly formulated the "Guangdong Provincial Experimental Action Plan for Systematic Promotion of Comprehensive Innovation Reform", systematically sorting out and putting forward 117 specific reform items, including 16 reform items authorized by the State Council and 101 reform items on provincial authorization. These policy arrangements provide policy and mechanism guarantees for the cultivation of growth poles in Guangdong, Hong Kong and Macao. Prompted by a series of government policies, Guangdong has formed an innovative "master plan" of "1 + 1 + 7", which makes Shenzhen and Guangzhou the leaders and seven national high-tech industrial development zones in the Pearl River Delta as the support for diffusing the coordinated development of east, west and north Guangdong.

(3) *The cooperation between industry, education and research in Guangdong, Hong Kong and Macao laid the foundation*

In June 2016, the "Innovation and Entrepreneurship Alliance of Guangdong, Hong Kong and Macao Universities", spearheaded by Hong Kong University of Science and Technology and co-sponsored by Macao University, Sun Yat-sen University, South China University of Technology, Guangzhou University of Technology and Guangzhou University, was formally established at the Fok Ying-tung Research Institute of Hong Kong University of Science and Technology in Nansha District, Guangzhou. In making efforts to enhance innovation cooperation, Guangdong Province is implementing an action plan for the Innovation Corridor and a sponsorship program for science and technology cooperation between Guangdong and Hong Kong. These programs seek to encourage the "moving out and beyond" of institutions of higher learning, research institutions and enterprises. To date, more than 240 overseas research organizations have been set up. At the same time, international science and technology plans to upgrade and enhance cooperation/collaboration will be implemented to support enterprises to set up R&D centers in countries and regions where there are extensive science and technology resources — via various means such as self-construction, mergers and acquisitions, joint ventures and cooperation — to acquire overseas technologies and to realize the achievements in Guangdong. In addition, we will focus on strengthening scientific and technological cooperation with Israel, the United Kingdom and Germany. Innovation platforms such as China (Guangdong) Pilot Free Trade Zone, China–Israel (Dongguan) International Science and Technology Cooperation Industrial Park, Jieyang China–Germany Metal Eco-city with a German Advanced Technology Promotion Center and German Advanced Equipment Domestication Center have been established.

(4) *Continuously increasing strengths of technological innovation*

In 2016, the number of high-tech enterprises in Guangdong was the highest in the country, reaching 19,857, with the Pearl River Delta region accounting for a very high proportion, reaching 18,880, and the growth rate was high, reaching up 78.8% year-on-year. Of these high-tech enterprises, Shenzhen and Guangzhou being the aggregation areas of high-tech enterprises in Guangdong, had 8,037 and 4,744, respectively. The number of high-tech enterprises in Guangzhou, Dongguan and Zhongshan increased rapidly by more than 100%, and more than 200 new research and development institutions had been established, including 154 provincial-level, new research and development institutions. In the innovation and entrepreneurship environment, 126 new incubators of science and technology enterprises were added in the Pearl River Delta region in 2016, totaling 491, and 311 had been included in the statistics for collective innovation space. Of these, 165 were national-level incubators, ranking 1st in the country. The Pearl River Delta has become the development "highland" with the most intensive innovation resources, the most advanced industrial development and the most active business incubation. It is also the core area for Guangdong Province to implement innovation-driven development strategies. On efforts to attract talents, the Pearl River Delta has implemented major human resource projects such as the "Pearl River Talent Plan" and the "Guangdong Special Support Plan". A total of 115 innovative and entrepreneurial teams and 88 leaders had been recruited. In 2016, patent applications and authorizations for inventions in the Pearl River Delta region grew at a rate exceeding 40%. The new national high-tech zones in the Pearl River Delta accounted for 0.07% of the province's land area, but it created one-seventh of the province's industrial added values, one-fifth of its business income and more than one-fifth of its net profit.

(5) *Location advantage and a "mature" and developed transportation network*

The external transportation network of the Guangdong–Hong Kong–Macao Greater Bay Area has emerged, forming a "three-dimensional" transportation network by sea, land and air. In terms of land transportation, major railway lines and corridors running across the east, west and north have been built in China, such as the Li–Zhan line (Litang to Zhanjiang), Beijing–Guangdong line, Jing–Jiu (Beijing–Jiujiang/Kowloon) line and Coastal Railways. Guangdong has opened an international land transport freight line from Shenzhen to Hanoi. With the construction of railways from Guangdong to Zhanjiang and Nanning, the railway transport capacity between the core areas of the Pearl River Delta and ASEAN has been enhanced. Through the national rail network, railway links between the central, southwestern regions and the northwest regions bridge the Eurasian continent. By the end of 2016, the total mileage of roads in Guangdong Province reached 218,000 kilometers, of which the highway mileage reached 7,673 kilometers, ranking 1st in the country. In air transport, Guangdong has Baiyun International Airport in Guangzhou, one of the three major hub airports in the country. Then there is also Shenzhen Airport, one of the major "backbone" airports. International routes generally cover most countries in the world. In 2015, the total passenger traffic volume of Hong Kong International Airport reached 68.5 million people, with a total cargo volume of 4.38 million tons and routes covering more than 200 countries and regions in the world. The cargo and passenger facilities owned by Macao International Airport can handle 6 million passengers and 160,000 tons of cargo annually. The routes of Macao International Airport cover mainly Asian countries and regions. In maritime transport, Hong Kong is the third largest container port in the world, with 9 container terminals and 24 docking berths and a throughput of 20.1 million standard containers (TEU [Twenty-foot Equivalent Unit]) in 2015. The ports of Guangdong Province have forged friendship and cooperation agreements with 29 foreign ports, opening 291 international container liner routes and 2,811 berths, of which 304 berths were for 10,000 tons and above. The annual cargo-handling capacity of Guangdong Province reached 1.67 billion tons, ranking 2nd in the country, with the annual throughput of containers reaching 59.481 million standard containers (TEUs), ranking 1st in the country. Guangdong, Hong Kong and Macao now have the largest passenger and cargo-handling capacities in the world.

(B) *Constraints on the development of growth poles in Guangdong, Hong Kong and Macao*

The development of growth poles in Guangdong, Hong Kong and Macao is facing some unavoidable constraints. On the issue of urban development, problems appearing in the growth poles include over-emphasis on urban construction but neglecting the nurturing of the quality of urbanization itself; long-term planning across cities lags behind economic development. The economic development of Guangdong, Hong Kong and Macao is also experiencing the impact of rising labor costs, decreasing land resources and weakening economic complementarity. It is therefore necessary to search, explore and establish new ways of development.

(1) *The formation of growth poles relies too much on administrative guidance*

The formation of China's growth poles relies too much on government intervention. Most government policies on the cultivation of growth poles are formulated at the provincial level and are implemented via the province concerned. It may be the case that the policymakers at the provincial level are not well-informed about the economic conditions of the towns and cities of their subordinates within each province. In addition, each of the cities in the province has its own interests to take care of. In order to achieve better performance targets, each city tries to strive for better provincial development planning for itself. It is not easy to coordinate the interests of each city within the province. The relevant industrial policies and industrial development planning at the municipal level are introduced based on the individual interests of each city or municipality. Because of the strong influence exerted by the government on economic activities, industries in the growth pole become homogenous or are getting more uniform and similar. There is little or low competition among the cities or urban areas, resulting in waste of resources and inefficient utilization: it will be difficult for them to produce or create their own comparative advantages. Additionally, attaching too much importance to the role of the government will weaken the establishment of a real market mechanism, which more or less distorts the functions of market mechanism in allocating resources.

(2) *Lack of coordination in the "matching" or "syncing" of institutional mechanisms between Guangdong, Hong Kong and Macao*

"One country, two systems" provides the basic institutional assurance, and it is the premise of regional economic cooperation between Guangdong, Hong Kong and Macao. However, the differences of system and policies between Guangdong, Hong Kong and Macao also aggravate the difficulties for economic cooperation among the three places. Although market economy has become the main mode of economic operation in China, the government still wields great power and influence over the economy. Hong Kong and Macao fully adopt the free market economic system, and the mode of economic operation facilitates self-regulation through the "rules of values", the relationship between supply and demand and the competition mechanism. The economies of Guangdong, Hong Kong and Macao are quite different in terms of social management, making it more difficult to coordinate cooperation among the three. Taking the construction of the Guangzhou–Shenzhen–Hong Kong passenger rail line as an example, the Guangzhou–Shenzhen section of the rail had already been completed in 2011. However, the Hong Kong section of the Guangzhou–Shenzhen–Hong Kong high-speed railway, originally scheduled to be completed in 2015, was delayed until 2018. Owing to the difference in decision-making and consultation mechanisms between Guangdong and Hong Kong, the construction of the two sections was not synchronized, and the construction cost of the Hong Kong section escalated. This delay greatly affected the high-speed rail. For another example, the implementation of the one-off special quota pilot scheme for transit for private cars in Guangdong and Hong Kong (commonly known as the "self-driving tour of Guangdong and Hong Kong") was sped up by administrative decision-making on the premise that Hong Kong would be able to enjoy the first phase of the pilot scheme and its people could first drive north to Guangdong for a short stay. In Hong Kong, the policies of the HKSAR government require public consultation and a large number of people in Hong Kong expressed discontent about outlanders coming in to "squeeze out" Hong Kong residents in using their public resources. It is therefore difficult to carry out proposals of providing convenience for all the people within the region.

There are great differences in industry standards and criteria for professional qualifications between Guangdong, Hong Kong and

Macao; there are great differences in assessment and evaluation standards in industries, resulting in the increase of the cost of doing business within the industries. The mutual non-recognition of qualifications of Guangdong, Hong Kong and Macao in the same industry affects the flow of personnel among regions and hinders the free movement or flow of resources within the region. For example, Hong Kong, Macao and Guangdong adopt different industry standards in science and technology service industries. Hong Kong and Macao follow international standards while Guangdong adopts domestic standards which means increases in the difficulties of cooperation in science and technology service between the three. In the fields of vocational and professional services, there is no uniform criteria and recognized qualification and certification. Mutual non-recognition policies between Guangdong, Hong Kong and Macao hampers the flow of high-tech talents within the three places. The different policies that are in place in the three regions make it very difficult to coordinate and carry out effective measures to integrate the development of the three places.

(3) *Dilemma of labor cost*

Low production cost and low prices have been the most important advantages of Guangdong's manufacturing industries in the past, making Guangdong a glorious manufacturing and production base for goods exported to the world. The rise and rapid development of "Made in Guangdong" manufacturing could not be separated from "low labor cost advantage". Guangdong Province became one of the largest labor-intensive regions in China, and the labor market was in a state of oversupply. Surplus labor from all provinces and cities in the country guaranteed low manufacturing costs in Guangdong. However, after years of rapid growth, Guangdong is now experiencing a wide range of labor problems, especially the shortage of skilled workers. This shortage of skilled labor is causing great difficulties to many labor-intensive enterprises. The shortfalls in the number of production workers in the Pearl River Delta region are mainly concentrated in some labor-intensive enterprises, numbering more than one million. At the same time, the cost of labor is also rising. In some provisions of the new Labor Contract Law safeguarding the rights and interests of workers, zero basic wages, reduced benefits, increased working hours and so on have become illegal means of reducing costs. In addition, in the new provisions of "temporary contract or contract for unfixed terms" for workers' welfare items, double overtime wages, paid marriage leave, sick leave and annual leave have greatly increased the cost of labor. In addition, the cost of living in Guangdong has been rising, pushing the cost of labor in Guangdong. Labor cost used to be an important supporting factor for Guangdong's economic development, but has now become a negative factor hindering Guangdong's economic growth.

(4) *Land supply is tight*

After years of rapid development, large numbers of residential, commercial and industrial parks in Guangdong have exhausted most of the usable land in Guangdong Province. There is very little land available in Shenzhen, Guangzhou and Dongguan and in other economically developed cities. Land has become a scarce resource. The cost of land has been soaring, rents have risen and there have been many land project auctions with astronomical price tags. It is no surprise that the operational cost of enterprises and the cost of living of residents have gone up. Additionally, the high costs have drastically reduced the number of projects deemed suitable for investment in the region. The land area of the Pearl River Delta is only 417,000 square kilometers and the land available for development is quite limited. Limited supply limits the development of new enterprises and large-scale projects in the region.

(5) *Weakening economic complementarity between Guangdong, Hong Kong and Macao*

After decades of development, Guangdong has established a comprehensive and a good division of labor system in many manufacturing industries by using its advantages in land, energy and the labor force, and it has formed an industrial agglomeration. The advantageous service industry of Hong Kong and Macao has also developed rapidly. However, after 1990s, with the diversification of Guangdong's foreign capital and the gradual establishment of its industrial system, the spillover effect of Hong Kong and Macao on Guangdong's economy has gradually declined. With the rising cost of production and living in Guangdong, there is increasing evidence of a convergence of economic structures between Hong Kong and Macao, Shenzhen, Guangzhou and other economically developed cities. This represents a direct conflict of interest which the development of Guangdong, Hong Kong and Macao faces. These are important issues that must be addressed if they are to carry out in-depth and effective cooperation. If there is no effective communication and coordination mechanism, there will be little or no motivation for cooperation, resulting in the lack of coordination and cooperation between the policies of the governments, in which case, each of the parties will "mind its own affairs" and conduct its own development regardless of the others. This situation is not amenable to the free flow of production factors, hindering the sharing of information. Such affairs is also not conducive to the effective allocation of resources within the region, and it also leads to the inability of Guangdong, Hong Kong and Macao to tap their own regional advantages, which will have adverse consequences for the overall development of the economy of Guangdong, Hong Kong and Macao.

(C) *Areas to make important breakthroughs in the development of growth poles in Guangdong, Hong Kong and Macao*

In order to attain sustainable development across the administrative regions of Guangdong, Hong Kong and Macao, we should not only take economic growth as the goal but also use scientific and technological cooperation of Guangdong, Hong Kong and Macao as the basis to change the mode of independent development to one of enhanced integration of industrial division and cooperation. We must try to realize the integrated development of science and technology, industry and finance across different administrative regions. We need to change the path of extensive development to one of intensive development and realize industrial agglomeration within the region. Maintaining the sustainable growth of Guangdong, Hong Kong and Macao is a systemic and complex project. We must make good use of the region's advantages and favorable conditions to realize the coordinated development within the region. We wish to achieve the "double synergistic" development, "the synergistic development of Guangdong, Hong Kong and Macao" and "the synergistic and coordinated development of science and technology, finance and industry", so as to realize the "1 + 1 + 1 > 3" effect.

(1) The system and mechanism of communication between Guangdong, Hong Kong and Macao must continue to be strengthened

Because of the differences and distinctions in the governance system, culture and law between Guangdong, Hong Kong and Macao, effective communication is indispensable in order to achieve the coordinated and synergistic development. The communication or contact between Guangdong, Hong Kong and Macao can be divided into two levels. At the first level, the communication between the governments focuses on the coordination of government policies, holding of regular and impromptu meetings between senior officials of the three places, consultation on important collaborative matters, coordinating matters of mutual interests, unification of schedule, improvement of coordination system, enhancement of the implementation of all parties and assuring the effectiveness of policy implementation. The second level is the non-governmental cooperation in which unfettered and free flow of key factors is promoted; the most effective allocation of resources is facilitated, their respective comparative advantages are explored, and problems that cannot be solved through government mechanisms solved — especially in judicial and social management. The integration of Guangdong, Hong Kong and Macao should be fostered, and a good social and cultural environment must be developed. We should establish and improve the cooperation between various industry and professional associations by establishing relevant cooperation platforms, in particular high-level dialogue platforms in the business and academic circles. We must also support the liaison and communication between cities and promote the coordinated development of the Greater Bay Area. The establishment of a regular exchange mechanism between Guangdong, Hong Kong and Macao industries is conducive to the establishment of unified and standardized industry standards and specifications. Different industries possess different particularities or uniqueness. Industry contacts and communication are more conducive to the free flow of elements within the industry. At the same time, information-sharing platforms, science and technology innovation service platforms and financial service platforms are to be established in various industries to reduce "information asymmetry". For example, general information can be obtained through public service platforms to serve general enterprises, thus making the whole market more open and transparent.

(2) *Promoting the free and unfettered flow of important factors and providing optimized allocation of resources*

In November 2015, the Mainland signed service trade agreements with Hong Kong and Macao separately to promote the liberalization of services trade between the Mainland, Hong Kong and Macao. The agreements formally came into force on June 1, 2016. Under the Agreements, the Mainland will open up 153 service sectors to Hong Kong and Macao, accounting for 95.6% of the WTO classification standards for service trades, of which 62 will be for national treatment according to Hong Kong and Macao. In the areas where Hong Kong uses the "negative" list, there are only 120 restrictive measures, 28 of which further relax access conditions. In cross-border services, culture, telecommunications and other areas where positive lists are used, 28 new "openness" measures have been added. Hong Kong will be accorded the most favorable treatment throughout the Mainland, that is, in future free trade agreements signed by the Mainland with other countries and regions, any measures more favorable than

CEPA provisions will apply to Hong Kong. In addition, a matching "package" management system commensurate with the negative list model will be established. Other than the restrictive measures reserved in the agreement and the establishment and change of companies and financial institutions in the telecommunications and cultural fields, Hong Kong service providers who invest in the service trade areas opened (as per the agreement) in the Mainland will have their contracts and articles of association for establishment and alteration changed to filed management. These measures greatly facilitate Hong Kong entrepreneurs' access to the Mainland market. Macao service providers can also enter the Mainland market through "commercial existence" to enjoy the same market access as Mainland enterprises. The service trade agreement is a free trade agreement in which the Mainland opens the field of services in a comprehensive way by means of pre-admission national treatment plus the "negative list" of access. It marks the general liberalization of services trade between the Mainland, Hong Kong and Macao.

The WTO divides the service sectors of the whole world into 12 sectors and 160 sub-sectors. By their numbers, 153 service sectors have been opened to Hong Kong and Macao in the Mainland, accounting for 95.6% of the sectors listed in the WTO. However, there are still some obstacles in the implementation of the opening-up measures. The real liberalization of service trade between Guangdong, Hong Kong and Macao has not reached a "formally open" level. Moreover, because the RMB is not freely convertible under capital accounts, capital has not yet been flowing completely freely. Other flows, including the flow of people, materials, institutional flow and information flow, have also been evidently restricted. Further efforts are needed to achieve the free flow of key elements and factors between the Mainland, Guangdong and Hong Kong and Macao.

(3) *Enhancing the power to industrialize science and technology*

Although the number of scientific and technological personnel in Guangdong Province leads China, there is a lack of top-notch professionals in high-tech industries. Although there are large numbers of scientific research professionals in various regions and territories, the depth of cooperation with enterprises is insufficient. Generally, most of them prefer academic research, and their creativity in science and technology is not manifested or reflected. The rate of achievement from the results of academic research is very low, even at the expense of wasting resources. This shortcoming limits the development of the science and technology industries.

Frequent exchanges and re-exchanges of scientific and technological knowledge, technology and information help reduce the cost of such exchanges. By sharing innovation infrastructure to enhance the effects of scale and spillover of scientific and technological innovation, establishing and improving the sharing system of scientific research equipment and scientific and technological information — and last but not least strengthening the public service function of the innovation platform — the problem of insufficient R&D resources in SMEs could be solved to provide support for innovation and entrepreneurship.

(4) *Achieving industrial "gradient transfer" in Guangdong, Hong Kong and Macao*

According to the gradient shift (or cascade) theory, most innovative activities involving new products, new technologies and new management methods, begin in high-gradient areas, and then gradually shift from high-gradient areas to low-gradient areas in a stepwise sequence. The industrial gradients of Guangdong, Hong Kong and Macao can be divided into three levels: (1) high-gradient areas of Hong Kong, Macao, Guangzhou and Shenzhen; (2) medium-gradient areas of Central and Eastern Guangdong; (3) low-gradient regions of Western and Northern Guangdong. Guangdong Province should make good use of the gradient hierarchy among the different areas and regions in the province to carry out technology and industry transfer in an efficient and orderly manner. The aforementioned transfer helps strengthen the economic links within the Guangdong–Hong Kong–Macao Greater Bay Area and foster the economic cycle within the Greater Bay Area. We will have to enhance the diffusion and driving functions of high-tech industries and service economy in high-gradient areas of Hong Kong, Macao, Guangzhou and Shenzhen, actively utilizing the advantages of geography, capital and technology and developing new industrial growth points and facilitating the transfer of industries and labor forces from high-gradient areas to Western Guangdong and Northern Guangdong. Low-gradient areas need to make full use of their comparative advantages to form the agglomeration effect of industries with comparative advantage and to promote their own economic development. It is necessary to cultivate and develop economic growth poles with their own characteristics in areas with different gradients.

(5) *Promoting the coordinated development of science, technology, finance and industry*

The existing problems in the Greater Bay Area of Guangdong, Hong Kong and Macao are as follows: insufficient extent of integration among science and technology, finance and industry; the transformation from science and technology to industry is not smooth; and the mutual support between finance and industry is not coordinated. Industrialization of science and technology requires financial support, but under the existing financial system, financial services are out of touch with the "innovation cycles" of enterprises. Lack of financial support and a low transformation rate from technology achievements to industry make science and technology remain at the level of scientific research. As such, science and technology cannot be transformed into real productive forces to drive the economy. First, financial institutions lack the ability to effectively evaluate technology. This is especially so for the main financing banks, wherein their stringent requirements of risk control will lead them to reject the financing requests of most technology companies. The establishment of an evaluation system for scientific and technological achievements will help reduce the information mismatch or asymmetry between financial institutions and scientific and technological enterprises, and it will enhance the ability of financial institutions to control the financing risk of scientific and technological companies. Second, we need to establish a multi-level financing system for science and technology, with innovative financial products and services tailored for different stages of science and technology research and development. This will ensure financial support from different financial institutions with different financial products for each stage of the technology development. We need to increase and speed up multi-level capital markets, develop and improve the equity transfer system for science and technology companies and cultivate professional institutions for science and technology investment. Third, the presence of a technology-integrated service platform will make technology a factor of production, the efficient flow of which among the parties facilitates the effective allocation of the scientific and technological resources.

The further promotion of the "Belt and Road" Initiative has created new opportunities for the establishment of a "Science and Tech Bay Area" in the Greater Bay area of Guangdong, Hong Kong and Macao. The promotion of "Belt and Road" Initiative is also inseparable from the support and cooperation of the Hong Kong and Macao Greater Bay Area. The Greater Bay Area is centered at the Pearl River estuary region, with its back leaning against the interior and facing the South China Sea. It is strategically located in the economic development area nearest to the countries along the Maritime Silk Road. The development of the Greater Bay Area is poised and oriented to the big "Belt and Road" market. The three places of Guangdong, Hong Kong and Macao need to ride on the "Belt and Road" Initiative to bring about more and new space for the innovation of science and technology industries to make it a global innovation "highland".

Chapter 6

Economic Radiating Effects of the Guangdong–Hong Kong–Macao Greater Bay Area in China Effects of the Guangdong–Hong Kong–Macao Greater Bay Area

Li Cheng

Shenzhen University

The city clusters of the Greater Bay Area refer to the former Pearl River Delta urban agglomeration, together with Hong Kong and Macao, forming a "9 + 2" group, with the Pearl River estuary as the core. Its specific spatial pattern can be described as "one ring, two fans, two screens and six axes". One of the most important parts is the ring, which is occupied by Hong Kong, Shenzhen, Dongguan, Guangzhou, Zhongshan, Zhuhai and Macao, forming the economic sphere of the Pearl River estuary.

The economic foundation of the Greater Bay Area of Guangdong, Hong Kong and Macao is mainly based in the core area of the Pearl

River Delta, which, together with Hong Kong and Macao, forms the Greater Bay Area economy. Therefore, the Greater Bay Area of Guangdong, Hong Kong and Macao first played the role of promoting the economy of the Pearl River Delta region.

The city clusters of the Greater Bay Area of Guangdong, Hong Kong and Macao refer to the former Pearl River Delta urban agglomeration, together with Hong Kong and Macao, forming a "9 + 2" group, with the Pearl River estuary as the core. Its specific spatial pattern can be described as "one ring, two fans, two screens and six axes". One of the most important parts is the ring, which is occupied by Hong Kong, Shenzhen, Dongguan, Guangzhou, Zhongshan, Zhuhai and Macao, forming the economic sphere of the Pearl River estuary. With this ring as the core and Guangzhou as the demarcated boundary, the urban sector (of one fan) along the eastern coast of the Pearl River estuary is formed, which covers the eastern part of Guangzhou, Dongguan Water Villages Economic Zone, Songshan Lake High-tech Zone, Huizhou Tonghu "Ecological Intelligence" Zone, Daya Bay New Zone and so on. Industrial parks with multi-form and multi-functions are arranged so as to form a spatial industrial layout with multi-growth poles to help accelerate the promotion of industrial transformation and upgrading of the eastern coastal areas. Next, the urban sector (of another fan) with Zhaoqing and Jiangmen as the boundary and the western area of the Pearl River estuary as the core — based upon the premise of preserving the good natural ecological environment of the region — is taken to be a springboard for opening up the economic and trade corridors of the southwest region and to help lead the population and industry to further agglomerate in the southwest of China through the integrated hub of airports, ports, rails and other modes of transportation, thus establishing an advanced equipment manufacturing belt. The "two screens or barriers" refer to the ecological barrier in the northern forest and mountain range plus the green ecological protection barrier on the southern coast. The six axes refer to strengthening the spatial connection between the Greater Bay Area and the surrounding areas with the establishment of six major county–city industrial development axes: (1) Hong Kong–Zhuhai–Gaolan Port–Daguanghai Port–Yangjiang–Western Guangdong Region; (2) Shenzhen–Zhongshan–Jiangmen–Yangjiang–Western Guangdong Region; (3) Guangzhou–Foshan–Zhaoqing–Yunfu–Southwest Region; (4) Guangzhou–Qingyuan–Shaoguan–Central Region; (5) Dongguan–Huizhou–Heyuan–Northeast Guangdong Region; (6) Shenzhen–Daya Circle Bay–Shanwei–Eastern Guangdong.

I. The Pearl River Delta has Become the Most Dynamic and Vibrant Region in China

The Greater Bay Area of Guangdong, Hong Kong and Macao will not only create a diffusion effect on the economy of its inner areas and Guangdong Province as a whole but its spillover effects will also reach the whole Pan-Pearl River Delta region. The Pan-Pearl River Delta is a concept formally put forward in July 2003. Like the Greater Bay Area of Guangdong, Hong Kong and Macao, it is also a "9 + 2" concept. The number "9" refers to nine provinces in South China, Southeast China and Southwest China, namely, Guangdong, Fujian, Jiangxi, Hunan, Guangxi, Guizhou, Sichuan, Yunnan and Hainan, while "2" refers to the two special administrative regions (SARs) of Hong Kong and Macao. The whole Pan-Pearl River Delta region covers nearly 20% of China's land area and contains one-third of its population, with its economic output exceeding one-third of the whole country. In 2004, the "Pan-Pearl River Delta Framework Agreement for Regional Cooperation" was signed and the Pan-Pearl River Delta Regional Cooperation was launched. In March 2016, the State Council issued the "Guiding Opinions on Enhancing Pan-Pearl River Delta Regional Cooperation", which further raised the issue of the overall requirements for deepening Pan-Pearl River Delta regional cooperation, signifying that Pan-Pearl River Delta regional cooperation entered a new phase. The whole Pan-Pearl River Delta region relies on the Greater Bay Area of Guangdong, Hong Kong and Macao as an important hub. Its sea outlets cover all ASEAN member countries and countries along the Maritime Silk Road. Most of the developing countries are those countries whose voices on international economic rules are weaker than those of China. In terms of overall economic positioning and economic layout, the economic functions of the Pan-Pearl River Delta are as follows: first, to export domestic capital, second, to import foreign capital and third, to reform the supply side of the economic equation. The Pan-Pearl River Delta region creates "outposts" for foreign capital to enter China, and also serves as the "back door" for the Chinese capital to enter the world. It could strengthen the regional cooperation at home and help conduct an overall plan to to further develop and open up coastal, riverside, border and inland areas.

The Greater Bay Area of Guangdong, Hong Kong and Macao not only involves the development of city clusters within the bay area but also entails coordinated development of cities in Guangdong Province and even the coordinated development of nine provinces in the Pan-Pearl River Delta region. Further integration and development of the "9 + 2" city clusters will enhance the power and range of diffusion of the Guangdong–Hong Kong–Macao Greater Bay Area as the growth engine of the Pan-Pearl River Delta. Therefore, the economic spillover analysis of the whole Guangdong–Hong Kong–Macao Greater Bay Area should be conducted from the inner, smaller "ring" of the Greater Bay Area to the middle "ring" of Guangdong Province, and then further to the Pan-Pearl River Delta area.

Taking the above points into consideration, this chapter shall focus on the following aspects to conduct research and analysis.

First, in talking about the economic radiation of the smaller "ring", we should consider the interior of the Greater Bay Area. As for the city clusters, they exhibit the phenomenon of having several centers of development. At the same time, owing to the different economic systems and the lack of top-level design and implementation of the "one country, two systems" imperative, there are obstacles in the communication and interactions among the central cities within the Greater Bay Area, seriously hampering the efficiency of the Greater Bay Area as the engine driving the economy of the Pan-Pearl River Delta. Meanwhile, Guangzhou and Shenzhen, as the two development and growth poles of the Pearl River Delta, are often regarded as competitors in their past economic developments. The efficiency of economic interaction between the two places and the achievements thereof need to be accurately evaluated.

Second, Guangdong Province must be taken into consideration when discussing the economic spillover of the middle ring. As Guangdong Province has been cut off into "two fans" by the Pearl River Delta, the economic development of the "two fans" lags far behind that of the Pearl River Delta. In recent years, the GDP growth rate in the Pearl River Delta has exceeded that of eastern, western and northern Guangdong, meaning that the economic disparities between the "two fan" regions and that of the Pearl River Delta will in time become even larger. Whether it is because of the increasing effects of economic agglomeration of the Pearl River Delta that have resulted in the loss of the important elements or factors or it is because of declining radiating power of the whole of Pearl River Delta, or both, are issues which we need to study in depth.

Lastly, for the economic radiation of the Guangdong–Hong Kong–Macao Greater Bay Area in the Greater Ring, one needs to begin from the whole Pan-Pearl River Delta region. The Pan-Pearl River Delta region covers the entire southern provinces of China, horizontally spanning the eastern and central regions, extending to the western regions of Yunnan and Sichuan. China's overall economy is characterized by a progressive decrease in economic levels from the east to the west. Therefore, the economic developments among the nine provinces in the Pan-Pearl River Delta are different. Moreover, we must note that the inherent factors of production for each possess their own characteristics. As an engine driving the growth of economy, the Greater Bay Area of Guangdong, Hong Kong and Macao produces different driving effects on the different provinces. In order to determine the economic spillover effect of the Greater Bay Area toward the nine adjacent provinces, the most important thing is to explore the role of the Greater Bay Area in the industrial transfer and upgrading of the nine provinces and to analyze the dominant position of the Greater Bay Area at the terminus of the industrial chain and its dominant position over production factors on the whole Pan-Pearl River Delta region.

II. Economic Radiating Effects within the Greater Bay Area

In researching the internal economic radiation of the Greater Bay Area, greater attention has been paid to the economic interaction between Hong Kong, Shenzhen and Guangzhou and their respective characteristics of economic development. The core issue is the internal integration in the Guangdong–Hong Kong–Macao Greater Bay Area. Because of the differential economic systems under "one country, two systems" and the obstacles in the exchange of talents, funds and technologies between the Mainland, Hong Kong and Macao, the development of the Greater Bay Area is bound to be different from that of other bay areas. The issues of internal coordination and integration are particularly critical. Owing to historical reasons and these obstacles and barriers, the agglomeration of the various resources in node cities has been hindered. Therefore, the biggest difference between the city clusters of the Greater Bay Area and other international urban agglomerations or city clusters is that there is no leading or dominant city, but there are three cities standing side by side, forming a belt. Therefore, the governance of this multi-center urban agglomeration is a particularly urgent problem to be solved in the Greater Bay Area. Although the geographical location of the Guangdong–Hong Kong–Macao Greater Bay Area conforms to the economic development of bay areas, because of the existence of several centers of development, it follows that the previous single-core or single-center concept of bay area establishment is not appropriate for the planning and development of the Greater Bay Area. We need to utilize the concept of multi-center urban agglomeration in urban economics as a theoretical framework for analyzing the economic characteristics of the Greater Bay Area in order to obtain results with greater practical significance.

In Europe, the theory of "poly-centricity" is more established in practice, and since 1999, the "European Spatial Development Outlook" has begun to promote the idea of multi-center urban clusters. Peter Hall and Kathy Pain organized an international research group to conduct an empirical study of "Polynet" in eight multi-center urban districts in Europe, through the publication of

"Multi-center Metropolis: Experiences of Having Urban Regions from Europe". The research results were published which provided case studies and ideas for subsequent research on multi-center networks. The research results indicated that the birth of world cities originated from the Advanced Producer Services (APS), which generated dominating networks in different levels of cities. Therefore, the network structures between city clusters or urban agglomerations have become the main areas of focus for studying urban agglomeration issues.

(A) *Analysis of the internal economic distribution patterns in the Greater Bay Area*

For an analysis of the diffusion effect of the Guangdong–Hong Kong–Macao Greater Bay Area on its internal economy, the following research methods will be adopted: first, we conduct accurate calculations of the economic distribution pattern of the Greater Bay Area; second, after determining the multi-center economic distribution patterns of the Greater Bay Area, we analyze the effects of economic interaction among the various centers; finally, upon establishing the spatial correlation of the regional economic growth among different regions in the Greater Bay Area, a spatial network of regional economic growth in the Guangdong–Hong Kong–Macao Greater Bay Area is to be established. Through the aforementioned pathways and steps, the economic dependence of each of the cities in the Greater Bay Area is analyzed, and the core economic radiation "ring" thereof is analyzed and interpreted in depth.

To study the distribution pattern of the internal economy, we must first analyze the classification of the size and categories of data of the cities within the Greater Bay Area. The following categories need to be given comprehensive assessment, viz the relevant city's economic development level, population, capital and other dimensions. Table 1 shows the GDP and population data of the cities within the city clusters of the Greater Bay Area of Guangdong, Hong Kong and Macao. The data are obtained from the 2016 *Guangdong Statistical Yearbook*, the 2016 *Hong Kong Statistical Yearbook* and the 2016 *Macao Statistical Yearbook*.

Table 1. GDP and population of the cities of the Greater Bay Area of Guangdong, Hong Kong and Macao.

	2000	2005	2010	2011	2012	2013	2014	2015
	GDP of cities (in 100 million yuan)							
Guangzhou	2,492.7	5,154.2	10,748.3	12,423.4	13,551.0	15,497.0	16,706.0	18,100.0
Shenzhen	2,187.5	2,187.5	9,773.3	11,515.0	12,971.0	14,572.0	16,001.0	17,502.0
Zhuhai	332.4	635.5	1,210.8	1,410.3	1,509.2	1,679.0	1,867.2	2,025.4
Foshan	1,050.4	1,050.4	5,622.6	6,179.7	6,579.2	7,010.7	7,441.6	8,003.9
Huizhou	439.2	803.9	1,730.0	2,094.9	2,379.5	2,705.1	3,000.4	3,140.0
Dongguan	820.3	2,183.2	4,278.2	4,771.9	5,039.2	5,517.5	5,881.3	6,275.1
Zhongshan	345.4	885.7	1,853.5	2,194.7	2,446.3	2,651.9	2,823.0	3,010.0
Jiangmen	504.7	801.7	1,570.4	1,830.6	1,880.4	2,000.2	2,082.8	2,240.0
Zhaoqing	249.8	435.1	1,088.4	1,328.8	1,467.7	1,673.4	1,845.1	1,970.0
Hong Kong	13,375.0	14,121.0	17,763.0	19,344.0	20,370.0	21,383.0	22,600.0	23,984.0
Macao	521.0	939.9	1,922.9	2,307.6	2,750.9	3,295.6	3,536.2	2,899.7
	City Population (in 10,000)							
Guangzhou	994.8	949.7	1271.0	1,275.1	1,283.9	1,292.7	1,308.1	1,350.1
Shenzhen	701.2	827.8	1,037.2	1,046.7	1,054.7	1,062.9	1,077.9	1,137.9
Zhuhai	123.7	141.6	156.2	156.8	158.3	159.0	161.4	163.4
Foshan	534.1	580.0	719.9	713.1	726.2	729.6	735.1	743.1
Huizhou	321.8	370.7	460.1	463.4	467.4	470.0	472.7	475.6
Dongguan	644.8	656.1	822.5	825.5	829.2	831.7	824.3	825.4
Zhongshan	236.5	243.5	312.3	314.2	315.5	317.4	319.3	321.0
Jiangmen	395.2	410.3	445.1	446.6	448.3	449.8	451.1	452.0
Zhaoqing	337.7	367.6	392.2	395.1	398.2	402.2	403.6	406.0
Hong Kong	666.5	681.3	702.4	707.1	715.4	718.7	724.1	730.5
Macao	43.0	47.4	53.7	54.9	56.9	59.5	62.2	64.2

From the GDP data, the growth rates of Guangzhou and Shenzhen were conspicuously outstanding, and their nominal GDP growth rate generally doubled every 5 years. Except for Jiangmen, the cities of the Guangdong–Hong Kong–Macao Greater Bay Area, which were originally cities within the Pearl River Delta, had their nominal GDP grow by 7 to 8 times in the past 15 years; Macao's economic growth rate was only five times, and Hong Kong's nominal GDP growth rate was only 1.7 in the past 15 years. Hong Kong began to rise economically only in the 1970s.

Before 1970, Hong Kong was nothing more than an insignificant British colony. Hong Kong's GDP in 1970 was HK$23.1 billion. Since then, its economy had grown by leaps and bounds. In 1980, it grew to HK$143.6 billion. In 10 years, its economic size soared 6 times, achieving a miraculous growth rate that doubled in less than 2 years. This golden decade laid the foundation for Hong Kong's industrial economy. After 1980, Hong Kong's economy continued to develop at a high speed for quite a long time. In 1990, its GDP was HK$599.3 billion, an increase of 317% compared to 1980. In 2000, its GDP was HK$1,337.5 billion, an increase of 123% over 1990. Although this growth rate was not as remarkable as the growth of the golden decade of the 1970s, it was not too slow. Hong Kong's economic growth has been slowing down rapidly since 2000. The main reason is that Hong Kong's manufacturing industry has been affected by the reform and opening-up in the Mainland. Many Hong Kong entrepreneurs have moved their industries to the Mainland and are quite satisfied with the policy of "processing of raw materials and samples, assembly of components and trade subsidies". There is no upgrade of the island's industries. By 1990, the ratio of the employed in the manufacturing sector to the total employed population fell to about 30%, and this figure fell to about 20% in 1995 and 12% in 2000. By 2010, it was only about 3%, an almost negligible figure. In absolute numbers of employed people, the total number of manufacturing workers in Hong Kong in 1980 was about 1 million, but by 2010 it was only slightly more than 100,000. The lack of manufacturing has led to the unsustainable growth of Hong Kong's economy. The high-end service industries represented by the financial industry possess the characteristics of high income and low employment. The scale of the financial industries and employment numbers cannot sustain the continued growth of Hong Kong's economy. In contrast, the industrial upgrading in Shenzhen and Guangzhou, located in the Pearl River Delta, appears more sustainable and reasonable. The industrial advantage of Guangzhou is reflected in commerce and trading, while the industrial advantage of Shenzhen is reflected in finance and Internet technologies. The fast-moving economic driving engines of the two cities have led their economies to be on an equal footing with Hong Kong. It is difficult to reproduce Hong Kong's economic boom. In order to further analyze the coordination of the urban development stages in the Greater Bay Area of Guangdong, Hong Kong and Macao, it is necessary to measure and compute the size and other relevant data of the cities. The most commonly used analysis method in the field of regional economics is the rank (or order) — size law, or Zipf's law.

The order size distribution was proposed by G.K. Zipf in 1949 and is a theoretical tool for studying the size distribution of the cities of a country or region. The urban size distribution reflects the distribution of urban population in different categories of cities in a country and is a measure used to examine the development of a regional urban system. According to Barabasi's (2002) definition of size distribution, in the model of size distribution, there are distributions with characteristic yardsticks and distributions without characteristic yardsticks. Chen Yanguang (2010) of Peking University applied the 2^n multiple method of mathematical analysis and proved that the distribution without yardsticks obeys Zipf's law. According to Zipf's law, the product of city size within a certain area and its rank order in all urban areas is a constant. The mathematical formula is described as follows:

$$P = C/S^\beta \, \beta \qquad P = C/S^\beta \cdots$$

where P is the indicator for the city size — generally based on the economic level or population distribution data; S is the ordinal number, that is, the rank of the city's size indicator among all regional cities; C is a constant and the value of β is the assessing standard under Zipf's law. When $\beta = 1$, this indicates that the cities in the region conform to the rank-size rule; $\beta > 1$ indicates that there is imbalance among the developments of the cities, and the specific manifestation is that the development is mostly concentrated in large cities and that the development of small cities is insufficient. This means that the resources and important elements of the region are concentrated in the core or main cities, with the surrounding cities being "out of touch" or not keeping in pace with the development of core cities. The core cities display more aggregating effects, without suitable or appreciable spillover effects, thus rendering the polarization of urban development to become more and more marked. The development of core cities and surrounding, peripheral cities could not forge effective linkages, and hence, the overall regional development would appear to be fragmented. When $\beta < 1$, this shows that the city sizes are well distributed and more balanced, a situation where large and small cities do not form polarization, with no particularly prominent city, and the overall regional development is balanced. However, this lack of core cities or the existence of inconspicuous core cities in the region makes it difficult to affect an agglomeration, and these affairs will also reduce the motivation of the core engine that drives and promotes regional development. The results of using Zipf's law to carry out calculation on the population of the city clusters of the Greater Bay Area of Guangdong, Hong Kong and Macao according to their economic development levels as indicators are shown in Figure 1.

As can be seen from Figure 1, with regard to the city clusters of Guangdong, Hong Kong and Macao, the value of β as measured by GDP is 1.5613 in 2000, and then the value of this indicator begins to approach 1 over time. This means that with GDP used as a city

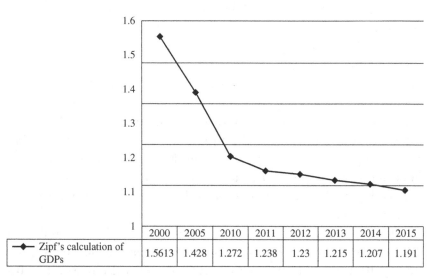

	2000	2005	2010	2011	2012	2013	2014	2015
—◆— Zipf's calculation of GDPs	1.5613	1.428	1.272	1.238	1.23	1.215	1.207	1.191

Figure 1.   Zipf's calculation of the GDP levels of the cities of the Greater Bay Area of Guangdong, Hong Kong and Macao.

size indicator to measure the urban agglomerations or city clusters of the level of imbalance due to extremely uneven development is decreasing year by year. Analysis of GDP data for the year 2000 shows that Hong Kong's GDP was much higher than that of Shenzhen and Guangzhou, accounting for more than 50% of the city clusters, but in the 15 years since, Guangzhou and Shenzhen have had higher GDP growth rate than Hong Kong. This situation to a certain extent achieves some form of balance in the overall economic development of Guangdong, Hong Kong and Macao. On the whole, the value of β in 2015 is 1.19, but the GDP ratio of other cities is still shrinking. This shows that the current balance of the overall urban agglomeration of Guangdong, Hong Kong and Macao is dependent on Hong Kong, Shenzhen and Guangzhou. The GDP levels of the three cities are about the same, and the GDP of the three cities accounts for about 70% of the total GDP of the urban agglomerations and city clusters of the Greater Bay Area. From this perspective, the trend toward equilibrium of economic development in the Guangdong–Hong Kong–Macao's Greater Bay Area stems from the balance of GDP in these three core cities, but in essence there is still uneven development. Next, the dimension of population is used to analyze the degree of equilibrium among the city clusters of the Greater Bay Area of Guangdong, Hong Kong and Macao. By calculations based on Zipf's law, the specific trends are shown in Figure 2.

According to Zipf's calculation, the population distribution of Guangdong, Hong Kong and Macao city clusters basically conforms to Zipf's law. Although the value of β showed a low in 2005, after 2010, its value remained in the range of [0.98, 1]. This shows that the development of Guangdong, Hong Kong and Macao's city clusters when using population as a dimension of measurement is more balanced, and its development trends are more reasonable and understandable.

By calculating the size of the city clusters, it is found that although the problem of unbalanced development has been quite greatly alleviated, on further analysis we discover the reason for this is that the slowdown of Hong Kong's economic growth has led to the

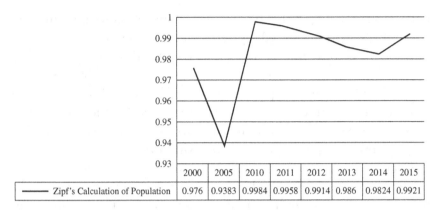

Figure 2. Zipf's calculation of the populations of city clusters in the Greater Bay Area of Guangdong, Hong Kong and Macao.

overtaking by Guangzhou and Shenzhen in the economic development curve by virtue of their own advantages and the preferential of national policies. All these have resulted in the three-city cluster comprising Guangdong, Hong Kong and Macao in the Greater Bay Area, with Hong Kong, Shenzhen and Guangzhou forming a "vertical, high-speed" economic development belt. For the next step, we are going to analyze the spillover effect of the three cities on the whole Greater Bay Area in the light of the position and status of the three core cities.

(B) *Evaluation of the status of the three major financial centers in the Greater Bay Area*

One of the major characteristic features of the economy in the Greater Bay Area is the developed high-end service industry, especially the financial service industry. Hong Kong, Shenzhen and Guangzhou, the three core cities of the Greater Bay Area, have all joined the list of global financial centers, according to the latest Global Financial Center Index (GFCI) released by the British think tank Z/Yen in March 2017. The evaluation of the global financial center rankings is based on a city's business environment, financial system, infrastructure, human capital and its reputation. The core cities of several major global bay areas are listed. Among them, New York ranked 2nd with 794 points, behind the number one — London — by only one point; Tokyo Bay Area's core city of Tokyo ranked 5th with 734 points and San Francisco of San Francisco Bay Area ranked 6th with 720 points. Of the three core cities, Guangzhou was listed in the global financial center ranking for the first time, at the 37th position with 650 points. Shenzhen ranked 22nd with 701 points, and Hong Kong ranked 4th with 748 points. Some of the criteria for inclusion in the GFCI list include rapid development, huge potential and financial industries with distinctive characteristics. The financial development in each of the three core cities possesses its own characteristics:

(a) Hong Kong's global financial index was 748. As an SAR of "one country, two systems", Hong Kong enjoys unique preferential policies. It is a world-renowned prosperous metropolis, an important international financial center, an international shipping center as well as an international trade center. It is known as a shopping paradise and has an irreplaceable position among neighboring countries and regions. In addition, Hong Kong is the third largest financial center in the world after London and New York.

(b) The advantages in cross-border finance and financial innovation possessed by Shenzhen are incomparable. Relying on the Qianhai Pilot Free Trade Zone, Shenzhen–Hong Kong financial cooperation can be further enhanced and there are opportunities for trial-and-error innovation in cross-border finance. The agglomeration effect of Shenzhen's financial industry is increasing. By the end of 2016, there were 50,900 financial-type enterprises registered in the Qianhai–Shenzhen–Hong Kong Cooperation Zone, accounting for 46.6% of all the enterprises in the Qianhai Pilot FTZ, and the total registered capital (including subscription) was 4.4 trillion yuan. Qianhai's cross-border RMB loans totaled 36.5 billion yuan, benefiting 171 enterprises in Qianhai.

(c) Guangzhou is vigorously developing direct financing with two-way interaction between finance and the real economy. Through the development of direct financing business, the financing cost of enterprises is reduced so the real economy is being actively developed. Up until 2016, the city's direct financing balance reached 1.35 trillion yuan, second only to Shanghai (1.48 trillion yuan), accounting for 60.65% of Guangdong Province's total. The proportion of direct financing in the financing for the whole society reached 52.3%, ranking 1st in large cities nationwide. Figure 3 shows the scores obtained by top 10 cities of the world and that of Shenzhen and Guangzhou in GFCI ranking released in 2017.

As far as financial centers are concerned, their core is the agglomeration effect of financial resources and the spillover effect of financial industries on the other industries. According to GFCI classification of financial centers, London and New York are classified as global financial centers, Hong Kong, Singapore and Tokyo are categorized as international financial centers whereas Shenzhen

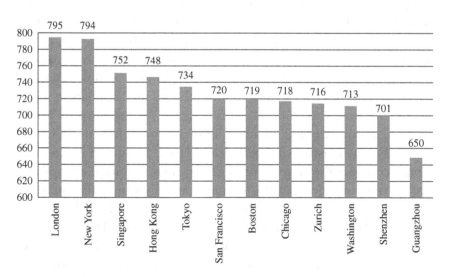

Figure 3. 2017 Global financial centre index rankings.

and Guangzhou are national financial centers. Taipei and other places with small or limited financial spillover effects are classified as regional financial centers. Financial centers such as Zurich Private Banking Center in Switzerland, Chicago Commodity Futures Center and Berlin Fund Management Center are categorized as "professional or specialist" financial centers. In the light of these different financial centers, this chapter seeks to comprehensively analyze the financial development levels of the city clusters of the whole Greater Bay Area through the indicators of financial competitiveness and to further outline the financial radiation capacity "road map" of the Guangdong–Hong Kong–Macao Greater Bay Area. Through the construction of strategic financial industry nodes, the diffusion overlap area, diffusion core area and diffusion peripheral areas are identified and targeted around the entire Guangdong–Hong Kong–Macao Greater Bay Area. We shall put forward financial development proposals to specifically correspond to the financial diffusion patterns of the Greater Bay Area.

Financial competitiveness indicators refer to a number of core indicators of GFCI, including the GDP level of the a city's GDP and the proportion of tertiary industry in its GDP. Only Hong Kong, Shenzhen and Guangzhou have been listed in the GFCI rankings, while other cities have not. For the city clusters of the entire Guangdong–Hong Kong–Macao Greater Bay Area, it is necessary to redesign a reasonable financial competitiveness index system to assess each of the cities so as to outline the financial radiation range of the core financial cities. Designs targeted for the purpose are to be made to measure the impact of financial competitiveness of cities within the city clusters of Guangdong, Hong Kong and Macao. We should consider the supply and demand relationship of economics, that is, the conditions of the demand and supply of the financial industry, and the size aggregation factors of financial industry that are more obvious than those of the other industries. The aforementioned three factors of size agglomeration are to be taken into consideration to comprehensively evaluate the financial competitiveness of cities within the inner cities of the city clusters. The conditions of demand for financial industries specifically refer to the level of the city's economic development, the economic system and the coverage of the hinterland economy; that is, the greater the demand, the higher the level of financial industry development there will be, and the higher will be the corresponding financial agglomeration effect and wider financial spillover effect. For the conditions of supply, they are evaluated from the perspective of level of supply of financial institutions' own funding, level of financial talent reserves, extent of financial advance, financial innovation, economic openness and financial system. The level of the financial agglomeration is more about analyzing the financial network structure within the cities. For example, the ratio of the number of employees in financial institutions to the total number of employed people, the increase in the value of financial assets to the added values of total assets, etc., reflect better the "health" of the entire financial industry. The proportion of the entire financial industry in the overall economic development level of the city is used to judge the extent of agglomeration of the financial industry. Based on the above analysis, the financial industry competitiveness evaluation index system as shown in Table 2 was constructed. Sources include data mainly obtained from the 2015 and 2016 *Guangdong Statistical Yearbooks*, the 2015 and 2016 *Hong Kong Statistical Yearbooks* and the 2015 and 2016 *Macao Statistical Yearbooks*. The yearbook of the year only shows the data for 2015, so all the data are more for 2015. At the same time, because there are differences in the method of computing and collecting data and different accounting systems between Hong Kong, Macao and the Mainland, there are deviations in the process of selecting indicators. Therefore, this chapter tries to select indicators that are consistent with statistical calibration, but deviations and disparities still exist. The deviations will inevitably cause certain errors in the measurement of competitiveness in the real financial industry.

The "level of financial demand" component reflects the level of financial demand for the economic operation of the entire city. Therefore, it needs to be measured from the overall economic development of the city. Only when the economy develops to a certain size and scale will the agglomeration effect of the financial

Table 2.   System of indicators for evaluating financial competitiveness.

Financial Competitiveness	
Level of Financial Demand	GDP per capita ($X1$)
	Per capita fiscal revenue ($X2$)
	Total fixed assets investment ($X3$)
Level of Financial Supply	Balance of local and foreign currency deposits ($X4$)
	Balance of local and foreign currency loans ($X5$)
	Value added to the financial industry ($X6$)
	Income of insurance premium ($X7$)
	Number of financial institutions ($X8$)
Level of Financial Agglomeration	Number working in financial industries/total employment ($X9$)
	Value added for the financial industry/ GDP ($X10$)
	Insurance density ($X11$)
	Number of listed companies ($X12$)

service industry be reflected. Through the promotion of financial demands, the financial industry's agglomeration and the increase in financial assets will be promoted, and a virtuous cycle will be formed thereby. As such, the three indicators of per capita GDP, per capita fiscal revenue and total fixed asset investment have been selected as the secondary (second level) indicators for measuring the level of financial demand.

The "level of financial supply" component reflects the level of financial industry development in a city. The most important indicator is the banks' deposits and loan business, which reflects the financial industry's ability to support the real industry. The aforesaid indicators also indirectly reflect the financial supply capacity. This book chooses the balance of local and foreign currency deposits and loan balances as research indicators. Additionally, the added values (or value added) of the financial industry and insurance premium income can be used to measure the level of development of the city's overall financial industry. Premium income is used to measure the insurance business of the entire city. The choice of this indicator is made because it reflects the health and level of the insurance industry in the city to a certain extent but the most important reason for this choice is the ready availability of data; also, Hong Kong and Macao share the same statistical standards or calibrations with the Mainland. Finally, the number of financial institutions indirectly measures the level of financial development and financial supply of the city.

The level of financial agglomeration reflects more the density of the financial network of the city. The ratio of the number of people employed in the financial sector to the total number of employed persons is selected as an indicator to gauge the level of financial agglomeration of the entire city. The ratio of the added values of the financial industry and the development level of the GDP of the whole city also indicates the proportion of the financial industry in the overall economic development, and these indicators better describe the level of financial industry's agglomeration for the whole city. Insurance density and the number of listed companies are also easily available and therefore selected to measure financial agglomeration.

According to the above indicator setup, EVIEWS is used to measure the 11 cities of the Guangdong–Hong Kong–Macao and Greater Bay Area city clusters using the factor (or component) analysis method, and their financial competitiveness is evaluated. The specific analysis results are as follows:

The first is the situation of reduced dimension. According to the Scree Plot diagram, upon component analysis, 12 secondary indicators are dimension-reduced and are finally merged into two common factors/components. The Scree Plot is shown in Figure 4.

As can be seen from Table 3, the cumulative variance contribution rate of the first common factor (component) after rotation is 71.23%, and the cumulative variance contribution rate of the second common factor (component) is 91.67%, indicating that the two common factors could be used to represent most of the information of the 12 second-level indicators, consistent with the results of the component analysis of the Scree Plot. After the variance of the loaded/weighted matrix is maximized and orthogonally rotated, the cumulative variance contribution of the first common factor

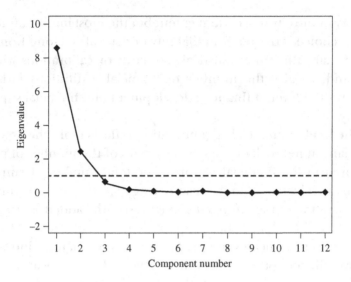

Figure 4.   Factor (component) analysis scree plot.

Table 3.   Variance contribution analysis.

		Initial Decomposition			Post Rotation	
Principal Component	Eigenvalue	Variance Contribution Rate (%)	Cumulative Variance Contribution Rate (%)	Eigenvalue	Variance Contribution Rate (%)	Cumulative Variance Contribution Rate (%)
1	8.548	71.23	71.23	7.732	64.44	64.44
2	2.451	20.44	91.67	3.267	27.23	91.67

(component) is 64.44%, and the cumulative contribution of the second common factor is 91.67%. Further analyzing the eigenvalues of the two common factors (components) after rotation, the eigenvalue of the first common factor is 7.732, the eigenvalue of the second common factor is 3.267 and since the eigenvalues of the common factors (components) after rotation are greater than 1, further analysis is based on scored data formed by the two common factors/components.

The rotation of components renders the principal component representative variable inconspicuous in the initial decomposition. By performing the rotation of components, the loaded matrix obtained by the orthogonal rotation method is more polarized, the principal component is easier to identify to facilitate analysis and the practical significance represented by the principal components can be obtained. The loaded matrix of components after rotation is shown in Table 4.

It can be seen from Table 4 that the first principal component has a large load on $X4$, $X5$, $X6$, $X7$, $X8$, $X9$, $X10$ and other indicators, while the second principal component is more loaded in $X1$, $X2$, $X3$, $X11$ and $X12$ indicators. According to the analysis, the first principal component is more representative of a city's financial indicator, while the second principal component represents one other type of a city's economic indicator — other than financial indicators — which can be called the "economy-supporting component". By the above calculations, the financial competitiveness rankings of the city clusters of Guangdong, Hong Kong and Macao can be obtained. PC1 and PC2, respectively, reflect the city's financial size–scale indicators and economic supporting indicators, and "Score" is the weighted score of the two. The higher the weighted score, the higher the city's financial competitiveness. The financial competitiveness of

Table 4. The loaded matrix of components after rotation.

Variable	PC 1	PC 2
$X1$	0.101516	0.839985
$X10$	0.866802	−0.381832
$X11$	0.264844	−0.691591
$X12$	0.178694	−0.664399
$X2$	0.177317	0.759865
$X3$	0.080322	0.815236
$X4$	0.894807	0.079302
$X5$	0.765006	0.056039
$X6$	0.823393	0.216625
$X7$	0.823393	−0.136928
$X8$	0.712231	−0.227873
$X9$	0.917115	−0.145608

Table 5.   Calculation of the competitiveness levels of the cities in the Greater Bay Area.

City	Component 1	Component 2	Total (Score)
Hong Kong	1.703324	−0.26137	1.441957
Shenzhen	0.580775	0.253873	0.834648
Guangzhou	0.852668	−0.05037	0.802299
Foshan	−0.09009	0.136636	0.046548
Zhuhai	−0.10168	0.077595	−0.02408
Dongguan	−0.08909	0.007766	−0.08132
Macao	0.007358	−0.22702	−0.21967
Zhongshan	−0.33867	−0.02418	−0.36285
Huizhou	−0.44094	−0.13914	−0.58008
Jiangmen	−0.449	−0.11642	−0.56542
Zhaoqing	−0.48012	−0.1801	−0.66022

each city in the Greater Bay Area of Guangdong, Hong Kong and Macao is shown in Table 5.

As can be seen from Table 5, cities with obvious financial diffusion capacity, that is, cities with a score greater than 0 (Foshan scored more than 0, but too close to 0, and that was mainly due to the higher scores in the economic supporting components — so the financial radiation capacity of Foshan is negligible) are Hong Kong, Shenzhen and Guangzhou. Cities with a total score less than 0 are cities in areas under the financial diffusion of core cities. As can be seen from Table 6, Hong Kong's financial radiating capability is far ahead of Guangzhou's. Shenzhen's financial radiation capability is slightly better than that of Guangzhou. Therefore, in the urban network structure with finance as the main indicator, Hong Kong is the core dominant city of the whole city clusters, while Shenzhen and Guangzhou play the role or carry out functions of secondary financial centers. The scores for financial competitiveness of other cities are much lower than those of the three cities, implying that they are much less competitive compared to the three cities. This result is consistent with the position of these cities under the radiating influence of the three core cities.

Table 6. Financial radiation range of the three financial centers of the city clusters of the Greater Bay Area of Guangdong, Hong Kong and Macao.

City	Financial Competitiveness Score	Financial Radiation Range (km)
Hong Kong	1.441957	111.27
Shenzhen	0.834648	93.17
Guangzhou	0.802299	90.86

(C) *Research on the "staggered" or differential, complementary development of the financial multi-center structure in the Greater Bay Area*

To study the inner diffusion effect of the Greater Bay Area of Guangdong, Hong Kong and Macao is to study the financial radiation capacities of the three cities. We compute the financial radiation radius for each of Hong Kong, Shenzhen and Guangzhou, using the computed radius to help us outline the map of financial location advantages or strengths of the whole Greater Bay Area. Upon this basis, we attempt to put forward different development strategies of financial services for each city.

The computation of the radius of the financial diffusion of each of Hong Kong, Shenzhen and Guangzhou is based on Wilson's (1967) spatial interaction model. This model solves the problem of calculating divergence in applying Newton's model to two-dimensional spatial interaction. The Wilson model is a rigorously deduced regional spatial interaction model based on the principle of maximum entropy, expressed in the following equation:

$$T_{ij} = KA_iD_j \exp(-\beta \, r_{ij}) \tag{6.1}$$

In this model, K is the normalization (or unifying) factor, whose value is generally 1; T_{ij} represents the total amount of resources that region i attracts from region j; A_i is the competitiveness level of resource elements (factors) for region i; D_j is the competitiveness level of region j's resource elements; β is the attenuation factor, which is chiefly affected by the distance based on the region's size or area; r_{ij} is the spatial distance between the ith city and the jth city. The Wilson model can be further simplified. The idea is to simplify the resource-level elements of the attracting area by adopting the simplified method of Wang Zheng (2002) to study the radiation capacity of the core nodes. The simplified formula is as follows:

$$\theta = D_j \exp(-\beta\, r_{ij}), \tag{6.2}$$

where θ is the threshold, whose actual significance is that when a city's financial competitive level drops to this level with some distance, it is taken that its financial radiation capacity is only up to that distance. Areas outside this distance are not affected by the financial radiation of the financial center. Taking the logarithm of Equation (6.2), we obtain the following equation:

$$r_j = (1/\beta) \times \ln(D_j/\theta) \tag{6.3}$$

According to Eq. (6.3), as long as the threshold is set, after the financial competitiveness of each city is measured, r_j can be measured according to the value of β, which is the financial radiation radius of city j. Referring to the conclusion of Wang Zheng (2002), for the value of β is obtained from the following equation:

$$\beta = \sqrt{\frac{2T}{t_{\max} \sum D_j}} \tag{6.4}$$

In Equation (6.4), T is the number of elements interacting in the region, and in the case of one region, this is used to indicate the number of cities in the city clusters in the region, so in this chapter, T has the value of 11. $t_{\max}$ reflects the number of financial centers within the city clusters. Among the city clusters of the Guangdong–Hong Kong–Macao Greater Bay Area, only Hong Kong, Shenzhen and Guangzhou can be regarded as real financial centers. Therefore, in this chapter, the value of $t_{\max}$ is 3. $\sum D_j$ is the sum of the administrative land area of all cities in the urban agglomeration; that is, the total area of the city clusters of

Guangdong, Hong Kong and Macao — the total area of the 11 cities in the Greater Bay Area of Guangdong, Hong Kong and Macao. Its overall area is 56,500 square kilometers. In the selection of the attenuation threshold, considering that Foshan's score on financial competitiveness is 0.0465, the threshold is set to 0.05, and cities with scores below this value are considered as cities without financial radiation capability. Once the financial radiation capacities of Hong Kong, Shenzhen and Guangzhou have dropped below this value, they will also be considered to have no more financial radiation capability. Based on the above analysis, the financial radiation ranges of the three major financial centers in the Greater Bay Area of Guangdong, Hong Kong and Macao are calculated as in Table 6:

The radiation radii (radiuses) of the core financial cities of the Greater Bay Area of Guangdong, Hong Kong and Macao have been computed as above. It can be found that there is an overlap of areas under financial radiation, including Guangzhou, Foshan, Dongguan, Shenzhen, Hong Kong, Zhongshan, Zhuhai and Macao — generally covering eight cities in the Guangdong–Hong Kong–Macao Greater Bay Area. Around this core diffusion area, it is necessary to divide the positioning of the regional cities in a specific manner so that the financial and real economies can be combined to form a mutually beneficial interaction between the two. In addition, owing to the greater number of financial centers in the region, if there is no proper planning and "staggered or complementary" development, a fierce intra-regional competition will take place. Excessive competition will not be conducive to the overall development of the city clusters or agglomeration of the Greater Bay Area.

In the overall national planning, the Greater Bay Area also covers three free trade zones in Guangdong Province, namely, Qianhai Shekou Free Trade Zone at the intersection of Shenzhen and Hong Kong, Zhuhai Hengqin Free Trade Zone at the junction of Macao and Zhuhai and Nansha New Zone at the intersection between Guangzhou and Zhongshan. From the positioning of the three major free trade zones, we can also see the top-level plan or design of China's differential developments for the entire Guangdong–Hong Kong–Macao Greater Bay Area. First, the functional positioning of Qianhai Shekou Free Trade Zone relies on enhanced cooperation between Shenzhen and Hong Kong, featuring international financial openness and innovation and focusing on the development of high-end services such as scientific and technological services, information services, modern finance and the establishment of a pilot zone as window for China's financial industry opening to the outside world. Second, the functional orientation of Nansha new district is to build a system of investment and trade regulations in line with international standards, focusing on the development of production services, shipping logistics, specialized finance and high-end manufacturing industries, building a comprehensive world-class service hub and creating an agglomeration of international high-end production services. Finally, the functional orientation of Hengqin New Area is on the in-depth cooperation between Guangdong and Macao, focusing on the development of tourism, leisure, healthcare, culture, science, education and high-tech industries: it is slated to become a cultural and educational pilot area and an international business service and leisure tourism base playing a new role in promoting the appropriate and diversified development of Macao's economy.

The differential positioning is based on the characteristics of each of the financial centers for which the three are "apportioned", positioning wise. Guangzhou borders Foshan, Zhongshan and Dongguan. The core industries of these three cities are all in manufacturing, especially Foshan's manufacturing industry. Foshan City is the only city in the Greater Bay Area of Guangdong, Hong Kong and Macao where the secondary industries account for a higher proportion of the overall economy than the tertiary industries. The financial center with Guangzhou as its core stresses more on production financial services. Guangzhou's pillar industries are advanced manufacturing and information services and business services industries such as automobile, electronics and equipment manufacturing. Its financial industry boosted GDP growth by 1.0% in 2016, making it the fifth pillar industry of Guangzhou. Making use of the resource advantages of headquarters and the strengths of administrative resources, Guangzhou should continuously expand its economic scale and enlarge its functions as a regional center and continue to consolidate its advantages in the banking and insurance industries by focusing on strengthening regional syndicated loans, notes/bills financing and fund settlement. Functions such as property rights transactions, commodity futures, financial education and research, development of headquarters finance and construction of financial business districts should also be emphasized. Therefore, in view of the urban development under the financial radiation radius of Guangzhou and the layout of Guangzhou's own industrial development, Guangzhou's financial services industry should be "more in touch with the real economy instead of relying on virtual economy" in its development direction, targeting the SMEs in its economic hinterland. The financial services should aim at universal or inclusive financial services, promoting the return of credit capital for "more real rather than virtual" entities, investing more in the real economy and effectively reducing the costs of financing of enterprises, especially small and microenterprises.

The two major financial centers of Hong Kong and Shenzhen should become more cooperative rather than competitive, because their markets are different. Hong Kong is more of an offshore center for the RMB taking on the role of an external bridge for Chinese companies to go global. Its unique talents, laws and economic and trade advantages play an important role for China's capital opening. Hong Kong is leading the Mainland in attempts to narrow the gap between China and developed countries by setting up a platform for connecting and joining domestic and foreign enterprises and capital. The existence and expansion of offshore markets is conducive to expanding the mutual access of financial institutions between the two places, relaxing the investment restrictions and increasing the scale of QDII and QFII, allowing more investors to participate in the market demands for cross-border financial transactions and reversing the direction of the open process of capital projects. Shenzhen has its unique strengths in innovation and financial technologies. In the 2017 global financial technology city scores issued by Deloitte, Hong Kong ranked 5th and Shenzhen ranked 30th in the world. We believe that joint efforts made by the two cities leading to the establishment of a financial technology center will have great potential. In January 2017, the two places jointly signed the "Memorandum of Cooperation on Promoting the Common Development of the Lok Ma Chau Loop", to jointly establish the "Hong Kong–Shenzhen Innovation and Technology Park" in the Lok Ma Chau Loop area to promote it as a high-end new engine for technological innovation. This new strategic fulcrum and platform for Shenzhen–Hong Kong cooperation will possess high international competitiveness.

As for the financial links, the opening of "Shenzhen–Hong Kong Stock Connect" on December 5, 2016 marked the successful connection of Shenzhen and Hong Kong securities markets. Shenzhen–Hong Kong Stock Connect will allow the Mainland's capital market to further open to the outside world under conditions of controlled risks, promoting the internationalization of the RMB and allowing Hong Kong to contribute more to the financial reform of the Mainland. In January 2017, new breakthroughs were made in financial technological innovation in Qianhai, Shenzhen: China Merchants Bank (CMB) used the first blockchain cross-border payment application technology in China to enable users of Shekou Free Trade Zone in Qianhai, Shenzhen, to make cross-border payment through Wing Lung Bank to their accounts in Hong Kong. Shenzhen–Hong Kong Stock Connect was launched at the end of December 2016. In order to strengthen Hong Kong's bond market, it is hoped that there would be a "Bond Connect" to open in 2017. Therefore, the role of Shenzhen–Hong Kong Stock Connect in the capital market is particularly important. Because of that, in the city clusters of Guangdong, Hong Kong and Macao, with Hong Kong being the offshore financial center and the core area of the Marine Silk Road, it needs to undertake the task of building an open economy for China. Shenzhen is an important bridge connecting Hong Kong to other regions of the Guangdong–Hong Kong–Macao Greater Bay Area and even entire inland areas. Shenzhen also has high-level financial services and innovative industries. It not only connects and "syncs" well with Hong Kong but also acts as a financial center and technology innovation center.

It has a very good radiation effect on the whole of the Guangdong–Hong Kong–Macao Greater Bay Area.

The Hengqin New Area has no core financial industry and it is more an area under financial diffusion. Because of the Pearl River estuary, the benefits of Shenzhen and Hong Kong's financial spillovers to the entire Hengqin New Area are relatively small. The completed Hong Kong–Zhuhai–Macao Bridge should improve this situation: a half-hour economic circle around the Pearl River estuary will take shape. Hence, the prospects for economic development of the area are to be anticipated in the future.

Looking at the radii of the financial radiation of the core cities in the Greater Bay Area of Guangdong, Hong Kong and Macao, we could discern two financial intersection "belts" or zones in the three core cities. One of the "belts" is the "removing virtual to go real" productive financial service belt with Guangzhou as the core spilling over to the manufacturing cities of the whole Greater Bay Area, and the other is the two-way cross-border financial diffusion belt formed by the financial superposition or "overlapping" of Hong Kong and Shenzhen. The two financial intersections are like the two wings of an airplane. One functions as the engine driving and promoting the development of the real economy while the other serves the "go global" strategy of development. The manufacturing cities of Foshan, Zhongshan and Dongguan in the two intersecting belts enjoy the full advantages of two-way superposing financial services. On the one hand, they can get the support of inclusive or universal financial services. On the other hand, they also obtain the financial support for high and new technologies in the "go global" type of enterprises through Shenzhen and Hong Kong. In other words, the development of the real economy is driven by the "two wings". This requires the two intersecting belts to achieve real differentiated development by way of correctly positioning their financial developments. For this to work, there must be reduced regional competition and a reasonable division of labor. Through the "staggered and complementary" development of the financial industries of the cities concerned, the three major financial centers will be able to really provide impetus for the economic development of the Guangdong–Hong Kong–Macao Greater Bay Area.

III. Economic Diffusion Effect of the Greater Bay Area on Cities in Guangdong Province

Being the number one economic province in the country, Guangdong Province has been at the forefront of economic development. The province has the Pearl River Delta, the engine driving national economic development. The further upgrading of the Pearl River Delta into the economic spheres of Hong Kong and Macao will further enhance its position as the engine for the new economic core of the Guangdong–Hong Kong–Macao Greater Bay Area. However, throughout Guangdong Province, the problem of unbalanced development between urban and rural areas has not been properly addressed and comprehensive solutions have not yet been found. In addition to the Pearl River Delta region or the Greater Bay Area of Guangdong, Hong Kong and Macao, there are three other regions in Guangdong Province: (1) the western wing or regions including Zhanjiang, Maoming and Yangjiang; (2) the mountainous region including Yunfu, Qingyuan, Heyuan, Shaoguan and Meizhou; (3) the eastern wing including Shantou, Chaozhou, Jieyang and Shanwei.

According to the data of the "Guangdong Macroeconomic Development Report (2016–2017)", Guangdong's eastern, western and northern regions are "entrenched" in the traditional development model: there is insufficient vitality in economic development and the economy faces great pressure of declining. The development of the Pearl River Delta is thriving pre-eminently, whereas in the east, west and north of Guangdong, developments are relatively slow. The GDP in the Pearl River Delta region increased by 8.1% in the first three quarters, but it was only 7.2% in the eastern, western and northern regions of Guangdong. The GDP of the eastern wing grew by 7.1%, the western wing by 7.3% and the mountainous region by 7.3%. Looking at the regional GDP growth rate variation figures, the disparities in regional growth rate had expanded after a long-term narrowing. According to the *Statistical Yearbook of Guangdong Province* in 2016, the GDP of the Pearl River Delta (excluding Hong Kong and Macao) was 6226.8 billion yuan; the development of Western Guangdong was the best, but with GDP of only 607.6 billion yuan; it was 543 billion yuan in Northern Guangdong and 491.1 billion yuan in mountainous areas. The eastern, western and northern regions of Guangdong added up to less than one-third of the GDP of the Pearl River Delta. Obviously, regional economic developments were extremely uneven. In this section, we shall analyze the situation of the unbalanced or uneven development in Guangdong Province and the economic correlation and extent and range of radiation of the Guangdong–Hong Kong–Macao Greater Bay Area as an economic growth pole over the other cities of Guangdong Province.

(A) *Overview of the economies of Eastern, Western and Northern Guangdong*

There are 21 cities in the Guangdong province, not counting Hong Kong and Macao. Owing to the difference in natural resource endowment, geographical location and the timing of policies and their implementation, there has been obvious and serious imbalance in the regional development in Guangdong Province. With the development of marketization, the agglomeration of industries, resources and labor force under the market mechanism, the economic disparities between the Pearl River Delta region and the eastern, western and northern regions of Guangdong were exacerbated. In 2013, Guangdong Province launched an overall and all-round strategy to step up the revitalization and development of the eastern, western and northern regions. However, over the past few years, overall the economic disparities still exist. According to the "Guangdong Macroeconomic Development Report", from the first quarter of 2012 to the third quarter of 2015, the coefficient of variation of quarterly GDP growth among cities narrowed from 31.5% to 7.3%, the degree of dispersion gradually narrowed, and the economy of each city flourished. The differences of the rates of economic growth diminished. However, beginning this year, the coefficient of variation of the growth rate of each city showed an upward expanding trend, from 11.0% in the first quarter to 12.4%

in the second quarter and to 13.3% in the third. In this chapter, several important economic indicators have been selected through the *Statistical Yearbook of Guangdong Province* (2015) for specific analysis. Detailed data are shown in Table 7.

As can be seen in Table 7, 79% GDP of Guangdong Province came from the Pearl River Delta region, only 7.7% from the western wing, 6.9% from the eastern wing and 6.2% from the mountainous regions of Guangdong. On industrial structures, the total proportion of the secondary and tertiary industries in the Pearl River Delta was 96.1%, with only 3.9% primary industries, of which the secondary industries accounted for 48.6% and the tertiary industries 47.5%. The primary industries in the western area accounted for 17.1%, while its secondary and tertiary industries accounted for 41.4% and 41.5%, respectively. Primary industries in the eastern region accounted for 9.2%, while the secondary and tertiary industries accounted for 52.5% and 38.3%, respectively, of the GDP. Primary industries accounted for 16.1% of GDP in the mountainous region, and the secondary and tertiary industries accounted for 40% and 43.8%, respectively. In terms of population, the Pearl River Delta population accounted for 54% of that of the entire Guangdong Province, the western area accounted for 14.6%, the eastern region accounting for 15.9% and the mountainous region accounted for 15.3%. In the proportion of exports, actual utilization of foreign capital, service industries above designated size and research expenditures, the Pearl River Delta region accounted for more than 90% of the total, and the fiscal budget revenue accounted for 86%. It can be seen that the Pearl River Delta region holds the vast majority of funds and spends the most in scientific research resources in the entire Guangdong Province. The funds, services and scientific research distributed in the other three regions are far less than those in the Pearl River Delta region, resulting in a very unbalanced ("lopsided") resource allocation.

In order to further demonstrate the geographical concentration of the development of cities in Guangdong Province, this chapter uses the Moran Index for analysis. The Moran Index is an analysis of the correlation between a city's own economic indicators and the

Table 7. Main economic indicators for cities of Guangdong province.

	GDP (in 100 million yuan)	Proportion of Secondary Industries in GDP (%)	Proportion of Tertiary Industries in GDP (%)	Population (100,000)	Exports (US$100 million)	Actual Utilized Foreign Capital (US$10,000)	Budget Revenue (100 million yuan)	Number of Service Industries above Designated Size or Scale	R&D Expenditure (10,000 yuan)
Guangzhou	18,100.4	31.6	67.1	1,350.1	811.7	541,635	1,349.47	6,333	2,122,613
Shenzhen	17,502.9	41.2	58.8	1,137.9	2,640.4	649,731	2,726.85	4,478	6,726,494
Zhuhai	2,025.41	49.7	48.1	163.41	288.11	217,787	269.96	561	434,013
Shantou	1,868.03	51.5	43.3	555.21	67.55	21,767	131.26	125	111,951
Foshan	8,003.92	60.5	37.8	743.06	482.05	237,726	557.55	651	1,929,893
Shaoquan	1,149.98	37.5	49.3	293.15	14.25	4807	85.23	132	114,858
Heyuan	810.08	45.7	42.7	307.35	28.33	14,425	67.48	51	24,141
Meizhou	959.78	36.7	43.7	434.08	22.72	7,130	103.59	40	22,510
Huizhou	3,140.03	55.0	40.2	475.55	347.75	110,499	340.02	359	597,225
Shanwei	762.06	45.8	38.7	302.16	15.78	9,958	28.83	38	50,323
Dongguan	6,275.07	46.6	53.1	825.41	1,036.1	531,982	517.97	1,175	1,267,890
Zhongshan	3,010.03	54.3	43.5	320.96	280.07	45,683	287.51	430	692,376
Jiangmen	2,240.02	48.4	43.8	451.95	153.72	87,940	199.01	199	387,361
Yangjiang	1,250.01	45.1	38.5	251.12	24.04	8,497	67.93	67	84,012
Zhanjiang	2,380.02	38.2	42.7	724.14	28.07	15,717	121.86	319	71,764
Maoming	2,445.63	40.9	43.3	608.08	10.99	17,190	113.92	168	133,088
Zhaoqing	1,970.01	50.3	35.1	405.96	47.66	139,447	143.36	114	192,157
Qingyuan	1,277.86	37.9	47	383.45	27.09	14,201	108.38	141	57,931
Chaozhou	910.11	53.2	39.7	264.05	27.64	2,044	47.2	46	51,109
Jieyang	1,890.01	59.6	31.5	605.89	67.04	3,929	77.4	71	108,194
Yunfu	713.14	42.6	36.5	246.0	13.6	5,451	58.7	29	25,596

same economic indicators of its neighboring, adjacent cities. Moran's $I > 0$ represents positive spatial correlation, and the larger the value, the more obvious the spatial correlation. Moran's $I < 0$ represents negative spatial correlation, and the smaller its value, the bigger the spatial difference. When Moran's $I = 0$, the space appears random. The weighted proportional (inner) vector product of the generalized Moran Index is expressed as follows:

$$I = \frac{n \sum_i \sum_{i \neq j} \omega_{ij} (y_i - \bar{y})(y_i - \bar{y})}{\left(\sum_i \sum_{i \neq j} \omega_{ij} \right) \sum_i (y_i - \bar{y})^2} \tag{6.5}$$

Here, y_i is an indicator of a country, $\bar{y}$ is the mean and ω_{ij} is the weighted matrix. In this chapter, the weighted matrix selected is a spatial distance matrix in which spatial data are constructed by defining the distance between different units in the area under study. The specific method of weighting is to measure the "surveyed and mapped" distance between the cores of the city. The higher the value of the Moran Index, the stronger the geographical aggregation, signifying the greater similarity of the proximity values. In this chapter, the economic indicator chosen is per capita GDP.

On analysis, we could see that areas with high per capita GDP in Guangdong Province are concentrated in the Pearl River Delta or the areas around the estuary of the Pearl River. In the periphery of the Pearl River Delta region, there are medium- and high-income areas, whereas in the two "wings" and mountainous areas, there are more low-income and medium-low income areas. The spatial correlation of per capita incomes in Guangdong Province is extremely high. In the previous section, we have analyzed the diffusion radiuses of the three core financial cities in the Greater Bay Area of Guangdong, Hong Kong and Macao. From the conclusion of the previous section, the effective financial diffusion radiuses of the three financial centers mostly cover the entire urban area (city clusters) of Guangdong, Hong Kong and Macao. The diffusion into the whole Guangdong Province is limited: the areas covered by the spillover form a layered ring structure, the concentrated core of which are the core cities of the Greater Bay Area. The second layer consists of the non-core cities of the Greater Bay Area — examples are Zhaoqing, Jiangmen, etc. Located in the outermost layer are the eastern, western and northern parts of Guangdong surrounding the entire urban area of the Guangdong–Hong Kong–Macao Greater Bay Area. The Moran Index for Guangdong Province has been computed, with specific results as can be seen in Figure 5. The Moran Index is 0.71764, indicating that there is a very strong spatial correlation between per capita GDP incomes in Guangdong Province.

On the economic development of the whole Guangdong Province, the government has also put forward a series of plans to redress the uncoordinated state or "disharmony" of regional development. The "double transfer" (i.e. transfer of labor and the transfer of industries) strategy proposed in 2008 was to transfer labor-intensive industries from the Pearl River Delta to the eastern and western regions and the northern mountain areas of Guangdong. On the one hand, labor from the eastern and western regions and the northern mountain areas of Guangdong were being transferred to

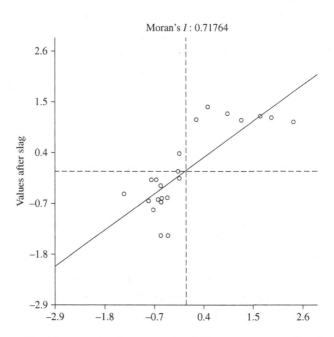

Figure 5.   Moran index for per capita GDP in Guangdong Province.

the local secondary and tertiary industries. On the other hand, some of the higher quality labor force was being transferred to the developed Pearl River Delta region. In the early stages of the implementation of the "double transfer" strategy, the industries in the Pearl River Delta had become better optimized and the industrial structure had been upgraded, while at the same time the eastern, western and northern parts of Guangdong had also taken over some industries transferred from the Pearl River Delta. However, after the first round of industrial transformation, owing to the decline of national economy — under the new normal circumstances — the industries undertaken by the eastern, western and northern parts of Guangdong were facing pressure of overcapacity and destocking. The pressure seriously impacted the follow-up and continuous development. Additionally, the low productivity of backward industries brought about inefficient production, shutdowns and suspensions under the economic downturn. These events led to the failure of the eastern, western and northern Guangdong regions to keep up with their industrial undertaking and they had thus missed the best opportunity for industrial upgrading. At the same time, as Eastern Guangdong is an important energy base, Western Guangdong is a national petrochemical energy base and Northern Guangdong is a raw material processing base — the heavy industries characteristics of eastern, western and northern Guangdong are becoming obvious. The "double transfer" strategy has not fundamentally changed and broken through the "unreasonable" situation of industrial structure in eastern, western and northern Guangdong. The paucity of financial revenue in the east, west and north of Guangdong implies that their economic development relies heavily on external financial support, and the efficiency of external financial support has a greater impact on its development. The three major financial cities in the Greater Bay Area of Guangdong, Hong Kong and Macao draw great attraction for capital. Especially in recent years, the investment in real estate has attracted a lot of capital. As a result, it is difficult for external capital to carry out large-scale investment in eastern, western and northern Guangdong; capital could not agglomerate, thus further hindering the development of eastern, western and northern Guangdong.

(B) *Analysis of the economic network structure of cities in Guangdong Province*

Since Guangdong's economic development is not balanced among different regions, in order to further study the Pearl River Delta and the upgraded city clusters of the Guangdong–Hong Kong–Macao Greater Bay Area to determine whether the economic spillover effect is greater for the surrounding, peripheral cities, or the economic benefiting effect on these city clusters is greater, a network structure based on the economy as its direction is to be constructed to analyze the urban agglomeration or city clusters of the Guangdong–Hong Kong–Macao Greater Bay Area, so as to find out whether the unbalanced development of Guangdong's economy will further deteriorate or is heading toward improvement. This section uses the network analysis method to study the network characteristics of the spatial correlation for economic growth among regions in Guangdong Province. To portray the spatial spillover effects between the regions is the key to outlining the spatial network of regional economic growth. Grunewald (2007) analyzes the spatial spillover effects among regions of China through the Granger causality test by constructing a vector auto-regression (VAR) model. On this basis, the research in this section translates inter-provincial data into various urban data of Guangdong Province. The economic auto-regression model of the economic level (GDP level) is constructed to examine the economic relations within Guangdong Province. Since the causality test obtained by the VAR model may be asymmetric, the test can better reflect whether the economic network relationship between cities is spillover or drawing attraction, or both, so a two-way network could be depicted. The constructed model gives a better analysis and opinion on the issue of feasibility.

With regard to the spatial network structure of regional economic growth, specific portrayal indicators include the following:

(1) network density; (2) network relevancy; (3) network rating and (4) network centrality.

1. Network Density

Network density is an indicator that reflects how close or loose the relevancy relationship of the entire network is. According to Scott (2007), network density should be obtained by the ratio between the number of relevancies and associations (coefficients) actually obtained by the entire network and the maximum number of relationships that can be possessed/obtained. The specific formula is as follows:

$$Dn = L/[N \times (N-1)], \qquad (6.6)$$

where Dn is the network density, L is the number of relevancies/associations actually obtained by the entire network and $N \times (N-1)$ is the maximum number of relationships that can be obtained.

2. Network Relevancy

Network relevancy reflects the reachability of the entire network, that is, it measures the point(s) of isolation of the entire network or the ratio of the number of unreachable points to the maximum number of relationships that can be obtained by the entire network. Its value is in the range $[0, 1]$, and the relevant formula is follows:

$$C = 1 - 2 \times V/[N \times (N-1)], \qquad (6.7)$$

where C is the reachability and V is the isolated point(s).

3. Network Rating

Network rating or grading is used to measure the proportion of core nodes in the network, and it is a measure of the rating of the network. A higher network rating means there exists nodes with highly dominant elements and the other nodes need to accept the spillover effect of the dominant node. It takes on value $[0, 1]$. A value of 1 indicates that the node existing in the network has the ability to control all the other nodes. A value of 0 indicates that there are no core nodes. K denotes the number of nodes with bidirectional effects in the network. $\max(K)$ is the logarithm of the largest possible symmetrically reachable point. The relevant formula to determine network rating is as follows:

$$H = 1 - K/\max(K) \tag{6.8}$$

4. Network Centrality

Network centrality is used to measure the position or status of each node in the network. According to Freeman (1979), network centrality refers to the ratio of the number of spillover associations between the node and other nodes n_i in the network to the number of the directly associated (relevant) relationship $N - 1$. The larger the value of this network centrality for this node, the higher dominance in the network will this node have over the rest. The formula for calculating the network dominance of the ith node is given as follows:

$$\text{De}_i = n_i/(N-1) \tag{6.9}$$

Similarly, the benefitting centrality in the network is used to analyze the spillover effect of the network node benefitting other nodes through the network benefit relationship, and the benefitting relationship coefficient n_i^* is directly related to the maximum possible relationship number $N - 1$. A large value would mean that the node in the network is a highly benefitting node. The formula for calculating the network dominance of the ith node is given as follows:

$$\text{De}_i^* = n_i^* /(N-1) \tag{6.10}$$

In order to measure the network relationship for economic growth between Guangdong Province and Hong Kong and Macao after the return of Hong Kong, this book uses the GDP of various cities in Guangdong, Hong Kong and Macao (1997–2005) as the variable data for measuring the spatial network of economic growth. VAR is used to establish a VAR model between the two cities. Through the ADF stability test, it is found that when the lag variable is selected for one term, the stability test could be used to perform the first-order scoring process on the total GDP data, and then the memory of the data itself is eliminated to form a stable time series; the Granger causality test is then performed. In this chapter, the threshold value chosen is 5%, that is, the significance test for rejecting the null hypothesis is 5%. The results of the detailed calculation are shown in Table 8.

Finally, through testing and inspection, it was estimated that there are a total of 134 economic associations or relevancy "coefficients". Since there are a total of 23 cities, the maximum number of relationships that can be obtained by being bidirectional is therefore $2 \times 23 \times 22 / 2 = 506$. The computed network density is 26%, indicating that the overall degree of relevancy between Guangdong and Hong Kong and Macao cities is not high. Because there is no

Table 8. Calculation of network relationships for economic growth in the Guangdong Province (including Hong Kong and Macao).

		Benefitting Relationships	Spillover Relationships	Total Relevancies	Benefitting Centrality (%)	Spillover Centrality (%)
Guangdong–Hong Kong–Macao	Guangzhou	9	9	18	40.9	40.9
	Shenzhen	6	11	17	27.3	50.0
	Zhuhai	5	5	10	22.7	22.7
	Foshan	6	4	10	27.3	18.2
	Huizhou	4	2	6	18.2	9.1
	Dongguan	4	5	9	18.2	22.7
	Zhongshan	4	4	8	18.2	18.2
	Zhaoqing	4	3	7	18.2	13.6
	Jiangmen	4	3	7	18.2	13.6
	Hong Kong	1	14	15	4.5	63.6
	Macao	1	1	2	4.5	4.5
Western Regions	Yangjiang	2	1	3	9.1	4.5
	Zhanjiang	2	1	3	9.1	4.5
	Maoming	2	1	3	9.1	4.5
Mountainous Regions	Zhaoguan	2	1	3	9.1	4.5
	Heyuan	2	0	2	9.1	0.0
	Meizhou	1	0	1	4.5	0.0
	Qingyuan	1	0	1	4.5	0.0
	Yunfu	1	0	1	4.5	0.0

Table 8. (*Continued*)

		Benefitting Relationships	Spillover Relationships	Total Relevancies	Benefitting Centrality (%)	Spillover Centrality (%)
Eastern Regions	Chaozhou	2	1	3	9.1	4.5
	Jieyang	1	0	1	4.5	0.0
	Shanwei	1	0	1	4.5	0.0
	Shantou	2	1	3	9.1	4.5

economic isolation point, that is, all cities are more or less affected by other cities, the overall network results indicate accessibility with network relevancy 1. The network rating is calculated to be 0.76, indicating that the spillover effects between cities in the network are greatly influenced by the status of the cities. The spillover effects of high-rating cities, i.e. cities with higher economic development levels, may be higher. This also indirectly explains the uneven development of the whole Guangdong Province and that the huge economic development inertia faced by economic restructuring are difficult to overcome by simply adjusting the overall economy through simple financial subsidies.

On further analysis of the cities, we find that Hong Kong is the most unusual or special. The main manifestation of Hong Kong's position is its economic spillover effect. Only two cities — Shenzhen and Hong Kong — exert mutual economic impacts on each other. As a city with the highest extent of spillovers, Hong Kong's outpourings of economic benefits are not proportional to the economic benefits it obtains. On the one hand, the differential economic system of "one country, two systems" leads to limited economic associations between Hong Kong and the Mainland. On the other hand, Hong Kong's substantive manufacturing industries have been transferred to the Pearl River Delta region as a whole, resulting in its great economic spillover effect. This also explains why Hong Kong's economic growth rate cannot keep up with the growth rate of the whole Pearl River Delta region. The economic spillover effects brought by the whole Pearl River Delta cannot be transmitted to Hong Kong because of the barriers created by the different economic systems. The spillover effects and benefitting effects of

Guangzhou average out the most. This is because Guangzhou is within the economic and financial radiation radius of Hong Kong and Shenzhen. Guangzhou mainly benefits from the city clusters of Guangdong, Hong Kong and Macao Greater Bay Area. At the same time, the adjacent cities such as Foshan, Dongguan and Zhongshan are mostly important manufacturing cities, so these cities do form good mutually beneficial interactions. Shenzhen has more spillover effect; looking around the vicinity of Shenzhen, the number of cities bordering Shenzhen is limited. Unlike Guangzhou, which borders many cities, Shenzhen only borders Dongguan, Hong Kong and Shanwei, so it receives less economic benefits than Guangzhou. However, owing to the rapid development of economy and the rapid advances of science and technology in recent years, a larger diffusion energy and a larger diffusion radius have been formed, so the economic spillover effect of Shenzhen is only less than that of Hong Kong and more than that of Guangzhou. Within the Greater Bay Area of Guangdong, Hong Kong and Macao, the cities of Zhuhai, Foshan, Zhongshan and Dongguan are at the second tier in the whole urban hierarchical network, and they may be considered as beneficiary cities even though they do have some spillover effects. However, overall we can see that the relationship network for the economic growth is still concentrated in the city clusters of the Guangdong–Hong Kong–Macao Greater Bay Area, and its extension is limited. Compared to the closely related situations of the cities in the Greater Bay Area of Guangdong, Hong Kong and Macao, the whole network in the east, west and north of Guangdong seems to be attached to the Greater Bay Area, which is more of an economic benefitting relationship, and the number of the cities benefitted is also significantly less than that of the cities in the Guangdong–Hong Kong–Macao Greater Bay Area.

(C) *Research on promoting the balanced development of cities in Guangdong Province*

This chapter analyses the reasons why it is difficult for the Greater Bay Area of Guangdong, Hong Kong and Macao to drive the development of the peripheral city clusters in the east, west and north of Guangdong Province. There are two aspects to the crux of the issue:

The multi-centers in the Guangdong–Hong Kong–Macao Greater Bay Area have led to these centers' respective planning and independent operation in economic development, without overall coordination and integrated conduct. There is therefore no advantage of overall planning, structure, function, system, industries and supporting facilities, thus making it difficult to form a centripetal force in the Greater Bay Area. The main problems relate to "fragmentation". First, regional space is fragmented and it is difficult to develop a strong and cohesive economy. Second, the institutional mechanism is fragmented and it is an onerous task to coordinate management. Third, policy measures are fragmented and it becomes difficult to share resources. Fourth, industrial functions are fragmented and it is difficult to optimize economic and industrial "matching packages". Moreover, the interactions between the two SARs of Hong Kong, Macao and the rest of the cities in the Greater Bay Area are limited and more unilateral or unidirectional. With the rise of the Mainland economy, the hollowing-out trend of Hong Kong's industries is becoming more and more evident. Without the support of the manufacturing industry and the wide hinterland of economic development, Hong Kong's position may further decline. Against this background, the central government had proposed to build Qianhai to strengthen the cooperation between Guangdong and Hong Kong. This proposal is not made just to take advantage of Hong Kong to realize Qianhai's own development but also to explore a new way to realize Hong Kong's long-term prosperity and stable development. Industrial integration is the key to cooperation between Guangdong and Hong Kong, and also the source of Hong Kong's competitiveness in the future. In order to strengthen the interaction between the two places, under the existing differential political and economic systems, it may be more effective to create a "match" or "coupling" between the two places through transitional regions. Specifically, Qianhai–Shekou Free Trade Zone and Hengqin New Zone, two free trade zones, were established to act as a middle "territory" to speed up the process of economic interaction between the two areas. As a pilot area of Shenzhen–Hong Kong cooperation, Qianhai could play an important role in agglomerating high-end, high-quality talents and high-quality capital. Hong Kong has a large number of professionals in finance, law, accounting, shipping and other fields. It is an international capital accumulation and distributing center. However, these professionals in production services and international capital rely on a huge manufacturing base to provide more rooms for development. In fact, with the decline of Hong Kong's competitiveness, there has been a phenomenon of narrowing of channels or reduction of opportunities for youths and the issue of insufficient space for career development. In contrast, Qianhai links the vast inland and hinterland. It has more room for economic maneuvers and flexibility. The RMB flowback "pipeline" or channel is unimpeded and the real economy is strong. It has many advantages that Hong Kong itself does not have or which Hong Kong will have difficulties in procuring. It can provide a big space for the development of specialist talents and huge liquidities for Hong Kong.

The next question is how can Guangdong, Hong Kong and Macao further promote development to the relatively backward eastern, western and northern areas of Guangdong Province? There are obvious "faults" in the economic developments of the Greater Bay Area of Guangdong, Hong Kong, Macao and eastern, western and northern Guangdong. Faults are caused by natural conditions and infrastructure, whereas the development imbalance is caused by the process of historical developments. To effectively promote the sustainable and stable economic growth of the less developed areas in the province and the region, we need to improve the infrastructure as well as the institutional rules and regulations of the less developed areas: we have to make good use of tax, finance, credit, scientific and technological supports and other policy measures. While implementing these conventional measures, we must also speed up the opening of economic channels with the Guangdong–Hong Kong–Macao Greater Bay Area. The strategy of the "double transfer" did achieve good results in the initial stage, showing that it's been an effective way to undertake industrial transfer from the Guangdong–Hong Kong–Macao Greater Bay Area. However, once the simple undertaking of the industrial transfer is impacted by economic fluctuations, this will inevitably lead to a relapse into the path of failure to undertake follow-up industries, finally leading to the breakdown of the economic chain of industrial linkages, further reducing the economic radiation radius of the Guangdong–Hong Kong–Macao Greater Bay Area. In view of the aforementioned problems, we should not just go through the industrial and economic corridors between the east, west and north of Guangdong Province and the Greater Bay Area of Guangdong, Hong Kong and Macao also make use of the high-level production services such as science and technology and high-end services in the Greater Bay Area of Guangdong, Hong Kong and Macao. In this regard, the leading position of Guangzhou in the production service industry needs to be better utilized, not only to undertake industrial transfer through industrial parks but also to help form a supporting production service industry in the surrounding areas. In addition to undertaking industrial transfer, Guangdong can also "provide blood for itself", i.e. through self-help in trying to achieve industrial upgrading. Additionally, multi-level cooperation and exchanges with the whole Guangdong–Hong Kong–Macao Greater Bay Area should be planned and implemented. Only in this way can we have closer links and achieve the coordinated development of the economy of Guangdong Province.

IV. The Economic Diffusion Effect of the Greater Bay Area on the Pan-Pearl River Delta Region

The Pan-Pearl River Delta region is designed to comprise nine provinces plus the Hong Kong and Macao SARs. As each province is a relatively independent, separate administration, the economic ties between the provinces are not as close as those between the cities. In order to coordinate the development of this super-large region straddling across the eastern, central and southwestern parts of China, we must break the shackles of administrative divisions through the layout of industrial chains. Therefore, studying the diffusion effects of the Guangdong–Hong Kong–Macao Greater Bay Area on the whole Pan-Pearl River Delta is to study the degree of industrial correlation and inter-relationship of the whole Pan-Pearl River Delta and to outline the economic diffusion effect of the Greater Bay Area on the whole Pan-Pearl River Delta by studying the transfer of industries of Guangdong, Hong Kong and Macao to the whole Pan-Pearl River Delta. Because the whole Pan-Pearl River Delta region is vast, there are large inherent, natural differences and different industrial advantages. It is an important entry point to analyze the economic diffusion effects of the Guangdong–Hong Kong–Macao Greater Bay Area on the Pan-Pearl River Delta based on industrial correlation. At the same time, the study can be conducted from the perspective of the industrial gradient and industrial transfer — how the Greater Bay Area provides a driving force to the Pan-Pearl River Delta regional economy. The aim is to coordinate the development of the whole Pan-Pearl River Delta region from the supply side and to offer effective solutions to the problem of overcapacity through rational and proper industrial transfer. It is hoped that the measures to be taken could promote industrial restructuring, reduce costs to enterprise, promote the development of strategic emerging industries and modern services, increase the supply of public goods and services and improve the adaptability and flexibility of supply structure to changes in demand.

(A) *An overview of the Pan-Pearl River Delta economy*

The development of the Pan-Pearl River Delta is not based on the Greater Bay Area of Guangdong, Hong Kong and Macao as a single engine driving its economy. In the Pan-Pearl River Delta, there are many city clusters and four free trade pilot zones in addition to the city cluster of the Greater Bay Area of Guangdong, Hong Kong and Macao. Therefore, the economic development of the whole Pan-Pearl River Delta should be a "linkage" or "associative" type of development with the industries as the core.

In the Pan-Pearl River Delta region, besides the city clusters of the Greater Bay Area, important city clusters include those of the

Strait's west coast, the city clusters around Poyang Lake, the city agglomeration of Changsha, Zhuzhou and Xiangtan, the city cluster of Chengdu and Chongqing and the city cluster around the northern Bay Areas. The second batch of pilot free trade pilot zones includes Guangdong Free Trade Zone and Fujian Free Trade Zone and the third batch includes Sichuan Free Trade Zone.

(a) Fuzhou, Quanzhou, Xiamen, Wenzhou and Shantou are the five central cities on the western coast of the Strait, which together drive the city clusters comprising 21 cities along the western side of the Strait. Compared with the Greater Bay Area of Guangdong, Hong Kong and Macao — a national-level urban agglomeration of city clusters — the city clusters on the western side of the Strait belong to a regional urban agglomeration. Its industries are mainly stone masonry and ceramics, water heating, kitchen and sanitation, footwear and light textile, machinery and equipment, and lighting and photoelectric information. The homogeneity of industrial structures and the convergence of the manufacturing structures of this city cluster of five cities are serious issues. Moreover, the industrial chain is too short, which is often the matching packaged industrial chain of the inner cities. This leads to low level of linking and correlation among the cities of this city cluster — a serious problem of vicious competition among them — affecting the coordinated development of the whole city cluster.

(b) The city cluster of Lake Poyang comprises Nanchang, Jiujiang, Jingdezhen, Yingtan and Shangrao, with Lake Poyang as the core. The pillar industries of Jiangxi Province are concentrated in this urban agglomeration around Lake Poyang. The industrial chain of the whole urban agglomeration penetrates more deeply, with a clear industrial division among cities, such as Jingdezhen's ceramics and household appliances, Shangrao's precision machinery processing industry, Yingtan's copper smelting industry, Nanchang's manufacturing industry and Jiujiang's petrochemical, shipbuilding materials, textile industries and so on. However, the development of the tertiary industries is relatively slow, and the urban industries urgently need upgrading.

(c) The Changsha–Zhuzhou–Xiangtan city cluster is located in the middle and eastern part of Hunan Province. The core cities are Changsha, Zhuzhou and Xiangtan. The three cities are situated around the Xiangjiang River in the pattern of the Chinese character "品". The three core cities are less than 20 kilometers apart and closely connected or associated. Changsha is dominated by electronic information, construction machinery, food and bio-pharmaceuticals industries; Zhuzhou's main industries are transportation, equipment manufacturing, non-ferrous metallurgy, raw chemical engineering materials and ceramics manufacturing; and Xiangtan is dominated by "black" or iron and iron alloy metallurgy, mechatronics and mechanical manufacturing, chemical fiber textile, raw chemical materials as well as refined chemical engineering. However, the overall strength of the Changsha–Zhuzhou–Xiangtan city cluster is not strong, its industrial structure is not good enough and the contradictions in the economic structures are still conspicuous: there is a lack of industrial agglomeration, which could drive the economy. There is also an absence of strategic pillar industries leading into the future.

(d) The Chengdu–Chongqing city cluster spans Sichuan Province and Chongqing City, with the Chengdu–Chongqing Economic Zone as its backing and the Chengdu–Chongqing Cities as its two core cities. In the development of industries, there are significant competition factors between the two cores. The main reason is that the issue of homogeneity — in the information technology industry and automotive industry — is quite serious: the competition between the two cores is greater than cooperation. The separation of administrative regions causes the industrial chain of this urban agglomeration to concentrate around the two core cities, with less interaction between the two. If we can break the administrative constraints posed by the regions, break the administrative division and implement proper and professional cooperation, this city cluster will certainly play a greater role in the West and indeed for the whole country.

(e) The Northern Bay Area city cluster is a national-level urban agglomeration approved by the State Council on January 20, 2017. The planned areas covered include Nanning, Beihai, Qinzhou, Fangchenggang, Yulin and Chongzuo in the Guangxi Zhuang Autonomous Region, Zhanjiang, Maoming, Yangjiang of Guangdong Province and Haikou, Danzhou, Dongfang, Chengmai, Lingao and Changjiang counties of Hainan Province. The urban agglomeration has a total planned land area of 116,600 square kilometers and a coastline of 4,234 kilometers. Relying on the advantages of the Northern Bay harbors, the Northern Bay city clusters have made great progress in petro-chemical, iron and steel, electronic information and other industries. However, the overall agglomeration capacity of the city clusters is not strong, and except for Nanning, other cities are obviously small in size and scale. This economic structural imbalance hinders to a certain extent the flow of production factors and the complementarity of economic cooperation among cities.

According to the China's Free Trade Zones, there are also the following differences in the positioning of Guangdong, Fujian, Hubei and Sichuan Free Trade Zones:

(i) Guangdong Free Trade Zone: Relying on Hong Kong and Macao, serving the Mainland and fronting the world, the Pilot Free Trade Zone will be built into an advanced demonstration zone for Guangdong, Hong Kong and Macao, an important hub for the 21st Century Maritime Silk Road in a new round of nationwide reform and opening-up.

(ii) Fujian Free Trade Zone: This FTZ aims to take full advantage of its position *vis-à-vis* Taiwan in taking the lead in fostering investments and trade liberalization with Taiwan, rendering the Pilot Free Trade Zone into a demonstration zone for enhanced cross-strait economic cooperation. Its frontline advantages of opening up to the outside world will be utilized to build a 21st century Maritime Silk Road core area.

(iii) Sichuan Free Trade Zone: This FTZ is mainly established to implement the requirements of the central government to increase the extent of opening up of the gateway cities in the western region and to build a strategic support belt for opening in the interior. It seeks to build an open inland economic "high ground" and to create synergy between the inland and coastal areas and along riverbanks.

(B) *Study on industrial gradients in the Pan-Pearl River Delta*

As regional economy is a comprehensive economic system, the level of industrial development among regions is affected not only by regional economic development but also by factors such as history, quality of labor, regional space and social ideology. Taken together, the superposed and overlapping distinct structures of industries among regions shape industrial gradients. An evident feature of industrial transfer in China is the proximity to the radius of industrial transfer, which is manifested in the short radius of general industrial transfer in China, whereby the proximity transfer is based on provincial administrative regions. This is because the regional economies of our country have high geographic linkages, that is, the economic development gaps of other provinces around the provinces with higher economic development level are not too big, a factor which provides convenience and a sound basis for industrial transfer. The neighborliness or proximity of the industrial radius also means that it is difficult to implement successfully planned strategies such as the development of the western regions; we should pay greater attention to the hierarchical and step-wise progress and development of the regional economies.

The provinces of the Pan-Pearl River Delta region have long had good cooperation among them. Except for Hainan Province, the economic development gaps between provinces are not obvious. Guangdong Province is an outstanding province; this province is used more as a transferor of industries. Considering that most of the industrial foundations of the Guangdong Province are concentrated in the city clusters of the Guangdong–Hong Kong–Macao Greater Bay Area, the analysis of the industrial transfer of the whole

Pan-Pearl River Delta is carried out to examine the industrial transfer of the Guangdong–Hong Kong–Macao Greater Bay Area.

This book analyzes the ideas of industrial transfer by referring to the statistical methods of Dai Hongwei's book *Research on Regional Transfer of Industries*. It analyzes the patterns of industrial gradients of the whole Pan-Pearl River Delta by constructing the industrial gradient coefficients. Considering the fact that the current industrial transfer is mainly concentrated in the secondary industries, we choose to describe the Pan-Pearl River Delta industrial gradient by using the data of industrial added values. Dai Hongwei's industrial gradient measurement method is conducted through two dimensions as follows:

The first is the comparison of labor productivity. The formula is given as follows:

Comparative Labor Productivity = The proportion of the value added of a certain industry in the region in the national value added for this industry/The proportion of employees in a certain industry in the region in the same industry for the whole nation (/means "divided by").

Second, the degree of specialized/professionalized production of the industry, generally characterized by location quotients. The relevant formula is given as follows:

Location quotient = The proportion of a region's particular industry's value added in the GDP of the region/The proportion of corresponding national value added for that industry in national GDP.

The industrial gradient coefficient is the product of the comparative labor productivity and the location quotient. In this chapter, the data from *China's Industrial Statistical Yearbook* (2016) are used to compute the industrial added values and total number employed and GDP of the nine provinces in the Pan-Pearl River Delta. The comparative labor productivity, location quotient and industrial gradient coefficient are then calculated. The results are shown in Table 9.

According to Table 9, the industrial gradient advantages of the Guangdong Province are mainly concentrated in the finance, wholesale and retail industries. It has no comparative advantage in

Table 9.   Calculation making use of data from the nine provinces of the River Delta.

Industries	Region	Added Values (100 million yuan)	Number Employed (10,000)	GDP (100 million yuan)	Comparative Labor Productivity (%)	Location Quotient	Industrial Gradient Coefficient
Industrials (Industrialization)	National	235,183	5,069	682,635	—	—	—
	Guangdong	30,259	981	72,813	0.66	1.21	0.80
	Hunan	10,945	122	28,902	1.94	1.10	2.13
	Jiangxi	6,918	138	16,724	1.08	1.20	1.30
	Sichuan	11,039	160	30,053	1.49	1.07	1.59
	Guizhou	3,316	43	10,502	1.68	0.92	1.54
	Yunnan	3,848	68	13,619	1.23	0.82	1.01
	Hainan	486	9	3,702	1.19	0.38	0.45
	Fujian	10,820	236	26,980	0.99	1.16	1.15
	Guangxi	6,540	76	16,803	1.85	1.13	2.09
Wholesale and Retail	National	66,203	883	682,635	—	—	—
	Guangdong	7,626	97	72,813	1.90	1.08	2.05
	Hunan	1,877	21	28,902	1.70	0.67	1.14
	Jiangxi	1,187	18	16,724	1.41	0.73	1.03
	Sichuan	1,871	31	30,053	1.30	0.64	0.84
	Guizhou	671	12	10,502	1.17	0.66	0.77
	Yunnan	1,335	25	13,619	1.15	1.01	1.16
	Hainan	441	6	3,702	1.10	1.23	1.35

	Fujian	2,046	28	26,980	1.55	0.78	1.21
	Guangxi	1,135	13	16,803	1.53	0.70	1.07
Traffic and Transportation	National	30,370	854	682,635	—	—	—
	Guangdong	2,928	83	72,813	0.76	0.90	0.69
	Hunan	1,291	24	28,902	1.14	1.00	1.14
	Jiangxi	736	21	16,724	0.75	0.99	0.74
	Sichuan	1,220	41	30,053	0.65	0.91	0.59
	Guizhou	920	12	10,502	0.71	1.57	1.11
	Yunnan	305	17	13,619	0.38	0.50	0.19
	Hainan	188	7	3,702	0.62	1.14	0.71
	Fujian	1,547	25	26,980	1.36	1.29	1.75
	Guangxi	803	20	16,803	0.87	1.07	0.93
Financial Industries	National	57,500	607	682,635	—	—	—
	Guangdong	5,757	46	72,813	2.69	0.94	2.53
	Hunan	1,104	24	28,902	0.99	0.45	0.45
	Jiangxi	897	13	16,724	1.53	0.64	0.98
	Sichuan	2,202	26	30,053	1.63	0.87	1.42
	Guizhou	607	9	10,502	1.52	0.69	1.04
	Yunnan	982	10	13,619	1.14	0.86	0.98
	Hainan	243	4	3,702	1.28	0.78	1.00
	Fujian	1,681	18	26,980	2.02	0.74	1.50
	Guangxi	1,018	13	16,803	1.65	0.72	1.19

industrialization and transportation. In fact, the industrial gradient of Guangdong Province is lower than that of the other provinces. As regards industrialization, production efficiency is low and although a location advantage is still present, it is the result of industrial transfer. However, the industrialization transfer is not complete, and even if its output value is relatively large, the efficiency is no longer comparable to Hunan and other provinces. Therefore, we can consider conducting the transfer of industries to Hunan, Guizhou and Guangxi with higher industrial efficiency to reduce the proportion of industrial production. For wholesale and retail trade, we can turn to Fujian — Fujian has certain advantages in efficiency and location. Because the number of industries in Hainan is too small, even though the industrial gradient is slightly higher than that of Fujian, it is more reasonable for the whole industry to transfer to Fujian, which has a better foundation. The advantages of Guangdong's financial industry are manifested chiefly in its high efficiency, which leads to a higher industrial gradient for the whole (financial) industry. We could consider transferring this industry to Sichuan, Guangxi and Fujian, because these three provinces have high industrial efficiency, while the location advantages are not evident. Transferring the financial industry can improve the location advantages of these three provinces, resulting in better industrial spillover effects.

Simple industrial transfer does not produce an immediate effect, because the market is more inclined to agglomerate. Industry transfer is often an act of the will of the government, so it is necessary to build an effective industrial transfer mechanism. With the government leading the way, we should set up a good industry transfer platform prior to industry transfer. With the behavior and actions of enterprises as the leading factors, production factors and naturally endowed resources as the carrier, we should be taking urban and even provincial cooperation as opportunities to promote industrial transfer from an advantaged region to a relatively backward region. Combined with the aforementioned problems of the city clusters analyzed earlier, the key issue to be addressed is the establishment of industrial chain for industrial transfer and upgrading in such a vast area. As a result of the "wishful thinking" of local governments, the homogeneity of industries within many city clusters, the short industrial chain and the concentration of supporting industries in the core cities have not formed an efficient and effective industrial chain, leading to vicious competition among the industries of cities and seriously affecting the efficiency of industrial upgrading. In view of this, the industrial transfer of Pan-Pearl River Delta should begin with top-level design; we should take into account the regional advantages and factors of natural endowment in coordinating the distribution of industries, stepping up the establishment of regional consultation mechanism to extend and refine the industrial chain by building a unified regional market. The idea is to carry out "staggered and complementary development" of provinces and to promote regional industrial transfer and integration through the reconstruction of industrial chains. All these are efforts made to promote industrial integration in the Pan-Pearl River Delta and achieve coordinated regional economic development.

Chapter 7

Strategic Positioning of the Greater Bay Area of Guangdong, Hong Kong and Macao

Chen Lijuan

Shenzhen University

The Greater Bay area of Guangdong, Hong Kong and Macao has been elevated to the status of a national strategic master plan and occupies an important position in the "Belt and Road" Initiative. The Greater Bay area is an important bridge connecting the countries along the "Belt and Road" Initiative. It is a cultural bond connecting English, Portuguese and overseas Chinese cultures. In addition, the Greater Bay Area of Guangdong, Hong Kong and Macao is also an important strategic locality for China's free trade zones (FTZs) that have been officially designated or are being negotiated or studied, such as the China–ASEAN FTZ and the China–ASEAN FTZ (upgraded version). Therefore, promoting the establishment of the Greater Bay Area will certainly accelerate the realization of major national strategies.

Since China's reform and opening-up, capital from Hong Kong and Macao has come into the Pearl River Delta region continuously, driving the economic development of the Pearl River Delta region. At first, the labor-intensive manufacturing industry of Hong Kong and Macao shifted to the Pearl River Delta. From then on, the industries of Hong Kong and Macao began to transform and their service industries developed rapidly. At this time, academic research and studies on cooperation between Guangdong, Hong Kong and Macao began to emerge. After that, with the return of Hong Kong and Macao to the motherland and China's accession to WTO, substantive cooperation ensued. With the signing of the CEPA agreement, "Guangdong–Hong Kong–Macao Cooperation Framework Agreement", "Outline of Pearl River Delta Development", "Guangdong–Hong Kong Cooperation Framework Agreement" and "Guangdong–Macao Cooperation Framework Agreement", the development orientation or positioning of Guangdong–Hong Kong–Macao regional cooperation at this stage was to establish a sub-regional cooperative economic entity. The aim at that time was to foster economic development of the three places of Guangdong, Hong Kong and Macao by taking full advantage of their comparative strengths.

I. The Gradual Rise of the Guangdong–Hong Kong–Macao Greater Bay Area Economy

With the development of economic cooperation between the three places, the economic structures of Guangdong, Hong Kong and Macao have undergone tremendous changes. Guangdong has forged closer relationship of cooperation with both Hong Kong and Macao, in the areas of transportation interlinks, industrial patterns and economic and trade cooperation. In 2014, in Shenzhen municipal government's "Work Report", the concept of the "Bay Area Economy" was for the first time put forward representing that it wished to make use of the economic cooperation between Guangdong, Hong Kong and Macao to promote the development of the Bay Area economy. In order to build a new pattern or situation of China's open economic system, China has implemented the "Belt and Road" Initiative, set up a Silk Road Fund and adopted a series of measures such as setting up the Asian Infrastructure Investment Bank (AIIB). These measures witnessed the transformation of China from participating in global economic integration to actively promoting global economic integration, and are strategically important for China to expand and broaden its opening up to the outside world. In March 2015, the declaration of "Vision and Action for Promoting the Construction of the Silk Road Economic Belt and the 21st Century Maritime Silk Road" jointly issued by the National Development and Reform Commission, the Ministry of Foreign Affairs and the Ministry of Commerce stated that the roles of open cooperation zones such as Qianhai in Shenzhen, Nansha in Guangzhou, Hengqin in Zhuhai and Pingtan in Fujian should be fully played and manifested and that the cooperation with Hong Kong, Macao and Taiwan should be enhanced so as to build the Greater Bay Area of Guangdong, Hong Kong and Macao into "leading troops and main forces" of the "Belt and Road" Initiative. It can be seen that the Greater Bay Area of Guangdong, Hong Kong and Macao has been elevated to the status of a national strategic master plan and occupies an important position in the "Belt and Road" Initiative. The Greater Bay Area is an important bridge connecting the countries along the "Belt and Road" Initiative. It is a cultural bond connecting English, Portuguese and overseas Chinese cultures. In addition, the Greater Bay Area of Guangdong, Hong Kong and Macao is also an important strategic locality for China's FTZs that have been officially designated or are being negotiated or studied, such as the China–ASEAN FTZ and the China–ASEAN FTZ (upgraded version). Therefore, promoting the establishment of the Greater Bay Area will certainly accelerate the realization of major national strategies. The role of the Greater Bay Area is irreplaceable. It is not only the need for Guangdong to "go global" and to continue to deepen reform but also the need for the development of Hong Kong and Macao. The establishment of the Greater Bay Area of Guangdong, Hong Kong and Macao has been unanimously recognized and accepted by Guangdong and Hong Kong and Macao, and it also forms an important part of the national implementation of major strategies.

All the world's famous bay areas have an open economic structure, strong agglomerating and spillover functions, efficient resource allocation capabilities, well-developed international network of contacts as well as pleasant living environments. They are important growth poles for the development of local regional economies and leaders in technological transformation. The world's three well-known benchmark bay areas — New York, San Francisco and Tokyo bay areas — all have developed their respective unique strengths over the years. The New York Bay Area is known as the "financial bay area" because the leading industry there is the financial service industry. It is the meeting place of the world's big banks, finance, insurance and other institutions. It is also the "core" hub and commercial center of world finance. San Francisco Bay Area is one of the world's high-tech R&D centers. Many high-tech companies like Apple and Google attract a large amount of venture capital, thereby making San Francisco Bay Area a place for accumulating venture capital. Tokyo Bay Area is known as the industrial bay area because it has a highly developed industrial base with advanced industries and is also the bay area with the highest number of Fortune 500 companies.

Along with the acceleration of China's reform and opening-up and the rapid economic development in recent years, the Greater Bay Area of Guangdong, Hong Kong and Macao as a forerunner and in its position as a pioneer has quietly become the fourth largest bay area in the world, and it is on its way to becoming the "fourth pole" of the world's bay area economies. First of all, the coastline of the Greater Bay Area of Guangdong, Hong Kong and Macao lies within important bastions of Northeast Asia and Southeast Asia, possessing the world's largest port cluster and the world's largest airport cluster. In 2016, the total economic volume of the Guangdong–Hong Kong–Macao Greater Bay Area reached 1.3 trillion US dollars, ranking 3rd in the four major bay areas, with import and export trade three times that of Tokyo Bay Area. The Guangdong–Hong Kong–Macao Greater Bay Area has a huge economic volume, and although its per capita GDP is at the bottom of the four bay areas, its GDP growth ranks 1st. Second, the entire Guangdong, Hong Kong and Macao city clusters possess a complete and comprehensive industrial system. Hong Kong is an international financial and logistics center. It is the world's freest economy and a high-end service industrial center. Macao's convention and exhibition industry and tourism are flourishing. Guangzhou and Shenzhen are innovative cities. The entire Pearl River Delta is also known as the "world factory" and "manufacturing center". The manufacturing industry is developed, and the proportion of the service industry in the Bay Area has already accounted for more than 80% .We could say that the Greater Bay Area has formed a complete and comprehensive industrial system with a "two-wheel drive" of advanced manufacturing and modern service industry, making it an important growth pole for China's regional economic development. Third, Hong Kong is an international financial center. Shenzhen is China's national financial center with strong financial leadership. Under the leadership of the two cities, the Greater Bay Area has so far attracted more than 70 of the world's top 100 banks. The HK Stock Exchange has surpassed the NY Stock Exchange to become the world's largest IPO market. Therefore, judging from the economic volume of the entire Bay Area, its industrial system, the level of development of the financial industry, and the development potential and innovation momentum of the Bay Area, it can be said that the Guangdong–Hong Kong–Macao Greater Bay Area already has all the conditions and requirements of a world-class bay area.

However, compared with the three other major bay areas, there is a big difference. The three other major bay areas are "homogeneous", all located in the same countries and in the same administrative areas but the situation is different for the Guangdong–Hong Kong–Macao Greater Bay Area. It is "heterogeneous". Each of Guangdong, Hong Kong and Macao belongs to a distinct and different administrative system and each is in a different customs and tariff zone. Guangdong, Hong Kong and Macao comprise two special administrative regions and free ports in Hong Kong and Macao, two special economic zones in Shenzhen and Zhuhai, and three pilot FTZs in Nansha, Qianhai, Shekou and Hengqin. The cooperation between Guangdong, Hong Kong and Macao belongs to cross-border cooperation under the "one country, two systems" imperative. Under these circumstances, the barriers caused by the systems hinder the deep integration between the three places and reduce the efficiency of regional integration. However, if the obstacles brought by the systemic and administrative differences can be tackled, the multiple economic systems superposed, the effects will be the generation of more economic powers and energies that could accelerate the marketization and internationalization of the Greater Bay Area.

With the above considerations in mind, when establishing the Guangdong–Hong Kong–Macao Greater Bay Area, we should be guided by the national "Belt and Road" Initiative. At the same time, by combining the Greater Bay Area with the establishment of the Guangdong FTZ, we must adhere to the rules for the economic development of the first-class bay areas and take efforts to make the Greater Bay Area the most economically viable and internationally competitive global technology innovation center, a financial innovation "mecca", an international logistics center, international economic and trade center, advanced manufacturing and service industry center and last but not least, a bay area with quality living environments. In conclusion, we seek to create a premier world-class bay area constituting heterogeneous SARs + Bay Area + FTZs with its own unique characteristics.

Based on the common economic characteristics of bay Areas, the construction of the Guangdong–Hong Kong–Macao Greater Bay Area requires continuously enhancing its global resource allocation function, making it an open international region. It is also necessary to build a high-end industrial system and to make it a development hub for the global economy. In addition, we need to have a highly developed innovation system in the Greater Bay Area in order to become a leading region of innovation and development. Finally, we need to facilitate a high degree of regional integration, so as to transcend the administrative boundaries and to bring about superposition effects.

II. Creating a New Global Center for Scientific and Technological Innovations in the Greater Bay Area

The world's first-class bay areas have first-class innovation capabilities. Innovation is the driving force of economic growth, and it's only through innovation that a nation could become strong and powerful. In the face of the new industrial revolution and the re-industrialization of the United States and Europe, we must pay attention to innovation: we need to keep up with the world's leading trends in science and technology, accelerate reforms and improve innovation capabilities and our core competitiveness. The construction of the Guangdong–Hong Kong–Macao Greater Bay Area as a high-tech innovation "highland" is not only the goal for development in the Bay Area but also an indispensable requirement for realizing the national strategy of innovation-driven development strategy to build a powerful world-class science and technology nation.

First of all, we recognize that the Greater Bay Area of Guangdong, Hong Kong and Macao has the ability to become a global innovation "highland". In terms of urban innovation capability, Guangzhou, Shenzhen and Hong Kong are well-known innovative cities. According to the "2017 China Urban Innovation Ranking", two cities in the Greater Bay Area, Shenzhen and Guangzhou, ranked 2nd and 4th, respectively. (Hong Kong and Macao are not included in the ranking.) In the "2017 Global Innovation Index Report" jointly published by the World Intellectual Property Organization and other organizations, the Shenzhen–Hong Kong region, with its "digital communication" as the main innovation field was ranked 2nd in the global "innovation cluster". Second, there are many universities and institutions of higher learning in Guangzhou and Hong Kong. Guangzhou has the highest number of universities in the Pearl River Delta, and Hong Kong has several world-renowned universities, such as the University of Hong Kong, the Hong Kong University of Science and Technology and the Chinese University of Hong Kong, which are capable of delivering high-quality scientific and technological talents to the Greater Bay Area, and these institutions also provide the Greater Bay Area with the results of science and technology R&D. Shenzhen has a mature and innovative entrepreneurial environment, and a number of world-leading high-tech companies such as Huawei and DJI have emerged — it is China's Silicon Valley. In 2015, the value added of Shenzhen's high-tech industry was 584.791 billion yuan, accounting for 33.4% of GDP;

the import and export volumes of high-tech products reached US$254.248 billion, and the research and development expenditure accounted for 4.05% of the city's GDP. The number of patent cooperation agreements reached 13,300. In addition, Shenzhen's innovation environment has also attracted many Fortune 500 companies to set up headquarters in Shenzhen — corporations such as Apple's South China Operations Center, Microsoft's Internet of Things Lab, Qualcomm Wireless Communications and Internet of Things Technology Exhibition Center, etc. These and other world-famous companies bring into Shenzhen innovative energies. Third, the developed industrial cities represented by Foshan, Dongguan, Zhongshan, etc., have built a huge industrial system that allows innovative inventions to become utilizable and developable to become industries.

The Stock Exchanges of Shenzhen and Hong Kong have provided important financial support for innovative enterprises in the Greater Bay Area. There are also numerous industry funds or foundations, venture capital, etc., which further drive the prosperity of the financial industry.

In 2016, Guangdong Province's research and development expenditures accounted for 2.52% of GDP. The total number of patent applications for the year reached 505,667; the total number of patent grants was 259,032, the number of patent cooperation agreements accepted was 23,574 and the output value of high-tech products was 5.9 trillion yuan, an increase of 10%. As can be seen from Figure 1, Guangdong's investments in high technology and output increased year-by-year.

It can be seen that the Guangdong–Hong Kong–Macao Greater Bay Area is fully capable of creating a high-tech industry leading zone second only to Silicon Valley of the United States. To build a global science and technology innovation "highland" in the Greater Bay Area, we need to build a highly open regional innovation system with effective and efficient division of labor and cooperation; we should build a global science and technology innovation platform and make an overall plan for the use of our innovative resources.

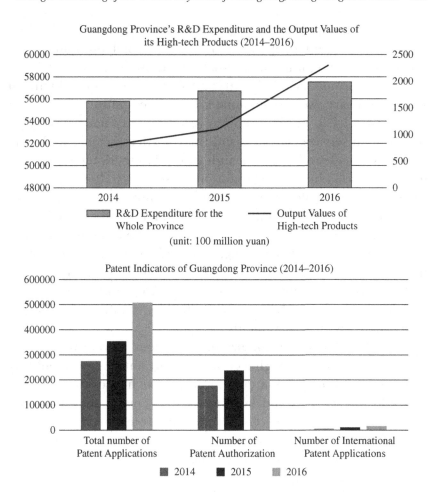

Figure 1. Science and technology indicators of Guangdong Province.

(A) *Building and perfecting the regional innovation system of division of labor and collaboration*

Taking advantage of the comparative strengths of the innovation factors of each city in the Greater Bay Area, a regional innovation network with Shenzhen, Hong Kong, Guangzhou, Macao–Zhuhai as the core innovation poles — coupled with the industrial innovation advantages of other cities in the Pearl River Delta — is to be established. These four core innovation poles should play a leading role in diffusing and promoting regional innovation and development, helping to expand cooperation in international innovation and actively integrating into the international innovation network.

Taking advantage of the strengths of Hong Kong's high-end service industry, we should establish service industry innovation centers and try to become innovative centers in financial services, professional services, business and trade services, science and technology services and logistics industries. Hong Kong should be utilized to aid in integrating innovative resources in the Greater Bay Area, and we should open up external innovation networks and carry out measures to connect the Greater Bay Area with foreign innovative resources. With several world-renowned schools and research institutes in Hong Kong, we would encourage these institutions to promote exchanges between universities, research institutes and enterprises within the Greater Bay Area, enhancing research and development capabilities and facilitating the transformation of scientific research achievements.

Taking advantage of Shenzhen's excellent innovative environment and its advanced high-tech industry advantages, we should lay emphasis on strategic emerging industries such as communication network, life sciences and healthcare, new energy, new materials, energy conservation and environmental protection, focusing on making breakthroughs in the emerging core technologies of these industries in order to gain the leading position in the world.

Relying on Guangzhou's Sun Yat-sen University, South China University of Technology, Guangzhou Branch of Chinese Academy of Sciences and research enterprises, we have achieved breakthroughs in the forefront of basic research, focusing on cloud computing, quantum communications, intelligent manufacturing, robotics and other core technologies.

Macao and Zhuhai both rely on universities such as Macao University and Zhuhai Campus of Sun Yat-sen University to achieve innovative breakthroughs in microelectronics, marine equipment and traditional Chinese medicine. At the same time, we should attempt to strengthen the ties of Macao with Portuguese-speaking and Latin American countries as well as improving the current contact networks to better connect the Greater Bay Area with the innovative resources of Portuguese-speaking and Latin American countries.

We should make greater efforts in making full use of the manufacturing advantages of other cities in the Pearl River Delta. We need to plan layouts for industrial parks, strengthen the connection with innovative cities and innovative resources and realize the commercial transformation of innovative achievements. For example, Dongguan shall make Songshan Lake Hi-tech Industrial Park as the center that connects Guangzhou's Science City in the north and Shenzhen's Nanshan District in the south, and it shall undertake to make use of the innovative resources of Guangzhou and Shenzhen to construct two "innovation belts" creating an "innovation corridor" straddling across the eastern coast of the Pearl River Delta.

We should aim at constructing a good and efficient regional innovation network of division of labor, work and cooperation. Under such innovation work, plus the free flow of innovation elements, we could conduct planning for the overall Greater Bay Area in establishing and sharing national scientific research institutions and R&D platforms. R&D centers should also be established in the Greater Bay Area, but duplication of construction must be avoided. We should make full use of local characteristics so as to produce the greatest innovation benefits.

However, if we want to establish a regional innovation system in which vital elements can flow freely, we need to innovate our mode and mechanism of cooperation. In 2008, the implementation of the "Outline of the Pearl River Delta Regional Reform and Development Plan (2008–2020)" provided policy assurance for regional cooperation and innovation between Guangdong, Hong Kong and Macao, accelerating the process of cooperation among the three regions. Subsequently, the signing of the "Guangdong–Hong Kong Cooperation Framework Agreement" and the "Guangdong–Macao Cooperation Framework Agreement" further bolstered regional cooperation between Guangdong, Hong Kong and Macao, thus encouraging the three places to work out the regional cooperation plan jointly through consensus and improving the mechanism for the joint meeting of the chief executive officers of the three places.

(B) *Building a global science and technology innovation platform*

At present, there are 6 national level high-tech parks, 2 national software parks, 12 so-called 863 bases, 1 national-level university science and technology park and more than 30 universities and research institutes with postgraduate training capacities in the Greater Bay Area. We should strive to encourage relevant institutions to tie up with major national science and technology projects and plans in building a national innovation platform in which contacts and exchanges between universities, research institutes and industries could be made and conducted smoothly. Additionally, a cooperation platform involving universities and research institutes, specialist colleges and key enterprises should also be built in order to comprehensively enhance the innovation cooperation of science and technology industries in all regions of the Bay Area, helping to realize the commercialization transformation of innovation from R&D to scientific and technological achievements.

In addition, for the Lok Ma Chau Loop area (which is adjacent to Shenzhen) in 2005, Shenzhen and Hong Kong had set up a joint team to conduct joint research on the feasibility of opening up the Loop area. For the present, the governments of Hong Kong and Shenzhen have signed the "Memorandum of Understanding on Hong Kong and Shenzhen's Cooperation in Promoting the Common Development of the Lok Ma Chau Loop Area", and they are committed to jointly developing the Lok Ma Chau Loop area into a "Hong Kong–Shenzhen Innovation and Technology Park". The parties had reached consensus as to the details of cooperation, development mechanism and the establishment of the Shenzhen–Hong Kong Science and Technology Innovation Cooperation Zone. Among others, the Agreement mooted the idea of establishing a key venture research cooperation base to attract top enterprises, research and development institutions and institutions of higher learning at home and abroad to house their operations there. The entire Science and Technology Park covers an area of 87 hectares, four times that of the Hong Kong Academy of Sciences. With the Loop's Regional Science and Technology Park as the center and by developing Shenzhen's Futian "bonded area" into a "Border Trade

Processing Zone" and by constructing Hao Ke Wei (or Hoo Hok Wai) (adjacent to the Loop) into a "Border Science and Technology Innovation Park", the three regions could jointly foster the development of Guangdong and Hong Kong innovative region and its platform.

(C) *Building a place where new innovations originate and spread to the world — a place that embraces the world*

Guided by the "Belt and Road" Initiative, we would encourage leading enterprises in the Greater Bay Area to set up R&D centers and product design centers through M&A, cooperation and joint ventures and to build innovative "carriers" such as international technology transfer centers and extension bases, science and technology parks and incubators. The establishment of international science and technology innovation centers and platforms in the Bay Area will attract transnational corporations to set up R&D centers in the Bay Area. The establishment of the long-term collaborative relationship between research institutions, institutions of higher learning and large enterprises in the Bay Area and world-class scientific and technological institutions will be encouraged. In this way, we could participate in globalization of science and technology, open up a global market for major scientific and technological achievements and comprehensively enhance the position of the Greater Bay Area as a Maritime Silk Road bridgehead with innovative spillover functions and capabilities.

(D) *Optimizing the innovative ecological environment of the Greater Bay Area*

To build an innovation engine in the Greater Bay Area, we need to optimize the innovative ecological environment in the Bay Area. We should encourage and support the establishment of venture capital funds originating from the societal capital in the Bay Area of Guangdong, Hong Kong and Macao. We need to support the innovation and upgrading of enterprises, stimulate the vitality of regional innovation and entrepreneurship, encourage the establishment of innovation and entrepreneurship platforms and promote mass entrepreneurship and innovation. We would take full advantage of Shenzhen's strengths in technological and financial development, strive to build Asia's largest venture capital center and encourage powerful venture capital enterprises to set up venture capital institutions and venture capital funds in countries along the "Belt and Road" Initiative. We have to introduce innovative talent policies and use our innovative atmosphere and those policies to attract domestic and foreign talents. By making use of the functions of capital markets in Hong Kong and Shenzhen, we can provide multi-channel financial support for innovative enterprises within the Greater Bay Area.

We should also lay emphasis on the functions and roles of the governments in formulating policy plans that serve to encourage innovative atmosphere, optimize innovative ecology and attract high-end talents. The government should spearhead the promotion of the cooperation between science and technology companies, universities and basic research platforms, so that high-end and high-quality talents of universities in the Bay Area would reside and remain in the Greater Bay Area. At the same time, the government should provide policy benefits on household registration, talents, education and tax incentives. Measures such as issuing green cards to high-end or highly qualified talents at entry and exit points should be implemented, so as to enable the free flow of talents inside and outside the Bay Area. One way to attract high-tech enterprises is through tax reduction or tax subsidies. Last but not least, governments must play a pivotal role in promoting cooperation between the government and technology companies, so as to incorporate science and technology into government affairs in areas such as public safety, transportation, education and employment.

III. Scaling New Heights in Financial Innovation in the Greater Bay Area

Finance is the core and pillar of the modern economy. It is through regional financial cooperation that capital is accumulated effectively. This is often done to promote the optimal allocation of capital and to provide effective financial support for regional economic development.

Financial cooperation has always been the emphasis of economic cooperation between Guangdong, Hong Kong and Macao. For this reason, Guangdong, Hong Kong and Macao have made a lot of efforts to promote financial cooperation. In 2003, the Mainland and Hong Kong signed the Closer Economic Partnership Arrangement between the Mainland and Hong Kong, which stipulates five measures for cooperation between the Mainland and Hong Kong in banking, insurance and securities, further opening up financial services in the trade sectors and making specific commitments in the areas of insurance, banking and securities. Subsequently, in 2004 and 2005, the "Supplementary Agreement" and "Supplementary Agreement II" on the Closer Economic Partnership Arrangement between the Mainland and Hong Kong were signed, respectively, which supplemented the ways of opening of financial services trade. The 2010 "Guangdong–Hong Kong Cooperation Framework Agreement" put forward more specific terms in the cooperation contents for financial cooperation. For the first time, it was proposed that Hong Kong's financial system would be taken as a leader in spearheading a regional financial cooperation with clear division of work supported by financial resources and services of cities such as Guangzhou and Shenzhen.

(A) *The Greater Bay Area has the foundation to build a financial innovation "highland"*

In the Global Financial Centers Index (GFCI) Report, both Hong Kong and Shenzhen were rated as Asian financial centers, while in the China Financial Center Report, Shenzhen was rated as a national financial center and Guangzhou was rated as a regional financial center. According to the latest issue of the "Global Financial Center Rankings", Guangzhou was listed officially as a formal official global financial center for the first time from the list of alternate financial centers. Hong Kong, Shenzhen and Guangzhou ranked 4th, 22nd and 37th, respectively. In the latest

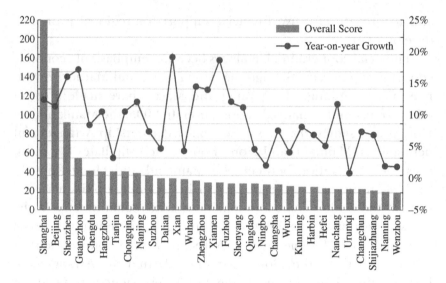

Figure 2.   China financial center index ranking.

Source: Financial Center Information Network.

issue of the *China Financial Center Rankings*, Shenzhen and Guangzhou ranked 3rd and 4th, respectively, and they were leaders in moving up the rankings (Figure 2).

According to the results of Financial Center Evaluation Network Questionnaire conducted by GFCI, among the 15 financial centers that are expected to further develop significantly, the top 6 are Shanghai, Singapore, Dubai, Hong Kong, Qingdao, and Shenzhen, with 5 of them from China and 2 from the Greater Bay Area of Guangdong, Hong Kong and Macao. It can be seen that the Guangdong–Hong Kong–Macao Greater Bay Area has the conditions and potential to build a financial "highland" or center, one which could compete with the financial industries of other bay areas of the world (Table 1).

(B) *Constructing regional financial networks*

To build a financial innovation "highland" in the Greater Bay Area, we first need to build a regional financial network, breaking down the institutional barriers within the Bay Area and promoting the

Table 1. Fifteen financial centers that could possibly increase their influence.

Financial Center	Number of Times/Occasions Cited in the Past 24 Months
Shanghai	119
Singapore	94
Dubai	78
Hong Kong	68
Qingdao	57
Shenzhen	55
Casablanca	38
Dublin	33
Luxembourg	31
Toronto	30
Gibraltar	24
Beijing	23
Busan	21
Istanbul	12
Abu Dhabi	12

Source: The 21st Issue of Global Financial Centers Index.

free flow of important financial elements in the region. We need to build a financial network taking Hong Kong as the financial leader, with support from Shenzhen and Guangzhou, and with other cities as the hinterland. This financial system network makes full use of the advantages of financial characteristics of various places in creating a new pattern or situation of financial cooperation.

Financial industry is Hong Kong's "advantaged" industry, with many financial talents and professionals, advanced financial management experience and a sound financial market system. In 2015, the International Monetary Fund and the World Bank reported that Hong Kong ranked 3rd in global financial center rankings and it is an important commercial and financial center in the world. Hong Kong is also the most open insurance market in the world. Of the top 20 insurance companies in the world, 14 are in Hong Kong, and the IPO market financing of the Hong Kong Stock Exchange has been a world leader long time running. Guangdong is a large economic and financial province, rich in financial resources, having strong financial demands and active financial markets. It is the natural hinterland to Hong Kong's international financial center and is also a relatively mature commercial banking center. Shenzhen is a relatively developed venture capital center, with strengths in its venture capital and private equity financing, while Macao and Zhuhai possess comparative advantages in bond markets and asset management.

Hong Kong should take advantage of its status as an international financial center to become a financing center for listing both domestic and foreign companies. At the same time, because of its geographical advantages, the listing and trading volume of RMB products in the Hong Kong Stock Exchange are huge, and it has comparative strengths in offshore RMB product trading and risk management — Hong Kong has become the most important offshore RMB settlement center and asset management center. Hong Kong should continue to expand its RMB-denominated and RMB-settled trade and financing business, making it an offshore center for the RMB in promoting the internationalization of the Chinese currency. In addition, due to its highly developed financial industry, Hong Kong is Asia's largest venture capital center. Through the use of this function, the introduction of Hong Kong's venture capital funds into other cities in the Bay Area will promote not only the economic development of the Bay Area but also the development of the financial industry in the Bay Area. Macao is a bridge between China and Portuguese-speaking and Latin American countries. It can use this advantage to build a commercial and financial cooperation service platform between China and Portuguese-speaking and Latin American countries via building a Sino-Portuguese RMB settlement center.

As a national financial center, Shenzhen should play the role of an extension and be supplementary to the functions of Hong Kong as an international financial center. First of all, we should actively "dock and couple with" Hong Kong's financial resources. Via breakthroughs in financial innovation, we should enhance the financial cooperation between Shenzhen and Hong Kong. Second, Shenzhen should serve as the "bridge" for RMB internationalization and the backup base or "reinforcements" of Hong Kong's RMB offshore center status. Shenzhen's role is akin to that of a bridge or intermediary for RMB's "go global" and "coming back". Mainland funds enter Hong Kong through Shenzhen, and Hong Kong financial institutions raise RMB loans to Mainland enterprises.

Shenzhen should also act as the national venture capital investment center. In 2010, the Shenzhen Municipal Government promulgated "Certain Provisions Pertaining to Promoting the Development of Equity Investment Funds". On this basis, it formulated supporting policies to create a conducive business environment for the development of venture capital institutions. While vigorously cultivating local venture capital institutions, it also helped bringing in internationally renowned venture capital institutions. Shenzhen should further promote the development of SME and Growth Enterprise Market (GEM) boards and strengthen the cooperation between Shenzhen GEM and Hong Kong GEM to promote the development of enterprises in the Greater Bay Area.

As a regional financial center, Guangzhou is the location for the branch of the Central Bank's (People's Bank of China) Greater Bay Area, head office of regional commercial banks and head office and regional branches of state-owned commercial banks. The China Banking Regulatory Commission (CBRC), China Insurance Regulatory Commission (CIRC) and China Securities Regulatory Commission (CSRC) have also set up provincial branches in Guangzhou. The presence of the aforementioned banking and finance institutions gives Guangzhou the advantage of having financial regional headquarters, thus attracting more financial regional headquarters to set up in Guangzhou, thus establishing Guangzhou as a regional financial headquarters center. With a sound banking system and huge trading volume, Guangzhou should step up the mutual establishment of institutions with Hong Kong and Macao banks and aggressively promote the integration of Guangzhou's banking and industries. Areas in which to develop industrial finance include automobile finance, logistics, shipping finance and real estate finance. Cooperation with Hong Kong's futures market should be strengthened and efforts must be made to strive for the establishment of an independent Guangzhou Futures Exchange and the establishment of a futures trading center.

(C) *Relying on FTZs and loop areas to promote financial cooperation and reform in the Greater Bay Area*

We should rely on the three FTZs of Qianhai in Shenzhen, Nansha in Guangzhou and Hengqin in Zhuhai to explore the construction of demonstration zones for cross-border financial cooperation, including financial R&D centers, futures trading centers, financial outsourcing service zones and financial industry parks, in order to "test the waters" on ways of promoting the reform of the financial system in the Mainland. First, we should encourage cooperation among the three places in banking, insurance and securities industries. We could relax the entry requirements ("threshold") for financial institutions in these industries and encourage cross-border establishment of these institutions. On the matter of cooperation in banking, banks within the three places of the Greater Bay Area should be encouraged to set up and facilitate cross-border interoperability, such as Guangzhou Development Bank (GDB) branches in Macao, and its representative offices in Hong Kong, and a number of branches of Hong Kong banks in Guangdong. Innovation in financial services should be encouraged to provide more convenient and affordable financial services for enterprises in both places, and RMB settlement business in cross-border trade should be developed. In 2009, Guangzhou, Shenzhen, Zhuhai and Dongguan became the "pilot" test cities for RMB settlement of cross-border trade in China, while Hong Kong and Macao became the first pilot test cities for RMB settlement of cross-border trade outside the Mainland. Banks from the three places could jointly carry out cross-border RMB syndicated loan business. Cooperation in the area of securities and funds is mainly manifested in QFII, QDII, cross-border M&A, overseas listing and so on. As for the insurance industry, Hong Kong's insurance industry is particularly well developed and is the most open insurance market (in the world). We therefore propose that Guangdong should further lower the threshold requirements of insurance access to Hong Kong, allowing setting up of mutual insurance institutions and promoting close cooperation between the insurance industries of the two places. Second, we should promote cross-border mergers and re-structuring of financial institutions in the Greater Bay Area by lifting restrictions on the proportion of shareholdings, such as China Merchants Bank's acquisition of the Hong Kong Ying Lung Bank. Third, we should support and encourage financial institutions in the Greater Bay Area to carry out cross-border business, to enrich and expand cross-border financial business modes, including deposits and loans, cash management, project financing, credit cards and so on. Fourth, we should promote cooperation and sharing of resources between the capital markets of Shenzhen and Hong Kong. In 2012, at a forum of the Shenzhen–Hong Kong Financial Cooperation Summit, it was proposed that qualified financial institutions and enterprises be encouraged to issue H-shares and RMB bonds in Hong Kong. It was also suggested that Hong Kong Stock Exchange and Shenzhen Stock Exchange should conduct bilateral stock trading to promote the integration of Guangdong, Hong Kong and Macao financial markets, allowing enterprises in both places to choose capital market financing without obstacles and barriers and in accordance with their needs. Fifth, the development of the bond market should be accelerated: Guangdong enterprises should be encouraged to issue bonds in Hong Kong and Macao to establish regional bond markets for the three places. In addition, cross-border financial services, including cross-border taxation business, cross-border e-commerce financing, online financing and other areas could also be developed to promote cooperation in financial infrastructure construction and payment services in the Greater Bay Area, thus establishing a regional financial network in the Greater Bay Area.

The Lok Ma Chau Loop area is considered to be the most ideal region for financial cooperation between Guangdong and Hong Kong. In 2008, the "two sessions" of Shenzhen City proposed that the Loop area should be established as a Shenzhen–Hong Kong financial city modelled after London's Finance City. The Loop area will be developed to become a special financial zone and a pilot zone to carry out financial reforms. Utilizing the special location of the Loop, we could first develop "border finance" that is open to the inland as a breakthrough for Guangdong–Hong Kong financial cooperation.

(D) *Promoting financial innovation in the Greater Bay Area*

Financial innovation is manifested mainly in system innovation, product innovation, subject innovation, tools innovation and innovation in other areas. It is imperative to implement our national innovation policy, attracting all kinds of important financial elements or factors and financial institutions to agglomerate and develop in the Greater Bay Area. In this regard, the State Council had promulgated the "National Strategic Emerging Industries Development Plan for the 13th Five-Year Plan", proposing that we should boost the innovation of financial products such as supply chain financing, science and technology insurance. Relevant legal provisions must be introduced and enforced so as to strengthen the protection of network information and information disclosure. The formulation of laws and regulations on network security and electronic commerce should be accelerated.

We should entrust the three major FTZs in Guangdong with exploring internationalized financial development and innovation. Internet technology is to be used to accelerate the integration of technology and finance, creating a new model of technology finance and intelligent financial services. An innovative financial service model should be adopted whereby intellectual property rights, benefits, rights to levy fees and financing of accounts receivable mortgages are practiced. We have to vigorously develop financial leasing business, promote investment and financing facilitation, establish RMB overseas investment, loans and funding projects and innovate cross-border RMB trading business. Additionally, we need to promote the issuance of multi-currency industrial investment funds, offshore business, cross-border asset mortgages and other related industries. We will encourage FTZs to try out financial innovation policies first and construct demonstration areas for financial innovation.

In the area of financial technologies, in the light of the rapid development of blockchains and artificial intelligence technology and their continuous penetration into the financial industry, the development of financial technologies has been accelerated, changing the traditional financial model. Financial technologies have been widely applied in intelligent investment, risk management and wealth management. Financial institutions are seeking collaboration with technology companies to create new financial products and services. Examples are Alipay, WeChat payments, "crowd-funding" and online loans, which expand the market capacity and which could make up for the shortcomings of traditional finance. In terms of financial services, financial technologies can provide cross-market, cross-regional and cross-institutional financial services to enhance the efficiency of financial services and to elevate user experience. Hong Kong, London, New York, Singapore and Silicon Valley are known as the top five financial technology centers of the world. We should leverage on the construction of the Guangdong–Hong Kong–Macao Greater Bay Area and Hong Kong's financial advantages to promote close cooperation in the field of financial technologies in the Greater Bay Area, rendering the Bay Area into a "highland" for the development of financial science and technology industries. The rapid development of financial science and technologies has also spawned a number of financial science and technology companies, whose function, *inter alia*, is to promote the cooperation between technology companies and financial research institutes, financial laboratories and universities, to help integrate the advantages of scientific research and industry resources, promoting the development of financial science and technology. On March 28, 2017, a domestic leading financial technology company, Hong Kong Financial Data Technology Co., Ltd. (FDT), signed a strategic cooperation agreement with (Shanghai) Academy of Artificial Intelligence (AIV) in Hong Kong to explore the full integration of financial artificial intelligence technologies and

Hong Kong's financial market. Both FDT and AIV have reached the international forefront of innovation in the field of financial technology. FDT has been a leader in the research and development of financial artificial intelligence, financial cloud computing, financial big data and financial intelligent investment technologies. Its cooperation with AIV is not only market driven but also supported by the policy of the Guangdong–Hong Kong–Macao Greater Bay Area. This will certainly enhance Hong Kong's competitiveness in financial science and technologies and consolidate its position as the world's financial science and technology center. For the Greater Bay Area, the cooperation between the two sides will certainly help the development of the financial market in the Bay Area and breed a "blue ocean" of financial science and technologies.

(E) *Making the Greater Bay Area a financial hub that is open to the whole world*

We should be guided by the "Belt and Road" Initiative in connecting ("docking") to the international financial platform by taking Hong Kong and Macao as the "matching" or "connecting" window. Hong Kong, located in the center of the "Belt and Road" Initiative, is an international platform for Guangdong's financial industry to go to the world. Its financing system is flexible and transparent, and the very act of a company listing in Hong Kong helps enhance its international reputation. We should support qualified financial institutions in the Greater Bay Area to speed up their layout plans of moving overseas and expansion into overseas markets. We would also create conditions for attracting overseas financial institutions to enter the Greater Bay Area, bringing in financial innovation and financial talents. The cities in the Greater Bay Area can build RMB overseas loan funds along the "Belt and Road" countries to provide investment and financing services for Bay Area enterprises. At the same time, we should support enterprises from the countries and regions along the "Belt and Road" route to enter the Greater Bay Area to issue RMB shares. We should guide enterprises set up capital operation centers in Hong Kong, so that Hong Kong will become an information and financing platform for "venturing out" enterprises. Meanwhile, Macao's role as a contact between the Mainland and Portuguese-speaking countries should be maintained and enhanced; a commerce financial service platform will be set up to provide financial services for the economic and trade cooperation between the Mainland and Portuguese-speaking countries.

IV. Building Advanced Manufacturing and Service Centers

Over the past four decades of reform and opening-up, Guangdong, Hong Kong and Macao have gone through several stages of regional cooperation, effectively bolstering the economic development of the three places while driving and radiating over the whole country. The Pearl River Delta has become the largest manufacturing base in the world, and Hong Kong and Macao have also achieved industrial transformation and upgrading: Hong Kong is now a modern logistics and financial industry center, Macao is a tourism and entertainment center and a regional business and trade service platform that integrates gambling, exhibition and leisure industries. Guangdong, Hong Kong and Macao have shaped their own industrial characteristics. In recent years, influenced by the international economic situations, the export trade of the Pearl River Delta has been hovering at low levels, while the domestic labor and energy costs have been rising progressively. Therefore, the original industrial development model of the Pearl River Delta is now unable to keep up with the pace of modern economic development and industrial transformation and upgrading is overdue. The development of modern service industries in Hong Kong and Macao is also limited by space. It is still necessary and appropriate to expand their development hinterland so as to consolidate the status of Hong Kong as a trade, shipping and international financial center and Macao as an international tourism center. Hence, we should remove obstructions and obstacles to regional cooperation between Guangdong, Hong Kong and Macao, innovate regional cooperation mechanism in the Greater Bay Area and promote industrial cooperation between

Guangdong, Hong Kong and Macao from the original "shop front and factory at the rear" mode of industries to transform it into a new stage of coordinated and synergized industrial development.

First, we should innovate the guiding functions of the government and strengthen the market-driven mechanism in the Greater Bay Area. Hong Kong's market mechanism is relatively mature and sound, but due to historical factors, the role played by our national government is still very noticeable. The Greater Bay Area needs to optimize the mode of cooperation and exchanges among governments at all levels. Planning for and taking cognizance of the competition among governments at all levels should be conducted comprehensively so that consensus could be reached. Planning for cooperation must take into account the Bay Area as a whole. Specifically, a coordination mechanism of cooperation between Guangdong, Hong Kong and Macao must be sought in which their respective conflicts of interests and regional market barriers are to be eliminated, so as to gradually achieve the uniformity of goods specifications in the Greater Bay Area and to achieve legitimacy of rules, regulations governing economic actions and contracts. The aforementioned steps will help promote the marketization process within the Bay Area and form a new situation of regional cooperation with unified markets and complementary industries. Second, we should innovate the mode of Guangdong–Hong Kong–Macao cooperation to improve its efficiency. Taking the common problems faced by Guangdong, Hong Kong and Macao — such as the control of ecological environment pollution — as an opportunity for cooperation, we should be able to solve all kinds of difficulties in cooperation through coordination, consultation and negotiation — thereby accelerating the process of regional cooperation between the three places.

The overall urban structure of the Greater Bay Area of Guangdong, Hong Kong and Macao can be divided into three levels: the core level comprising nine cities in the Pearl River Delta and two cities in Hong Kong and Macao. The second level — covering Guangdong, Hong Kong and Macao — are the other cities in Guangdong excluding the nine cities in the Pearl River Delta — which provide a broad economic hinterland for the Greater Bay Area. The third level of the Bay Area urban regions extends eastward to Fujian, Taiwan, westward to Guangxi, Guizhou, Yunnan, etc., and extending northward to Jiangxi, Hunan and other areas. In other words, the Greater Bay Area of Guangdong, Hong Kong and Macao is a bay area with strong hinterland advantages. At the same time, the Northern Bay Economic Zone and Southeast Asia are to the west of the Greater Bay Area, which connect to ASEAN. To achieve internal diffusion and to promote hinterland development, emphasis must be placed on external linkages and seizing the commanding position of the global industrial chain.

(A) *Establishing a win–win industrial development system for cooperation in the Greater Bay Area*

After several stages of cooperation and development, Guangdong, Hong Kong and Macao have entered a phase of deepened cooperation and development. Driven by the port-harbor cluster group, different industrial clusters have been formed in the whole Greater Bay Area, each taking full advantage of its respective industrial strengths. "Staggered and complementary" development of industries has occurred, and in building a win–win industrial development system for cooperation in the Greater Bay Area. Guangzhou and Shenzhen could take advantage of their achievements in technological innovation and R&D advantages, focusing on high-tech and emerging industries such as communications, new energy, new materials, cloud computing, intelligent manufacturing, robotics, energy conservation and environmental protection. At present, Shenzhen has incubated a number of hardware technology enterprises such as DJI's UAV, LinkSpace Aerospace, Guang Chi Science, etc. Shenzhen is also the world's largest consumer electronics manufacturing base. Relying on its pioneering advantage as international free port, Hong Kong is building a modern service industry system with financial industry and science and technology consultation service industry as the leading industries. Macao should focus on exhibition, tourism and trade service industries. The manufacturing industries of Dongguan, Foshan, Zhongshan, Huizhou, Jiangmen and Zhaoqing have gained a certain reputation in the world; they focus on the development of advanced manufacturing industries, such as IT industries in Dongguan, manufacturing of electric home appliances in Zhongshan and ceramics in Foshan.

Guangzhou and Shenzhen, with their high-tech and new industries, should help drive the upgrading of industries in Dongguan, Zhongshan, Foshan and other cities in the Pearl River Delta. Specifically, the two advanced cities should transfer their tech know-how achievements in high-end manufacturing for takeover by the afore-mentioned, less developed cities for planned large-scale production. Hong Kong could provide professional and high-end services for the industries aforementioned. Meanwhile, Macao's exhibition industry could provide a platform for products, projects and exhibitions. In this way, the connections between the different places are strengthened. Collaboration and rational division of labor are the themes of the times in creating a benefits-sharing, collaborative and mutually supporting industry chain in the Greater Bay Area.

(B) *Building advanced manufacturing centers*

To build an advanced manufacturing center with international influence, we first need to follow closely the direction of development of the world's science and technology and the industry, and we need to develop leading, "pillar" industries. Second, we select a new generation of information technologies, green environmental protection, biological sciences, high-end equipment manufacturing, new energy, new materials and other industries and strive to achieve break-throughs in the key, core technologies; we need to cultivate strategic emerging industries and enhance the added values of the industrial chain. Third, as there are not just high-end industrial clusters such as communication and electronic information, new energy vehicles, UAVs, robotics within the Greater Bay Area but also medium- and low-end industrial clusters engaged in petrochemical industry, apparel, shoes and hats, toy processing, food and beverage in

Dongguan and other places, we therefore propose that the tax exemption policy be offered to industries with high technology content and added values, so as to encourage medium- and low-end industries to move into high-end manufacturing and production. Fourth, we should establish a high-level technology import and export trading platform to promote industrial technology exchange, undertake outsourcing business — focusing on software outsourcing business — and promoting industrial technological innovation. Fifth, we have to improve the development quality of the manufacturing industry in the Pearl River Delta, cultivate advanced equipment manufacturing industry and enhance the ability of industrial "matching and connection", thus strengthening coordinated development. Our goal is to promote the upgrading of the manufacturing industry from being big to becoming strong. In 2016, the value added of Guangdong's advanced manufacturing industry reached 1,573.978 billion yuan, an increase of 9.5% (Figure 3).

(C) *Creating modern service centers*

We note that the proportion of the service industry in other major bay areas of the world is very high. So, if we want to "match up" with

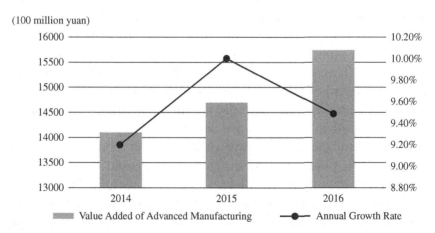

Figure 3. Advanced manufacturing industries of Guangdong Province, 2014–2016.

international industries, Guangdong, Hong Kong and Macao should also intensify efforts to develop their high-end service industries. The strongest industrial strength of Hong Kong and Macao lies in their service industries, which should play a leading role in promoting the development of the industries for the whole bay area. First of all, Hong Kong is the world's financial, trade and logistics service center. Macao is the most attractive gambling and tourism center in the world. It is also an important business and trade service platform of the Greater Bay Area. We should take advantage of the strengths of Hong Kong and Macao to develop trade services, formulate policies to promote investment in Hong Kong and Macao services in the Pearl River Delta, facilitate the entry of Hong Kong and Macao services into the Pearl River Delta and accelerate the development of service trade in the Pearl River Delta. And since the Pearl River Delta borders a large number of hinterland cities, Hong Kong and Macao should take the Pearl River Delta as a springboard to promote their service industries to enter the inland areas. Second, the Pearl River Delta should strengthen their opening up to Hong Kong and Macao's service industries, taking in professional talents, encouraging the establishment of accounting, legal, consultation and other professional service institutions in the Pearl River Delta, thus promoting the growth of service industries in the Greater Bay Area and accelerating the construction of a modern industrial system.

The Greater Bay Area could focus on information, logistics, finance and other industries for close cooperation. Not only does Guangdong have a well-developed manufacturing industry but it is also the place where many of the world's computer, communication equipment products and software are manufactured. Hong Kong is well developed in both software and hardware, so there is a large market for collaboration between the two sides in the information industries. In financial services, Hong Kong could cooperate with enterprises in the Pearl River Delta by providing them with accounting and financial audit services in line with international standards and specifications. It could also provide internationally recognized legal opinions and commercial disputes mediation and arbitration services.

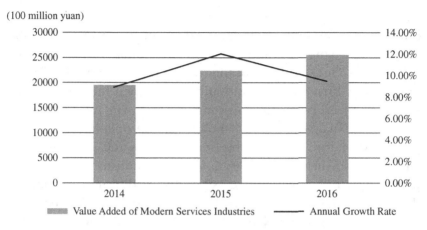

Figure 4. Modern service industries of Guangdong 2014–2016.

Finally, we should develop modern service trade, develop service industries based on the Internet and Internet of Things, promote the construction of information services and improve e-commerce systems in areas such as logistics, credit and payment. In 2016, the added values of modern service industries in Guangdong Province reached 2,556.817 billion yuan, with an annual growth rate of 10.4% (Figure 4).

(D) *Promoting industrial transformation and integration in the Greater Bay Area by considering the FTZs as pilot projects*

Only by enhancing the reform and transformation of the mode of economic development and breaking the bottlenecks of the traditional mode of development can the Greater Bay Area achieve greater and more development space in a series of future global industrial changes. A FTZ is a platform integrating reform, opening up and innovation. Guangdong's pilot FTZs have been established with high standards in order to explore the mechanism of enhanced industrial cooperation between the Pearl River Delta and Hong Kong–Macao. FTZs should be built into demonstration zones of deep cooperation between Guangdong, Hong Kong and Macao, and they are the vehicles promoting the industrial transformation and upgrading of the Bay Area. Currently, there are three FTZs listed in Guangdong, namely, Shekou in Shenzhen's Qianhai, Nansha in Guangzhou and Hengqin in Zhuhai. The three major FTZs need to make full use of the "trial and experiment first" policy to carry out "first or trial" innovation, to deepen the reform of the system and to serve as the forerunners of reform and opening-up. First of all, Guangdong's FTZ should expand opening up to Hong Kong and Macao, eliminate barriers to access and policy obstacles and promote the close integration of the industries of the three places. Based on the industrial strengths of different regions, the three FTZs should be developed in staggered and complementary manners. Guangzhou's Nansha should focus on the development of shipping logistics, international trade, shipping finance and other production services, creating a service hub dominated by production services. Shekou of Qianhai in Shenzhen should focus on the development of strategic emergent services such as finance, information services, modern logistics, with emphasis on promoting industrial cooperation with Hong Kong. Hong Kong's high-end service industry should be introduced into Shekou. For Zhuhai's Hengqin, its development focuses on tourism, leisure, business and finance industries, with emphasis on expanding industrial integration with Macao to build an international business and financial platform. Second, we should make use of the free business environment of the FTZs to promote the development of cross-border finance, cross-border e-commerce and cross-border purchase and procurement. The free flow of industrial elements and factors in Guangdong, Hong Kong and Macao are to be accelerated, industrial innovation and transformation stepped up and the cooperation of service industries enhanced.

(E) *Expanding the opening up of the Greater Bay Area industries under the guidance of the "Belt and Road" Initiative: A new paradigm*

The Greater Bay Area of Guangdong, Hong Kong and Macao is a strategic node along the road map of the "Belt and Road" Initiative, and Hong Kong and Macao are important windows to the outside world for the Greater Bay Area connecting the Mainland to the "Belt and Road" countries. It is an important bridge through which the Pearl River Delta and Mainland enterprises get abroad and foreign enterprises get in.

Hong Kong is a well-known free port in the world. According to the index of economic freedom and the report on the world economic freedom, Hong Kong is rated as the freest economy in the world. It not only has a long, close relationship with European and American markets in business and trade but also has frequent economic exchanges with Southeast Asian countries. Macao, on the contrary, has close economic and trade contacts with Portuguese-speaking and Latin American countries. It is a world-class leisure tourism center and a platform for business cooperation between China and Portuguese-speaking and Latin American countries. Entrusting the three major FTZs to "dock" or connect with Hong Kong's status as an international financial center and shipping center, and together with Macao's commercial and trade service platform, the Greater Bay Area will be made a "Belt and Road" open hub.

First of all, we must create a free and welcoming "drawing in" business environment in the Greater Bay Area. For 22 consecutive years, Hong Kong has been ranked the world's freest economy, with freedom of business, trade, finance, a sound legal system, and its business operations are most compatible with international practice, specifications and regulations. The Pearl River Delta region should learn from Hong Kong's experience in the internationalization, legalization and marketization of its business environment. Measures must be taken to accelerate the Pearl River Delta's compliance with international standards in terms of quality, technology, safety, environment and labor. The Pearl River Delta region should enhance its adaptability to high-standard international specifications and stipulations and create a good business environment that is in line with international standards and regulations, so as to increase its attractiveness to transnational corporations to establish R&D and regional HQs in the Pearl River Delta. Or it could at the very least promote the cooperation between Bay Area industries and foreign industries, thus bringing foreign high-tech, cutting-edge innovation and bringing about the transformation of the Greater Bay Area industries and enhancing the ability of the Greater Bay Area industries to participate in high-level international competition.

Second, we should accelerate the reform of the management system of "go global" enterprises in the Greater Bay Area and enhance the competitive advantage of international economic cooperation in the Greater Bay Area. Hong Kong has a mature service industry, and hence, it can provide international professional services such as accounting, design, law, finance and consultation for enterprises to "go global". For example, Hong Kong's developed financial industry could provide investment and financing services for overseas investment of the Pearl River Delta enterprises, and it could also set up RMB investment loan funds to provide financial and trade services to all countries and regions along the route of "Belt and Road" Initiative. Hong Kong could also provide legal consultation for enterprises to go out and help solve international disputes, encourage industries with comparative advantages such as household appliances, light industry and electronic information in the Pearl River Delta to go out and invest in factories overseas, supporting industries such as petroleum, chemical and building materials to establish production bases overseas and improving the quality of overseas investment. e-commerce is another area to develop — it opens up international market space for enterprises. We will build overseas marketing networks and overseas commodity and goods marketing centers so as to expand their international market space and promote enterprises to "go global". We should allow the Zhuhai–Macao Business and Trade Service Cooperation platform to fully and effectively carry out its functions in providing various professional services for industrial cooperation between China and Portuguese-speaking countries and Latin American countries.

V. Building a World-Class International Logistics Center

Guangdong, Hong Kong and Macao already possess the conditions to become an international logistics center. First, the urbanization and transportation infrastructures are good and reasonably efficient. Currently, the whole Guangdong–Hong Kong–Macao Greater Bay

Area is well served by three world-class ports: the ports of Hong Kong, Shenzhen, and Guangzhou. At the same time, there are also large domestic ports comprising Dongguan Port and Zhuhai Port. Hong Kong Port, in particular, is one of the busiest and most efficient international container ports in the world. It is also the "hub port" in the global supply chain. Its container throughput has been ranked among the top in the world. Ranked just behind Shanghai and Singapore in 2011 and 2012, the Hong Kong Port remains the third largest container port in the world. And Hong Kong has always been a management model for private enterprises in adopting and maintaining the free port policy with its high customs clearance rate of goods, free access to foreign exchange and of course it is a world-renowned free port. There are five main airports in Guangdong, Hong Kong and Macao, including Hong Kong, Guangzhou, Shenzhen, Macao and Zhuhai. At the same time, the second airport in Shenzhen and the new, high passenger volume flight routes airport in the Pearl River Delta are being planned. The Greater Bay Area is also speeding up the construction of railway networks, highway networks, intercity rail networks and urban rail networks, and it is promoting the formation of a "one-hour living circle" within the Greater Bay Area. Currently, the planning and construction of the second Humen Bridge, Fujian–Shenzhen High-speed Railway and Guangzhou–Shantou High-speed Railway are under way. Sea, land and air entry and exit points or ports are also accelerating the integrated construction and innovating the process of customs clearance and improving the efficiency of customs clearance at the entry and exit points. Second, in terms of logistical volume, the total value of the logistical inflow and outflow of goods in Guangdong Province in 2014 accounted for 8% of the country's total value, and the total value of cross-border logistics was 6.61 trillion. Therefore, both in terms of urbanization and transportation infrastructure construction, as well as in terms of logistical volume, the Greater Bay Area has already met the basic conditions for becoming an international logistics center.

However, there is still a big gap and a long way to go for it to become a first-class international logistics center. To make it into a world-class logistics center, we must first promote the integrated planning of transport infrastructure in the Greater Bay Area, making it a functionally complementary port and shipping, air and aviation hub, as well as a railway and multimodal transport hub. At the same time, we must accelerate the layout of information infrastructure, logistics services and supply chain management, so as to enhance the international competitiveness of the logistics industry. Second, there must be collaborative cooperation or synergy within the Guangdong–Hong Kong–Macao Greater Bay Area in which the component regions work together to strengthen the construction of external transport networks to connect to the world.

(A) *Strengthening the interconnectivity of the transportation infrastructure in the Greater Bay Area*

First of all, we should further strengthen and facilitate closer cooperation between the Pearl River Delta and Hong Kong and Macao in major infrastructure. We need to promote the uniform construction of major infrastructures in the Greater Bay Area, improve information infrastructure and build a modern and comprehensive transport system. In so doing, we must attempt to innovate cross-border infrastructure construction in Guangdong, Hong Kong and Macao and conduct overall planning of port and harbor construction in accordance with the principles of complementary advantages and mutual benefits, aiming to achieve win–win situations. We should strive to strengthen the eastern and western ports of the Pearl River estuary in terms of optimization and integration of port resources. We should form a port group or cluster with complementary functions and "staggered" development, so as to avoid chaotic competition and repeated or duplicated construction. At the same time, we will have to actively develop modern shipping and freight services such as e-commerce, finance, information, consultation and trade to enhance the collaborative functions of the shipping industry in the Greater Bay Area — we have to improve the overall quality of the international shipping services in the Bay Area.

Second, the existing airports in the Pearl River Delta should be expanded and rebuilt. The airports involved are Baiyun Airport in

Guangzhou and Bao'an Airport in Shenzhen, the second Guangzhou Airport, Nansha General Airport and Huizhou Airport (second phase). The expansion and rebuilding are necessary to optimize the general layout and conditions of the airports in the Pearl River Delta in promoting the cooperation between airports in the Pearl River Delta and Hong Kong and Macao Airports. Another aim is to build a "multi-layer" or "multi-level" air transport system in the Greater Bay Area. In addition, it is necessary to enhance the information, finance and consultation and other package capabilities of the airport groups in the Greater Bay Area and to expand the matching aviation service market.

Third, we need to establish for the Greater Bay Area a "rapid public transit network" and to carry out the overall planning of the layout of the railway, highway and road networks in the Bay Area, including the planning and construction of a high-speed road network, urban rail network and intercity rail network, thus strengthening the interconnectivity and coordination between cities. We wish to foster the formation of a fast "one-hour living circle" in the Greater Bay Area.

Finally, we should improve the multi-directional passage network in the Greater Bay area, promote the "docking" or "coupling" of railways, highways, ports and airports. We should strive to build an integrated transportation network of air and sea routes and rapid transit networks, realize the "zero-distance" transfer of passenger transport and the "seamless connection" of freight transport, enhancing the dispersal capacity of ports and airports, promoting the integration and unification of transportation in the Bay area and improving the efficiency of integrated transport services.

In the area of transport interconnection, planning should take into account the whole of the Greater Bay Area to realize the "staggered and complementary" development of airports and ports in Guangdong, Hong Kong and Macao. Disorderly or chaotic competition must be avoided; instead, we should build and share transport infrastructures and avoid duplication of construction and waste of resources. Currently, Guangzhou's planning center is in Nansha. It is expected that Guangzhou will build Nansha General Airport by accelerating the construction of rail transit and high-speed expressways. Zhongshan is planning its rapid metro construction with Guangzhou; Dongguan is planning the "coupling" with Shenzhen, Huizhou is connecting to Fujian–Shenzhen Railway while Guangzhou–Shantou High-speed Railway is connecting Guangzhou, Shenzhen, Dongguan, Heyuan, Shanwei and other key cities. In addition, Huizhou is planning the second phase of its airport and constructing the airport economic zone to build a new "main flight route" (flight with high volume of passengers) airport. Meanwhile Zhuhai will build a multi-level comprehensive transportation hub system in the Greater Bay Area by making use of the Hong Kong–Zhuhai–Macao Bridge and the undersea tunnel of the Hong Kong–Zhuhai–Macao Bridge.

(B) *Promoting the construction of a transport network in the Greater Bay Area that connects to areas outside the bay area and building a transportation hub that connects to the outside world*

Guided by the "Belt and Road" Initiative, the Greater Bay Area of Guangdong, Hong Kong and Macao must possess the ability to connect with the world. Only when there is free flow and transfer of information, logistics and capital — to be allocated to all parts of the world through it — can the Greater Bay Area become a logistics hub. To build the "Belt and Road" logistics hub, we must build a comprehensive logistics corridor and network system founded on Guangdong, Hong Kong and Macao, which at the same time, spreads to the Asia-Pacific region and is global in its orientation. It is not only a shipping center but also an aviation center. What is more, it is also going to be a multimodal transport center for rail, shipping and air, creating a logistics and supply chain management center commensurate with commercial and capital flows.

We should take the "Belt and Road" Initiative as indicating the strategic direction when promoting the construction of Guangdong, Hong Kong and Macao international passageways, deepening the cooperation and "coupling" between the ports of Guangdong, Hong Kong and Macao and the ports and airports along the 21st

Century Maritime Silk Road and actively develop international air freight and shipping networks for Southeast Asian, European and American countries. We should develop offshore trade and entrepot trade, making the Greater Bay Area the hub of the Asia-Pacific supply chain, and enhance its function in international transfer of goods, info, capital, etc. We should speed up the transformation and upgrading of ports, increase the proportion of international transshipment business, establishing an international procurement and distribution platform and forming a regional production service center and an integrated transport hub for the Asia-Pacific region. We also need to enhance the global shipping center role of the port group of the Greater Bay Area, actively expand international air cargo and passenger transport network along the "Belt and Road" countries, explore and open up direct flights and increase the number of airline flights. Second, we will open up the international freight trains to the countries along the "Belt and Road" Economic Zone. We should enhance and expand their international airport radiating functions and cooperate with Guangxi and Yunnan in promoting the interconnection of land transport with the Pan-Pearl River Delta and ASEAN, strengthening the "docking and coupling" with the South Asia and ASEAN "Pan Asian Railway" passageways. We would encourage domestic transport enterprises such as shipping and aviation enterprises to set up overseas bases and subsidiaries, expand the opening of low-altitude flights within our territory, develop civilian helicopter services, etc. We must constantly enhance the radiation function of our international airports. We should take advantage of the strengths of the developed information industries and agglomeration of the information enterprises in Shenzhen and its surrounding cities to accelerate the integration of Internet technology and transportation. We need to set up a transportation information service platform that promotes the connection of transportation and information service and which improves the function of information interconnection and intercommunication in the Greater Bay Area. At the same time, we have to build the core nodes of international information network, strengthen the function of international information port nodes, optimize the layout of seaports, landports and airports in the Greater Bay Area, strengthen the integration of ports, innovate the mode of port customs clearance and improve the efficiency of passenger and cargo customs clearance.

It is also necessary to establish an international logistics industry chain on the basis of cross-regional cooperation and joint construction of transport infrastructures among the three regions of the Greater Bay Area of Guangdong, Hong Kong and Macao. Bonded warehousing logistics bases and container hub stations must be built. We should attempt to create a regional international procurement, distribution and transfer center. Commensurate with our policy for "bonded areas", we shall transform the Greater Bay Area into an international trading platform connecting domestic and foreign markets. It is also going to be an agglomeration area for the flow of cargo, information, orders and capital. Our goal is to strengthen the international trade integration function of the Guangdong–Hong Kong–Macao Greater Bay Area and realize it. We would facilitate the circulation of trade, industry and capital in the Greater Bay Area.

VI. Building an International Economic and Trade Center in the Greater Bay Area

(A) *To create a good and conducive business environment in the bay area and enhance the integrating function of the Greater Bay Area in international business and trade*

Because of its excellent geographical location, low taxation, professional services, good financial environment and a sound and comprehensive legal environment, Hong Kong's business operations are transparent and encounter less government intervention — it is recognized as an ideal business city of the world. It has attracted many multinational corporations to set up their Asia-Pacific headquarters, leading incidentally to the gathering of science, technology and talented professionals in Hong Kong and further promoting the development of Hong Kong's economy and commerce. Through years of trade with the Mainland and other countries, Hong Kong's standing as an international financial center, trade, shipping and information center has been strengthened, and Hong Kong's status has effectively promoted insurance, transportation, warehousing and consultation industries in the Greater Bay Area. The concomitant development of consultation and other related service industries within the Greater Bay Area has injected new vitality into Hong Kong's economy and consolidated its position as an international business center. Macao is also an important commercial and business service platform. It has advantages in gambling, tourism and exhibition industries. It has been serving as a bridge between the Mainland and Portuguese-speaking and Latin American countries in information communication, intermediary services and overseas Chinese services, providing a platform for technical cooperation and exchange between the Mainland and the outside world.

The Pearl River Delta region should rely on its FTZs, industrial parks, logistics parks and "tax bonded areas" to accumulate science and technologies, professionals, finance and other essential elements and factors. It should deepen cooperation and exchanges with Hong Kong and Macao in business and trade, talents, education, finance and transportation and help facilitate the radiating effects of Hong Kong's financial and logistics industries. Macao's convention and exhibition industries, tourism, culture and education industries are industries which could be spread to other cities in the Greater Bay Area. In order to improve the international trade integrating function of the Greater Bay Area, enterprises or institutions are to be introduced from Hong Kong and Macao for enterprises in the Greater Bay Area to "dock" or "form coupling" with the international business regulations of Hong Kong and Macao, thus optimizing the business environment of the Greater Bay Area.

(B) *To foster economic ties and trade exchanges between the mainland and foreign countries with help and assistance from Hong Kong and Macao*

We should take full advantage of the position of Hong Kong as an international trading center with its advanced information technology to gather domestic and foreign trade institutions, to promote the development of Hong Kong's trade economy, and at the same time to drive the development of the trading economy of the whole Greater Bay Area. Relying on the advantages of Hong Kong as a "shopping center", we could open up two market channels or "passageways" at home and abroad to promote the integration of domestic and foreign trade. With the help of Hong Kong's high-end and high-quality service industries, we could build up our own service industry agglomeration platform to provide professional services for economic and trade exchanges between the Mainland and other countries, such as providing Hong Kong-standard accounting and financial auditing services for the listing and financing of Mainland enterprises in Hong Kong, providing internationally recognized legal opinions for the expansion of Mainland enterprises to cooperate with overseas companies and offering good experience in international dispute mediation and arbitration between the Mainland and other countries.

Macao has a flourishing gambling tourism industry and it possesses certain advantages in developing the exhibition industry. Macao has established the Exhibition and Conferencing Associations to assist Portuguese-speaking and Latin American countries to enter the Chinese market. In recent years, Macao has devoted itself to the improvement of tourism infrastructure, as well as to the training of exhibition professionals and the establishment of an international tourism conference center. Macao serves as a service platform for business cooperation between China and Portuguese-speaking countries. It serves as a link between the Mainland and Portuguese-speaking and Latin American countries and serves as a bridge for Mainland enterprises to venture abroad and to "import" foreign enterprises. It will also be the Sino-Portuguese trade and economic cooperation exhibition center, Portuguese-speaking countries' food distribution center as well as the Sino-Portuguese SME business service center, which will develop into a product exhibition center, an international convention and exhibition and an expo center in China for Portuguese-speaking countries as well as related countries along the "Belt and Road" route.

The advantages of Hong Kong and Macao as the economic and trade cooperation platform for small and medium-sized enterprises in the Greater Bay Area lie in the fact that the legal mechanisms of Hong Kong and Macao's commercial and trade operations are close to international benchmarks. Macao provides a lower operating cost of business, and at the same time, life there is relatively relaxed, which contrasts with the tense and fast pace of life and work in Hong Kong. Therefore, Hong Kong and Macao can complement each other as commercial and trade platforms for small and medium-sized enterprises.

In 2016, the total import and export volume of Guangdong Province was 6,302.947 billion yuan, accounting for 25.9% of the total national import and export volume, while that of Hong Kong was 7,596.6 billion yuan. We should utilize Hong Kong and Macao's positions as international trade centers and international business platform to build a Greater Bay Area national import base and create an import trading platform for consumer goods and important industrial raw materials in the Bay Area. We shall build a technology import and export trading platform in the Greater Bay Area and build a national Product Design and Trade Promotion Center, making full use of these platforms to promote the economy and trade exchanges between the Greater Bay Area and countries along the "Belt and Road" route (Figure 5).

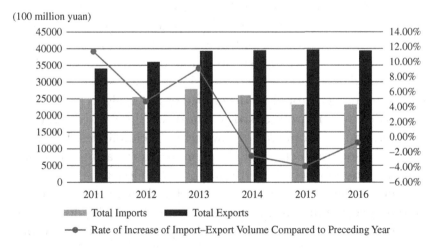

Figure 5. The import–export volume of Guangdong and its growth rate 2011–2016.

VII. Creating a Quality Life or Living Sphere within the Greater Bay Area

In order to attract talents and professionals, the Greater Bay Area has to build itself into a highly livable, habitable and tourist-friendly city cluster with ecological civilization, a beautiful environment with cultural richness. Hence, we should promote the integration and development of cultural and business tourism in the Greater Bay Area, develop a green and low-carbon economy, build a "highland" for pooling talents and create high-end tourism, so as to form a high-quality living environment in the Greater Bay Area, thus accelerating the accumulation of talents, science and technology industries in the Greater Bay Area.

(A) *Developing a Green and low-carbon economy in the Greater Bay Area*

First, we should tighten pollution control. We shall focus on stepping up the treatment of heavily polluted rivers and cleaning up coastal areas, especially those in the Pearl River Delta region where manufacturing industry is very developed. We need to strengthen cooperation and exchanges on water pollution control among Guangdong, Hong Kong and Macao and promote the joint treatment of water pollution in the three places. Second, we should foster the transformation and upgrading of industries that cause pollution. Enterprises whose pollution or emissions exceed the safety standards should be banned or transformed. High-end service industries should be developed aggressively to increase the proportion of tertiary industries. Third, we should accelerate the research and development of low-carbon technologies, build low-carbon pilot projects and implement zero-carbon emission demonstration projects. Fourth, we should build a multi-level transport network and innovate green travel and commuting modes to help reduce carbon emissions of vehicles. Fifth, we should establish green finance, carbon emission trading platforms and carbon pricing centers.

(B) *To cultivate, enhance and exploit the effects and influence of education in the Greater Bay Area; to build up talent pools and to speed up the agglomeration of talents*

We should integrate educational resources in the Greater Bay Area, encourage universities in Guangdong, Hong Kong and Macao to set up branch campuses or to establish schools in disciplines and areas of their respective strengths and encourage universities to build research institutes or scientific research centers with high-end and high-tech prestigious enterprises in different regions. We shall promote the construction of university towns and talent training bases in different regions, actively introduce world-class universities and disciplines from abroad, and cultivate the international influence of Greater Bay Area education so as to attract high-end talents at home and from abroad.

In addition, we should improve the system of medical insurance, entry and exit requirements, taxation and pension systems in the Greater Bay Area, establish an international talent policy, actively attract innovative talents and high-level personnel at home and from abroad and build Guangdong, Hong Kong and Macao Bay Area as a region for innovative and high-end talents as well as an area for international talents to congregate.

(C) *Creating a world-class international tourism brand*

The Greater Bay Area of Guangdong, Hong Kong and Macao is not only a symbol of economic development but also a region for leisure tourism, drawing strong attraction from tourists. For the three major bay areas of the world, their tourism products, supporting facilities and the number of tourists are all at the forefront of the world's tourism industry. The Greater Bay Area of Guangdong, Hong Kong and Macao does have the foundation for building a leading tourism industry. It has distinctive tourism routes, comprehensive and public infrastructure and supporting "traveling, touring, food, shopping and entertainment" service elements — fulfilling the needs of international passengers for leisure and business. Hong

Kong has incomparable advantages in terms of "humanistic" or "cultural and social" tourism resources. It is an international metropolis that integrates Chinese and Western cultures. Its culture, education, social life and architecture are characterized by diversity and internationalization. It is also known as a shopping and food paradise. It attracts a large number of domestic and foreign tourists. Macao's tourism industry is its pillar industry, because it is also a place where Eastern and Western cultures converge, and its lifestyle, architecture, etc., show pluralistic cultural characteristics. In addition, Macao's gambling industry is an important magnet attracting a large number of tourists. It is known as one of the three largest casino cities in the world. Currently, it also possesses strengths in developing business exhibition tourism activities. The Pearl River Delta is also very rich in tourism resources, and Guangdong has a large inland hinterland and could connect the inland with the tourism resources of Hong Kong, Macao and other countries.

To create international tourism brands of the Greater Bay Area, we must first overcome the institutional barriers between Guangdong, Hong Kong and Macao and promote the enhanced cooperation of the tourism industries of the three cities. For example, we could learn from, rely on and make the developed yachting industry of Hong Kong and Macao and other high-end tourist activities as key collaborative projects to accelerate the construction of pilot yachting areas in the Greater Bay Area. It is necessary to facilitate the customs clearance policy of Guangdong, Hong Kong and Macao in opening up the tourist corridors of the three places, to connect the tourism resources of the three places and to promote the interactions and movements of tourism institutions, tourist agencies and staff and tourism-related services in the Greater Bay Area. We aim to promote the agglomeration of tourist industries, creating high-quality tourism products and routes, promoting the assimilation of tourism into the Greater Bay Area of Guangdong, Hong Kong and Macao and, at the same time, connecting to the rich tourist resources of the interior of Guangdong Province and its hinterland.

Second, in promoting the integration of tourism resources in Guangdong, Hong Kong and Macao, we should take full advantage of the strengths of tourism in each of the three places, implement "staggered and complementary" development to complement each other's functions. Hong Kong is the world's shopping center, and it is mainly developing its shopping and leisure tourism. Macao's current development goal is to build a world-class tourist resort integrating leisure, entertainment and gambling. Guangdong's main niches are its natural ecological resources, historical and cultural advantages — all of which should be used to develop ecological, leisure and cultural tourism with local characteristics. Differential developments should be carried out in the three areas to build a tourism system in the Greater Bay Area.

Finally, we should establish an international tourism cooperation sphere and use the opportunity provided by the "Belt and Road" Initiative to connect the tourism resources of the Greater Bay Area to the opportunities offered by the "Belt and Road" Initiative. The Maritime Silk Road was originally a cultural road map with rich cultural tourism resources. The Greater Bay Area can entrust the Pilot FTZs to strengthen the cooperation between domestic and foreign tourism resources and tourism projects, simplify the visa procedures for cruise ships and yachts and establish the Bay Area International Tourism Pilot Zone, develop Maritime Silk Road tourism products and high-quality "boutique" or "specially tailored" tourist routes with the help of the harbor cruise ports of Hong Kong and Shenzhen. We could also utilize the platforms offered by the "Guangdong International Tourism Culture Festival" and the "Guangdong International Tourism Expo" to establish an international tourism cooperation sphere.

Bibliography

Breiger Ronald: "Structure of Economic Interdependence among Nations", *Continuities in Structural Inquiry*, 1981.

Brun Jean Francois, Combes Jean Louis and Renard Mary Francoise: "Are There Spillover Effects Between Coastal and Noncoastal Regions in China?" *China Economic Review*, Vol. No. 2, 2002.

Cassi Lorenzo, Morrison Andrea, Ter Wal Anne L.J.: "The Evolution of Trade and Scientific Collaboration Networks in the Global Wine Sector: A Longitudinal Study Using Network Analysis", *Economic Geography*, Vol. No. 88, 2012.

Cha Zhenxiang and Charlie: "Research on the Economic Tracks of Shenzhen's Development in the Bay Area", *Journal of Shenzhen Vocational and Technical College*, Vol. No. 4, 2014.

Chase-Dunn Christoper and Grimes Peter: "World Systems Analysis", *Annual Review of Sociology*, 1995.

Chen Xiaodan, Tang Tianjun, Che Xiuzhen, *et al.*: "Research on the Strategy of Environmental Improvement in Shenzhen Bay Area from the Perspective of Bay Area Economy", *Special Regions Economy*, Vol. No. 12, 2014.

Chen Xiongbing and Zhang Zongcheng: "Re-discussing Granger Causality Test", Research on *Quantitative Economics Technology and Economics*, Vol. No. 1, 2008.

Cheng Yao: "Trends and Policy Measures to Address the Issue of Moving Populations Against the Background of Healthy/Wholesome Urbanization", *Economic Geography*, Vol. No. 4, 2012.

Deng Zhixin: "The Establishment of Shenzhen Free Trade Zone under the Economic Development Strategy of the Bay", *Special Regions Economy*, Vol. No. 12, 2014.

Everett, M.: "Textbook at Essex Summer School in SSDA", *Social Network Analysis*, 2002.

Freeman Linton C.: "Centrality in Social Networks: Conceptual Clarification", *Social Networks*, Vol. No. 1, 1979.

Groenewold, Nicolaas, Guoping Lee, and Anping Chen: "Inter-regional Spillovers in China: The Importance of Common Shocks and the Definition of the Regions", *China Economic Review*, Vol. No. 1, 2007.

Hu Hao, Jin Fengjun, and Wang Jiao'e: "Research on Spatial Patterns and Spatial-temporal Evolution of China's National Historic and Cultural Cities", *Economic Geography*, Vol. No. 4, 2012.

Ju Limeng: "Empirical Research on Subject Body Functions by Regions in Underdeveloped Areas — Taking Jiangxi Province as an Example", *Economic Geography*, Vol. No. 4, 2012.

Krackhardt David: "Graph theoretical dimensions of informal organizations", *Computational Organizational Theory*, 1994.

Li Guoping, Wu Aizhi and Sun Tieshan: "China's Regional Spatial Structure Research: Review and Prospects", *Economic Geography*, Vol. No. 4, 2012.

Li Jing, Chen Shu, Wan Guanghua and Fu Chen Mei: "Spatial Relevancy and Interpretation of Regional Economic Growth in China: Based on the method of Network Analysis", *Economic Research*, Vol. No. 11, 2014.

Li Rengui and Zhang Wenguang: "Practices of French Growth Pole Strategy and Enlightening Revelations Thereof ", *Development Research*, Vol. No. 7, 2012.

Lin Jianfang: "New Chapter of 'Cumulative Strengths' in the Construction of Comprehensive Transport System in the Greater Bay Area of Guangdong, Hong Kong and Macao", *China Transport and Communication News*, Vol. No. 3, 2017.

Liu Huajun, Zhang Yao, and Sun Yanan: "Spatial Network Structure of China's Regional Development in and its Time Lag Changes: An Analysis Based on DLI Index", *Chinese Population Science*, Vol. No. 4, 2015.

Liu Huajun, Zhang Yao, and Sun Yanan: "Spatial Network Structure of Regional Development in China and Its Influencing Factors-based on Interprovincial Development and People's Livelihood Index 2000–2013", *Economic Review*, Vol. No. 5, 2014.

Liu Jianing: "Guangdong's Practice of 'Three Integrations' of Technology, Finance and Industry", *Southern Economics*, Vol. No. 9, 2015.

Liu Yanxia: "Research and Enlightening Revelations on Economic Development of Bay Areas at Home and Abroad", *Urban Insight*, Vol. No. 3, 2014.

Long Gen Ying: "Measuring the Spillover Effects: Some Chinese Evidence", *Papers in Regional Science*, Vol. No. 1, 2000.

Long Gen Ying: "Understanding China's Recent Growth Experience: A Spatial Econometric Perspective", *The Annals of Regional Science*, Vol. No. 4, 2003.

Long Yongjun and Yang Qingyuan: "Research on the Urban Economic Spatial Impact of Chongqing", *Economic Geography*, Vol. No. 5, 2012.

Lu Zhengge: "The Bay Area Economy: A Bright Transition to Reveal the Transformation of a Mature City", *City Memories*, Vol. No. 4, 2014.

Lu Zhiguo, Pan Feng, and Yan Zhenkun: "Research on the Economic Comparison of Global Bay Areas and Comprehensive Evaluation Thereof", *Science and Technology Progress and Policy*, Vol. No. 11, 2015.

Lu Xu, Ma Xueguang and Li Guicai: "Research on Urban Network Spatial Patterns in the Pearl River Delta-based on the Layout of International High End/Advanced Producer Service Industries", *Economic Geography*, Vol. No. 4, 2012.

Lun Wenbao: "Comparative Analysis of Silicon Valley and Zhongguancun". www.lwbao.com.

Oliveira Márcia and João Gama: "An Overview of Social Network Analysis", *Wiley Interdisciplinary Reviews-Data Mining and Knowledge Discovery*, Vol. No. 2, 2012.

Pan Jie and Zhang Shou: "Modes of Financial Cooperation between Guangdong, Hong Kong and Macao since the Reform and Opening-up: Review and Prospects", *International Economic and Trade Research*, Vol. No. 9, 2014.

Pan Wenqing: "Spatial Spillover Effects of Regional Relevancy/Linkages and Economic Growth in China", *Economic Research*, Vol. No. 1, 2012.

Schiavo, Stefano, Javier Reyes, and Giorgio Fagiolo: "International Trade and Financial Integration: A Weighted Network Analysis", *Quantitative Finance*, Vol. No. 10, 2010.

Smith David A. and White Douglas R.: "Structure and Dynamics of the Global Economy: Network Analysis of International Trade 1965–1980", *Social Forces*, Vol. 7, No. 4, 1992.

Snyder David and Kick Edward: "Structural Position in the World System and Economic Growth, 1955–1970: A Multiple Network Analysis of Transnational Interactions", *The American Journal of Sociology*, Vol. 84, No. 5, 1979.

Su Hua, Chen Weihua and Chen Wenjun: "The Income Disparities between Urban and Rural Areas in China Under the Effects of the Productivity Factors and Allocation Thereof", *Economic Geography*, Vol. No. 4, 2012.

The World's First Internet Museum, "History of Silicon Valley", 2015. http://www.techcn.co.

The World's First Internet Museum, "Silicon Valley Ills", 2015. http://www.techcn.co.

Tu Wenming and Cao Bang: "The Realization Mechanism of Growth Pole Strategy and the Reconstruction of China's Practice Model", *Contemporary Finance and Economics*, Vol. No. 9, 2012.

Wang Hai: "Coastal Innovation Growth Poles Lead China's Economic Transition and Upgrading", *Modern Economic Research*, Vol. No. 4, 2015.

Wang Hongbin: "Bay Area Economy and Chinese Practice", *China Economic Report*, Vol. No. 11, 2014.

Wang Qiang: "Discussions on the Construction and Development Direction of Human Economic Geography Disciplines — Summary of the Symposium on the Future Development of Human Economic Geography in 2012", *Economic Geography*, Vol. No. 4, 2012.

Wang Xiaoyu: The Polarization and Diffusion/Dispersal Effects of China's Regional Growth Poles, Jilin University, 2011.

Wasserman, Stan and Faust, Katherine: "Social Network Analysis: Methods and Applications", *Journal of Women's Health*, Vol. 91, No. 435, 1994.

Weng Zhangmei: Research on Issues of Innovation and Development of Yang Pu Science and Technology Park, Tongji University, 2017.

White, Harrison C., Boorman, Scott A. and Breiger, Ronald L.: "Social Structure from Multiple Networks: Block Models of Roles and Positions", *The American Journal of Sociology*, Vol. 81, No. 1, 1976.

Wu Lijuan, Liu Yuting, and Cheng Hui: "A Review and Evaluation of the Research on the Dynamic Mechanism and Key Contents of Overall Urban-Rural Development Planning", *Economic Geography*, Vol. No. 4, 2012.

Wu Zhe: "The Total Industrial Output of High-tech Enterprises Leaps to National No.1 Position", *Southern Daily*, Vol. No. 4, 2017.

Xu Aiyu: Research on the Transformation of Manufacturing Industries in Guangdong Province, Jinan University, 2011.

Ye Mingue: "The Characteristics and Influencing Factors of the Migration of China's Economic Center from 1978 to 2008", *Economic Geography*, Vol. No. 4, 2012.

Zhang Qing and Felmingham Bruce: "The Role of FDI, Exports and Spillover Effects in the Regional Development of China", *Journal of Development Studies*, Vol. No. 4, 2002.

Zhang Youyin, Gu Jing, and Huang Heqing: "Spatial Differential Analysis of the Structural Changes in China's Regional Tourism Industry", *Economic Geography*, Vol. No. 4, 2012.

Zhu Ming: "A Look at Xiongan's Future Positioning from the Development History of Silicon Valley", *Securities Times*, Vol. No. 4, 2017.

Zuo Liancun and Liao Zhe: "Research on the Joint Innovation Zones of Guangdong, Hong Kong and Macao", *Industrial Economics Review*, Vol. No. 1, 2010.

Index